Bringing Human Rights Education to US Classrooms

Bringing Human Rights Education to US Classrooms

Exemplary Models from Elementary Grades to University

Edited by Susan Roberta Katz and Andrea McEvoy Spero

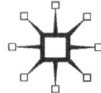

BRINGING HUMAN RIGHTS EDUCATION TO US CLASSROOMS
Copyright © Susan Roberta Katz and Andrea McEvoy Spero, 2015.
Softcover reprint of the hardcover 1st edition 2015 978-1-137-47112-3

All rights reserved.

First published in 2015 by
PALGRAVE MACMILLAN®
in the United States—a division of St. Martin's Press LLC,
175 Fifth Avenue, New York, NY 10010.

Where this book is distributed in the UK, Europe and the rest of the world, this is by Palgrave Macmillan, a division of Macmillan Publishers Limited, registered in England, company number 785998, of Houndmills, Basingstoke, Hampshire RG21 6XS.

Palgrave Macmillan is the global academic imprint of the above companies and has companies and representatives throughout the world.

Palgrave® and Macmillan® are registered trademarks in the United States, the United Kingdom, Europe and other countries.

ISBN 978-1-349-50088-8   ISBN 978-1-137-47113-0 (eBook)
DOI 10.1057/9781137471130

Library of Congress Cataloging-in-Publication Data

    Bringing human rights education to US classrooms : exemplary models from elementary grades to university / edited by Susan Roberta Katz and Andrea McEvoy Spero.
    pages cm
    Includes index.

    1. Human rights—Study and teaching—United States. 2. Education, Humanistic—United States. I. Katz, Susan Roberta, editor of compilation. II. Spero, Andrea McEvoy, editor of compilation. III. Title: Bringing human rights education to United States classrooms.

JC571.B693 2015
323.071'073—dc23   2014040001

A catalogue record of the book is available from the British Library.

Design by Newgen Knowledge Works (P) Ltd., Chennai, India.

First edition: April 2015

10 9 8 7 6 5 4 3 2 1

We dedicate this book to Maya Angelou (1928–2014), Yuri Kochiyama (1921–2014), and Nelson Mandela (1918–2013), whose long lives were devoted to making this world a more humane place, and to all the teachers who stand on their shoulders.

Contents

List of Figures and Tables   ix
Foreword   xi
Acknowledgments   xvii

Part I   Overview of Human Rights Education

1   Building a Human Rights Education Movement in the United States   3
Felisa Tibbitts

2   The Challenges and Triumphs of Teaching for Human Rights in US Schools   15
Susan Roberta Katz and Andrea McEvoy Spero

Part II   Pedagogical Tools

3   Each One, Teach One: The History and Legacy of the Black Panther Party for an Elementary School Audience   31
Jessie Blundell

4   The Right to an Adequate Standard of Living: Human Rights Education in the Elementary Classroom   47
Erin Brennan

5   Bringing to Life Human Rights Education in the Science Classroom   65
Annie S. Adamian

6   Challenging Islamophobia in the Middle School Classroom: Using Critical Media Literacy to Teach Human Rights   87
Kelly Delaney

7	*Tout moun se moun* "Every Person Is a Human Being": Understanding the Struggle for Human Rights in Haiti *Victoria Isabel Durán*	107
8	Know Your Rights: Understanding the Universal Declaration of Human Rights *Jacqueline Fix and Puja Kumar Clifford*	129
9	Teaching *The Crucible* through Human Rights *Barbara J. Arduini*	149
10	Reframing a Community College Social Problems Course through a Human Rights Perspective *Lindsay Padilla*	169
11	Teaching and Learning Asian American Leadership: A Human Rights Framework *Melissa Ann Canlas*	187
12	Female Genital Mutilation: A Pedagogical Tool to Explore Global Violence against Women *Onllwyn Cavan Dixon*	209
Afterword: Will Human Rights Education Be Decolonizing? *K. Wayne Yang*		225
Notes on Contributors		237
Index		241

Figures and Tables

Figures

7.1	A Soccer Game in a Tent City	124
7.2	Sunday Afternoon	124
7.3	Paving New Roads	125
7.4	What Is Under Construction?	125
7.5	Tent City Port-au-Prince One	126
8.1	Handout: Lesson Three, Handout One: What Is a Human? What Are Human Rights?	144
8.2	Handout: Lesson Three, Handout Two: Frayer-Style Vocabulary	145
8.3	Handout: Lesson Six, Handout Three: Circle Notes (Scaffold)	146
8.4	Handout: Lesson Six: Circle Notes (Challenge)	147
12.1	Diagram: Female External Genitalia	215
12.2	Diagram: FGM	216

Tables

5.1	Handout 1: Sizing up a Cell	81
5.2	Handout 2: Race—The Power of Illusion	82
5.3	Handout 2 Part 2: Race—The Power of Illusion	83
5.4	Handout 3: Genetics Research Article	84
9.1	Unit Block Plan	156
10.1	Course Schedule	181

Foreword

Human rights. What a simple, clear, universal concept with which humanity could very well be served, if we applied it universally, and more importantly, if we taught it to young people as part and parcel of their educational experience. This book takes a bold, creative step in that direction, ensuring that young students understand the deep impact of viewing the issues that surround them through a human rights lens.

As I reflect on my own educational and social activist journey, I see clearly how human rights issues impacted my entire life. Coming to the United States from Mexico as a young girl and growing up in a farmworker family in the Central Valley of California in the early 1960s, I was living every day the lack of adequate housing, adequate job conditions, adequate pay, and union representation. We were already living what at that point were violations of human rights. Like so many other immigrant children, I entered school without knowing English and was misplaced in special education classes. Once I mastered English, I excelled academically and ultimately graduated from high school as a top honors student and leader.

I enrolled at the University of California, Santa Cruz, where I actively participated in the Chicano student movement and was part of a nascent consciousness about the Latin American revolutionary movements of the day. Together with other fellow students we founded the Third World Teaching Resource Center and initiated an independent Latin American Studies major that is now the UC Santa Cruz Latin American/Latino Studies Department. After graduating in 1973, I traveled to Argentina where I became part of the progressive wing of the Peronist movement. While in Argentina, I was jailed and tortured as part of a massive effort by the Argentine right-wing government to suppress the Left oppositional movement.

Even with this personal history, for many years I did not have the consciousness of the human rights framework or the language of "human rights" because it had not been part of my schooling or political discussion. I was not aware of the Universal Declaration of Human Rights (UDHR) until 1976 after being released from jail in Argentina and returning to the United States. When I first read the UDHR, I found it to be a wonderful tool and was comforted to know that other people had thought about and codified universal rights. Similarly, the examples in this book show the power of codifying for young people both the definitions as well as practices of this kind of understanding of human rights.

Besides being able to look at my own life differently, I also saw the inherent power of the human rights framework in educating and mobilizing others to take action against human rights violations worldwide. When I came back to the United States, I was working in Washington, DC, for the Argentine Commission of Human Rights, specifically on defending my fellow Argentinian prisoners and denouncing the violation of human rights in that country. We based a large part of our work to cut off military aid to Argentina on the groundbreaking Harkin Amendment, which the US Congress passed after the 1973 overthrow of Allende in Chile. Thanks to this amendment, we could argue effectively that the United States should not provide public funds to countries violating the human rights of its citizens. We were able to talk to people about the fact that their tax dollars were being misused to send military aid to Argentina, a country that practiced illegal detention and torture. Once they became aware of this fact, people wanted to stop US support of military dictatorships. Ultimately, we succeeded in ending military aid to Argentina through the use of the Harkin Amendment as well as leveraging the grassroots movement formed during my imprisonment. It was a relatively small victory with huge consequences.

Also we were able to use the UDHR as an organizing tool in responding to people's questions: "So what did you all want in Argentina? What were you fighting for?" And we answered by explaining that Argentinians were like everyone else in the world in wanting a good life for their family and community, with adequate education, housing, financial resources, the ability to create, and so on. Therefore, the underpinnings of universal human rights provided a mechanism to name and identify violations, to hold governments accountable, and to build a sense of international community.

The youth in the US classrooms portrayed in this book have responded similarly to how I did in discovering the UDHR. They innately know about violations of human rights because they live that reality every day. And just like I did, they find the written words in the UDHR to be comforting in the validation of their own experience. I applaud the teachers in this book who are doing this work and bringing it to the personal lives of the students—or anybody else—because that is what evokes the biggest understanding and empathy—the personal connection to an issue. Because if you understand your own humanity and your own human rights, and if they are being violated, then you, more than likely, will go on to that next stage of understanding. You will grow to care about and want to act on the injustice taking place when your own and other people's rights are being violated.

My own conception of human rights has developed and changed over time. I have come to understand that ultimately it is about our humanity, about the basic right to be who you are. This has been an integral part of my evolution as a queer person. At times I have denied this part of my being, hiding it, and trying to place it elsewhere; yet it has personally been such a central part of my activism and life. But being in the Left political movement for many years, either as an activist in the Chicano movement, the Latin America solidarity movement, or the socialist party-building movement, this issue of Lesbian Gay Bisexual Transgender Queer (LGBTQ) rights was never dealt with well.

For many years my understanding was to consider sexuality as "just personal"—something that had to stay to the side because we had more important work to do in the struggle. The ideology of the Left, not just in this country but worldwide, was that we had to submerge the personal. Many of us did exactly that, until finally we came to understand and incorporate what the early feminists had been saying all along—"the personal is political." I am really glad to see that LGBTQ rights now are front and center in the media; in this one area, we really have seen much progress.

Also now there is more consciousness in our movements in terms of the intersection of our issues, whether race, gender, sexuality, or immigration status. I am pleased to see that. I have always felt as if I have lived my life in silos—as a Chicana, as a woman, as a Leftist, as a queer person. Like other movements (except those we have formed ourselves), the LGBTQ movement has been very white and male-dominated. But now I see a growing consciousness of intersectionality, reflected in campaigns such as support for the undocuqueer, where undocumented queer people come out and organize and advocate both as immigrants and as queer. In many instances the undocuqueer are forcing the immigrant rights organizations and LGBTQ rights organizations to work together and take up these issues in ways they had not done before.

So in my own personal understanding and conception of human rights over time, I have come to a fuller understanding and appreciation for how we can make our movements stronger by seeing human rights from various perspectives. This progression is reflected in the leadership training that we do at Chicana Latina Foundation, which is to highlight the power of your personal story. You start with your personal story. And that leads you to have an understanding of other people that are going through some of the same things. Developing this collective consciousness then moves forward to collective action, to social action, and on to a social justice movement.

In some ways this storytelling process that we use is very similar to human rights education (HRE) in that it provides students with important tools to understand the lives of others and then go back to the self. I emphasize the importance of starting with the students' personal story and offering activities for the students to express their own personal experiences; these stories can be expressed in art, in song, in poetry, in short stories or novels. What matters is that the students can express their personal story and then share them in order that others can hear them.

In the Chicana Latina Foundation we have seen that this process really does develop empathy and builds a sense of collectivity. When our documented students hear the stories of our undocumented students and their particular struggles—constant fear of deportation, inability to access resources, separation from family members—they come to understand and develop empathy for experiences that are not their own, but that touch them and propel them to be part of the movements that address these issues. I really am convinced that this works. And teachers need to guide the students to ask the important questions, to help move the students away from victimization and toward action: "The fact that five of you have experienced violence in your neighborhoods, what does this reflect? What does this say about the neighborhood? What does this say about the local government? What does it say about the educational system? What are the things that we could change?"

The social action the students take can be something seemingly simple yet very powerful in its impact and implications. If the problem is nutrition, they can organize a local farmer's market. If the problem is neighborhood violence, they can propose community patrols and set up a meeting with the Chief of Police and city officials to provide spaces and recreational resources for young people. The goal is to identify a social action totally connected to the students' own personal story. No matter the issue, whether creating an arts program, getting rid of some liquor stores, or addressing gender violence, your personal story is an incredibly powerful point of entry to understanding and taking action.

What I see with the examples in this book is that the teachers are the messengers and carriers of these important concepts: how to defend human rights, and how to stop violations of human rights. No matter whether you have been a victim of human rights violations or not, you can always be a carrier. Maybe you have not suffered as others have, and that's great. People should not have to suffer. In the Chicana Latina Foundation, we always want to make sure that we do not inadvertently set up a hierarchy of sad stories, implying the sadder the better. Those sad stories need to be shared, but everyone needs to see themselves as carriers of empathy, of understanding through their own personal story.

After I spoke to the University of San Francisco Human Rights Education class in 2007 about my personal story as a political prisoner in Argentina, the students commented that this was a powerful experience that profoundly impacted them. They appreciated the discussion, primarily because I was sharing my personal experience of torture and imprisonment; through that one story they were able to feel and empathize with the pain and repression suffered by thousands. Often people get the most motivated and moved to do things after hearing someone's personal story, no matter if the speaker is from Rwanda or from their own neighborhood. The transformative part, whether international or local, comes from making the individual connection.

And this is one of the great things that HRE can do—always connecting the global back to the personal. Many people may still think, "Oh, human rights, they're talking about international issues. Right?" We must emphasize that yes, we are talking about the human rights of people around the world, including the ones that are so crucial here that have to do with our society and the future of our community.

Through making a personal connection, people can begin to see how honoring human rights is in their own self-interest. For example, the Latino population in California is now 40 percent of the state, yet Latino youth experience a huge dropout rate. This small representation of a sizeable and significant part of our population in the educational system affects not only that particular community, but also everyone living in California. It is in everyone's interest that the Latino community has access to the educational levels that will help break the cycles of poverty. So it is paramount that everyone sees access to quality education "for all" as a basic human right. Aside from defending human rights from an altruistic perspective, we have to understand the ramifications, the impact, and the consequences of violations of human rights. Even if they do not impact us, what are the consequences? Teachers need to keep this in mind; for example, what happens when low-income and Latino residents are getting evicted from the Mission? What happens then to the future of the community? What happens to that fabric of the community that has been so important? How does it touch you? All of these things for the most part end up touching us all one way or another.

The human rights framework offers us a way to the future, especially since right now our world is complex, yet we are increasingly intertwined and connected to each other. The good thing is that we can be aware so much more globally of all the various issues. On the other hand, we cannot lose sight of the fact that we have to look at our own lives and we have to look at the United States. That is why it's so important for the HRE framework to focus on people's lives in our immediate community. We need to codify that understanding and the definitions so that we may move from the local to the global.

Perhaps one activity teachers could develop is involving their students to create a Declaration of Human Rights in the United States. We have the Universal Declaration, but what is specific to the United States? In the process, students could look at what is happening now that was not happening 20–30 years ago, like the wealth gap. This kind of framework has been missing and yet could teach so much because it is based on people's personal experience. With the appropriate pedagogy, teachers can guide students to a more universal understanding. A human rights lens allows us to understand that these economic issues of education, health care, and jobs are human rights.

At the same time we cannot lose sight of the basic human right to live our lives freely and in the pursuit of happiness. This right is something that has for so long been denied of LGBTQ folks, solely on the basis of sexual orientation or gender identity. And yet we have seen unprecedented movement forward. Five years ago, we could not have predicted the growing support for LGBTQ rights. After Proposition 8 (constitutional amendment opposing same sex marriage) passed in California in 2008, we thought we had 50 more years of struggle ahead of us. But the fact is that people can evolve and can transform their thinking. Working with young people and then seeing that transformation is possible is what gives me hope. And ultimately, I would say that as humans, we can see the potential for evolution and transformation.

I believe this book will be a valuable tool for teachers who want to engage students in critical thinking about human rights and how their own lives are affected by the protection or the violation of those rights. Teachers can use this book and become the carriers of this message: "Don't be disengaged yourself. Look at your own personal story. How can YOU carry the message of human rights?"

And I hope that in doing this work there is an element of joy for the students and the teachers. I would emphasize the joy of life, the joy of working with people, the joy of having victories, be they small or big. Joy will carry you through to ensure that fulfillment of human rights is possible.

Olga Talamante

Acknowledgments

This book is a true labor of love, nurtured by the commitment of so many colleagues, activists, teachers, and scholars who have dedicated their lives to the fulfillment of human rights for all. To name everyone would take up more pages than the chapters of this book, but we want to acknowledge those who have supported our work, either openly or behind the scenes.

To all the contributors to this book who poured their heart and soul (as well as blood, sweat, and tears) into their chapters: Scholars Annie S. Adamian, Barbara Arduini, Jessie Blundell, Erin Brennan, Melissa Canlas, Onllwyn Dixon, Kelly Delaney, Victoria Durán, Jacqueline Fix, Puja Kumar Clifford, Lindsay Padilla, Olga Talamante, Felisa Tibbitts, and K. Wayne Yang. Cover artist Natalia Anciso.

To human rights educators in the United States: Nancy Flowers who pioneered HRE in the United States and generously contributed to our USF library; Karen Robinson, former Education Director of Amnesty International, who unknowingly ignited the spark to bring HRE to USF.

To the University of San Francisco: USF Jesuit Foundation, USF Human Rights Collaborative, especially Professors Rob Elias and Stephen Zunes of Department of Politics, former president Stephen Privett, S. J., who lives and breathes human rights as a Jesuit; Provost Jennifer Turpin, and the Provost's Office, which supports USF faculty in the New York University Faculty Resource Network where this all began.

USF School of Education: Current Dean Kevin Kumashiro; former dean Walter Gmelch; Associate Dean Elena Flores; Associate Dean Christopher Thomas; International and Multicultural Education (IME) Department: Associate Dean Shabnam Koirala-Azad, Professors Emma Fuentes, Monisha Bajaj, Rosita Galang, Ruth Kim, Stephen Cary, Betty Taylor, Brad Washington, Sedique Popal, and Jackie Reza. Attorneys Kathy Roberts,

Shonali Shome, Michelle Leighton, and educator Rita Maran who taught the International Human Rights Law for Educators course. All the dedicated and passionate IME students, with special thanks to those enrolled in the first HRE pilot class in Spring 2007, including former Graduate Merit Scholar, Dr. Aaron Horn. Much gratitude to IME doctoral students who helped in the preparation of this manuscript: research assistant Victoria Durán for coordinating multiple aspects of the production process, and Patricia Barthaud for her thorough editing. Former IME program assistant Connor Cook; Professor Rick Ayers of Teacher Education who critiqued our co-edited chapter; Thanh Nguyen of Department of Leadership Studies whose smile lights up our day; Amy Lean Fogliani and Lisa Klope who always cheer us on.

USF School of Law: Former dean Jeff Brand and Professor Connie de la Vega, who invited Professor Katz into the new territory of human rights law.

Palgrave/Mcmillan: San José State University Professor Jason Laker who went out on a limb and first encouraged us to submit our proposal; Mara Berkman and Sarah Nathan, our editors, who solidly supported us throughout the process. The two blind reviewers who moved us miles ahead with their constructive feedback. Suzanne Sherman Aboulfadi, who prepared the index.

Bay Area social justice and human rights organizations: Sandy Sohcott, Ellen Sebastian-Chang, Sarah Crowell, John Nepomuceno and his students at Fremont High School of The World As It Could Be; Teachers 4 Social Justice; Amnesty International; Clayborne Carson and The Martin Luther King, Jr., Research and Education Institute; Jennifer Kim and the staff of the Ella Baker Center for Human Rights; David Gonzalez of the San Francisco LGBT Community Center; Jack Weinstein and Milton Reynolds of Facing History and Ourselves; Cliff Mayotte and Claire Kiefer of Voice of Witness; *Social Justice* journal; *Peace Review* journal; and the generous staff of Café Leila in Berkeley, California, where the editors often met and wrote.

Bay Area activists, teachers, and artists who were inspirational guest speakers in the Human Rights Education class over the years: Evan Bissell, Richard Brown, MamaCoatl, Victor Diaz, Suzie Dod (RIP), Trevor Gardner, David Gonzalez, Ericka Huggins, Antonia Juhasz, Jennifer Kim, Carlos Mauricio, Zachary Norris, Leah Piepzna-Samarasinha, Robert Roth, Roger Hill of the film *Flying Paper*, and David Zlutnik of the film *Occupation Has No Future*.

Other notable individuals: Professors Carl Grant of the University of Wisconsin-Madison, and Jabari Mahiri of the University of California,

Berkeley, for their encouragement to publish this book. Chia-Ry Chang, Victoria Durán's student at Calero High School in San Jose, who submitted her beautiful artwork.

Finally, our beloved families and dear friends who gave us the space and stamina to see this book through to the very end. Especially the love and support of Jason, Ella, and Maya Spero. We love you all!

PART I
Overview of Human Rights Education

CHAPTER 1

Building a Human Rights Education Movement in the United States

Felisa Tibbitts

Introduction

The concept of human rights is widely recognized but perhaps poorly understood in the United States. Most people will recognize the term, but few are able to explain what "human rights" are, or what it means to them. This situation is troubling, suggesting that at the grassroots level human rights values are not being tapped to their full potential in promoting social change.

Teachers committed to both a humanistic approach and the power of education to promote individual agency and social transformation have begun to embrace human rights education (HRE). The international HRE movement itself began to gain steam in the 1990s and has continued to evolve and expand ever since. This chapter presents a brief overview of the history of the HRE movement, both internationally and in the United States, as an introduction for the case studies of this book.

The Human Rights System

The history of HRE is linked with the evolution of international human rights standards. In layperson's terms, human rights can be defined as those basic standards essential for people to live in dignity as human beings. Human rights standards are legally codified in international treaties. Some treaties (also known as conventions or covenants) that may be familiar include the International Covenant on Civil and Political Rights (1966), the International Covenant on Economic, Social and Cultural Rights (1966) (granting the rights to education, health, housing and a livable wage), the Convention on the Rights of the Child (1989), and the Convention against Torture (1984). International treaties are developed by the United Nations Human Rights Council; once passed by the UN General Assembly, governments then have the option to voluntarily sign and ratify the treaty. The international human rights system is based on this simple principle: states sign human rights treaties, voluntarily commit themselves to uphold them, and are then held accountable through self-reporting to the United Nations and independent observation of watchdog agencies, their own citizens, and members of the international community.

Human rights are sometimes contested because of the historical circumstances under which the 1948 Universal Declaration of Human Rights (UDHR)—the document that was to become the basis for the entire international human rights legal system—was written. In the late 1940s, the newly formed United Nations did not include many of the countries that exist today. Since that time, international human rights standards have evolved to reflect a more diverse understanding of human rights, reflecting the expansion of UN members and new ways of thinking over the past 60 years. Although the idea of "individual rights" remains central, "collective rights," for example, has now entered into international legal standards, in part through the influence of indigenous peoples. The addition of new human rights standards—including the right to HRE—continues to be debated in the UN Human Rights Council, and such debates are more rigorous and authentic when they take into account more diverse perspectives.

International human rights standards are also resisted at times because of the claim that they are universal, a claim that can be accompanied by teaching human rights in a top-down and hegemonic manner with little knowledge or respect for local culture. Human rights educators have the very unique challenge to *offer* to learners the "power of human rights" through its legal standards and its widely accepted value system without *imposing* this framework. This is successfully achieved through methodologies that reflect the praxis of emancipatory, or transformative, learning as well as sensitivities to local context and culture.

The case studies presented in this book represent examples of both. In chapter 3, Blundell describes a primary school unit that links the history of the Civil Rights Movement in the United States with the history of Bay Area human rights activism as exemplified in the Black Panther Party. Delaney (chapter 6) as well as Fix and Kumar (chapter 8) have developed curriculum at the middle school and high school levels, respectively, that use the UDHR to help students develop a critical consciousness about human rights and oppression, drawing on the students' own life experiences. These chapters illustrate the impact of HRE when brought down to the local level and when integrated with students' daily realities.

The Right to Education and HRE

The right to education is a central human right and an end in itself: it ensures that humans can reach their full potential and claim their other rights, and it offers protection and structure in times of instability, aiding those most vulnerable, especially children, to enjoy their basic needs and build the best foundations for a better future. The right to HRE, and related potential content, is an aspect of this right to education.

States are duty bound, as stipulated in the UDHR, the International Covenant on Economic, Social and Cultural Rights, and in other human rights instruments, to ensure that education is aimed at strengthening respect for human rights and fundamental freedoms. HRE is an international movement to promote social change in accordance with the human rights values of freedom, equality, and justice through awareness about human rights and the procedures that exist for the redress of violations of these rights.

The United Nations defines HRE as,

> all educational, training, information, awareness-raising and learning activities aimed at promoting universal respect for and observance of all human rights and fundamental freedoms and thus contributing, inter alia, to the prevention of human rights violations and abuses by providing persons with knowledge, skills and understanding and developing their attitudes and behaviors, to empower them to contribute to the building and promotion of a universal culture of human rights. (United Nations General Assembly, 2011, Art. 2, para 1)

One of the outstanding outcomes of the efforts of human rights educators since the 1990s has been to reclaim the practice of human rights so that it is no longer the purview of only lawyers. This has come about through linking the message of human rights to social change efforts that are happening at the grassroots level in communities and through the socialization that takes place in schooling systems.

Beginning with the adoption of the UDHR in 1948, the United Nations and its specialized agencies formally recognized the right of citizens to be informed about the rights and freedoms contained in the documents ratified by their countries—the right to HRE itself. Since then, numerous policy documents developed by UN-affiliated agencies, international policymaking bodies, regional human rights bodies, and national human rights agencies have referenced HRE, proposing that human rights themes should be present in schooling.

Although in 1974 the United Nations Educational, Scientific and Cultural Organization (UNESCO) adopted a document explicitly supporting education for human rights (UNESCO, 1974), it took two more decades before interest in HRE would be revived in any serious manner within the United Nations. The World Conference on Human Rights, which took place in Vienna in 1993, is considered to be a landmark event for recognizing HRE and was followed by the establishment of the United Nations Decade for Human Rights Education 1995–2004 (United Nations General Assembly, 1994). In 2005, with the conclusion of the UN Decade for HRE, the Office of the UN High Commissioner for Human Rights launched an ongoing and more focused World Programme with a Plan of Action for Human Rights Education, which aspires to elicit improved cooperation from governments, as well as cross-cutting support from UN bodies (United Nations General Assembly, 2005). The first phase of the UN *World Programme for Human Rights Education* asks governments to ensure that HRE is integrated within the schooling sector (United Nations Office of the High Commissioner for Human Rights, 2005).

In 2011, the General Assembly passed the strongest policy instrument yet—the UN Declaration on Human Rights Education and Training (DHRET). Although falling short of establishing a judiciable right to education, the DHRET says: "Everyone has the right to know, seek and receive information about all human rights and fundamental freedoms and should have access to human rights education and training" (United Nations General Assembly, 2011, Art. 2, para 1). The Declaration also reaffirms that states have the primary responsibility to promote and ensure HRE, though in practice it is civil society organizations that have engaged most enthusiastically in HRE. Advances in international HRE policy are in large part due to the establishment of the Office of the UN High Commissioner for Human Rights in the mid-1990s and the launching of the Decade for Human Rights Education. These initiatives coincided with the strengthening of the human rights movement worldwide in the 1990s through a dramatic increase in the number of human rights organizations. Many of these nongovernmental organizations (NGOs) began to carry out human rights education and training, particularly in the immediate post-authoritarian environments of Central and Eastern Europe and South Africa. In the decade before in Latin America and the Philippines, grassroots organizations had been carrying out HRE in the nonformal education sector. These earlier experiences with popular education methodologies influenced international HRE practices, in particular through the writings of the Brazilian educator Paulo Freire.

Key Features of HRE

Human rights education and training comprise all educational, training, information, awareness raising, and learning activities aimed at promoting universal respect for and observance of all human rights and fundamental freedoms. HRE is strategically viewed as contributing to the prevention of human rights violations and abuses by providing persons with knowledge, skills, and understanding and by developing their attitudes and behaviors to empower them to contribute to the building and promotion of a universal culture of human rights (United Nations General Assembly, 2011, Art. 2, para 1). This definition is not specific to the school sector and, in fact, the United Nations proposes HRE for all sectors of society as well as part of a "lifelong learning" process for individuals (United Nations Office of the High Commissioner for Human Rights, 1997). This definition is quite broad, which can be seen as an asset, as human rights educators are then challenged to develop programming specifically suited for the learning environment where they are working.

This book illustrates such choices made by University of San Francisco graduate students working in educational settings from the primary school level to higher education. In chapter 5, Adamian demonstrates how the human rights lens can be brought into a seventh grade life science classroom by applying bioethics to core science concepts and using methodologies that reflect democratic practice. In chapter 10, Padilla presents the ways in which her community college sociology course adopts a human rights framework to engage students in service-learning activities with vulnerable populations. HRE encompasses education: (a) *about* human rights, which includes providing knowledge and understanding of human rights norms and principles, the values that underpin them and the mechanisms for their protection; (b) *through* human rights, which includes learning and teaching in a way that respects the rights of both educators and learners; and (c) *for* human rights, which includes empowering persons to enjoy and exercise their rights and to respect and uphold the rights of others (United Nations General Assembly, 2011, Art. 2, para 2). These three aspects of HRE emphasize that the processes of and conditions for teaching and learning are of equal importance in supporting the "learning" of human rights and the internalization and application of the associated values.

HRE has both legal and normative dimensions. The *legal dimension* deals with content about international human rights standards as embodied in the UDHR and in treaties and covenants to which countries subscribe. These standards encompass civil and political rights, as well as social, economic, and cultural rights. In recent years, as mentioned earlier, collective and environmental rights have been added to this evolving framework.

This law-oriented approach recognizes the importance of monitoring and accountability in ensuring that governments uphold the letter and spirit of human rights obligations.

The legal content can be introduced beginning in secondary school, although at the upper primary school level, children can be introduced to human rights in a developmentally appropriate manner: that they and all children have rights related to their human dignity that have been written into law in the Convention on the Rights of the Child (United Nations 1989), that their government has "signed up" for this treaty, and that it involves everyone knowing about children's rights and helping to promote them—including children in relation to their classmates and others in the school. In chapter 4, Brennan demonstrates how fiction and nonfiction readings carried out by young children can be used to foster discussion and understanding of basic needs and an adequate standard of living (UDHR, Article 25).

The normative content of HRE has to do with crosscutting principles that can be applied in the daily life of the school. Education should be provided in a way that is consistent with human rights, including equal respect for every child, opportunities for meaningful participation in decisions that affect their interests, freedom from all forms of violence, and respect for language, culture, and religion (UNICEF and UNESCO, 2011, p. 4). Schools and classrooms that embody HRE foster participation, self-expression, communication, cooperation and teamwork, and discipline processes that affirm the human dignity of students and educational personnel. The human rights principles of equality and nondiscrimination, participation and empowerment, as well as transparency and accountability, together constitute a value system that can be applied in daily practice in the classroom and in the policies and practices of the overall schooling system, as part of a rights-based approach.

HRE provides skills, knowledge, and motivation to individuals to transform their own lives and realities so that they reflect human rights norms and values. For this reason, interactive, learner-centered methods are widely promoted, consistent with the praxis of emancipatory and transformative education. The following pedagogies are representative of those promoted by HRE practitioners:

- *Experiential and activity-centered*: involving the solicitation of learners' prior knowledge and offering activities that draw out learners' experiences and knowledge
- *Problem-posing*: challenging the learners' prior knowledge
- *Participative*: encouraging collective efforts in clarifying concepts, analyzing themes, and engaging in the activities

- *Dialectical*: requiring learners to compare their perspectives and values with those offered by authoritative sources
- *Analytical*: asking learners to think about who benefits or is disadvantaged by values and practices found within culture and wider society
- *Healing*: promoting human rights in intrapersonal and interpersonal relations
- *Strategic thinking-oriented*: directing learners to set their own goals and to think of strategic ways to achieve them
- *Goal and action-oriented*: allowing learners to plan and organize actions in relation to their goals (Asia-Pacific Regional Resource Center for Human Rights Education, 2003).

HRE and Schools

Although the UN treaty system places the responsibility on governments for protecting, respecting, and fulfilling human rights, the UN definition of HRE suggests that it is the actions of individuals that contribute to building the "culture of human rights." It is bringing these values "down to earth" in the classroom and school setting that breathes life into human rights promises, because such values can be reflected immediately in our personal relationships. The promise of human rights, like that of peace, is one that can never be completely fulfilled. However, it can be approached step by step. This is the special responsibility of the educator: to recognize how human rights values can be promoted in teaching and learning processes—even in national environments where human rights abuses are glaringly apparent—and how to empower the learner with the hope and capacities to promote human dignity.

Perhaps the most prevalent form of HRE programming is aimed at the schooling sector, though it can take place informally with youth and vulnerable populations and within training programs geared for professionals, such as teachers. International governmental organizations and NGOs have since the 1990s engaged in HRE in the schooling sector in collaboration with the relevant departments of education. Increasing numbers of countries are reporting some degree of inclusion of HRE in national curriculum frameworks, though the quality and depth of implementation are rarely systematically studied.

In rare instances, courses with an explicit human rights focus are offered in a school curriculum, as is the case at the School of Education of the University of San Francisco (USF). More commonly, human rights themes are embedded within required or optional subjects, such as the humanities or social sciences, or linked with the theme of citizenship. Educational policies that identify and validate human rights include national curricular frameworks, which may link human rights values and associated civic and intercultural competencies; and special policies encouraging a "transversal" approach to human rights, with integration of human rights values into existing subjects and school practices. In many countries, ministries authorize HRE and allow teachers to address it in their open hours, according to their interests and often with the support of NGOs. Ideally, HRE is mandated and validated within required teaching, such as in South Africa.

In order to facilitate the inclusion of HRE in curriculum, core competencies for high schools were elaborated by the regional human rights and security organization, the OSCE Office for Democratic Institutions and Human Rights (OSCE ODIHR, 2012) in consultation with other inter-governmental bodies and HRE experts. Here is a sampling of these learner outcomes.

Knowledge/Understanding

- Core human rights standards, such as the UDHR and the UN Convention on the Rights of the Child (UNCRC). Depending upon the national context, the Convention Relating to the Status of Refugees might also be referenced, as well as specific rights such as the child's right to protection that apply in the contexts of conflict, disasters, and poverty.
- Critical human rights challenges in our schools, communities and societies, and factors that contribute to supporting/undermining the enjoyment of human rights.
- Current or historical human rights issues or movements in our own country context or the world, and individuals and groups that contributed to upholding human rights.

Attitudes/Values

- Respect for oneself and others based on the recognition of the dignity of all persons and of their human rights.
- Acceptance of and respect for persons of different race, color, language, age, disability, sex, gender, religion or belief, national, ethnic or social origin, property, and other differences, with awareness of one's own inherent prejudices and biases and endeavoring to overcome these.
- Openness to reflecting and learning so as to improve personal behaviors aligned with human rights principles.
- Compassion for and solidarity with those suffering human rights violations and those who are the targets of attacks resulting from injustice and discrimination.

Skills/Action

- Take an active part in discussions and debates, participating sensitively and constructively on controversial human rights topics.
- Identify and apply strategies for opposing all forms of discrimination and bullying.
- Network and collaborate with others in advocating for human rights.

These HRE learner outcomes can be used to influence the presence of HRE in school curriculum. Regardless of the presence of HRE in national or state curriculum, it is the educator who will decide the shape and practice of HRE. Many decisions need to be made. For example, across the wide range of human rights standards, which rights will be of greatest relevance and interest to students? How can human rights be introduced in such a way that it will "speak" to the values of learners and move them to promote and defend the principles that human rights represents? This was precisely the task posed to the educators enrolled in the HRE graduate course at USF, the results of which are presented in the forthcoming chapters. Before turning to these examples and discussion of the USF graduate program in chapter 2, the next section presents highlights of HRE efforts in the United States over the past 20+ years.

A Brief History of the US Human Rights Education Movement

US schools have traditionally provided students with an understanding of civil and political rights through the treatment of the Constitution and the Bill of Rights. US students will, over the course of their schooling, most likely learn about the Civil Rights Movement and possibly about other social movements, such as Women's Rights. This exposure to rights, however, is truncated from the broader range of rights found in the UDHR and international standards. People in the United States typically equate civil rights with human rights with no sense of how the international human rights system works or relates to life in their community.

Policy research carried out by HRE advocates within academia in the late 1990s confirmed what activists already knew a decade earlier: US schools had little curricular space for HRE. Banks' 2001 study revealed that fewer than half of all 50 states had mandates for the inclusion of human rights content in compulsory education. Moreover, many of these mandates were linked to curriculum subtopics (e.g., study of the Holocaust and genocides) that were more narrowly focused than the definition offered by the UN Office of the High Commissioner for Human Rights. No information existed on the amount of time individual classroom teachers actually devoted to human rights instruction, or the degree to which such instruction was informed by accurate and current information on the topic (Banks, 2001). In a subsequent study in the United States, Stone (2002) found that while the majority of states referenced human rights in their teaching standards, systematic integration of HRE rarely occurred in the nation's classrooms.

Domestic organizations eager to rectify this situation include a dedicated group of civil society organizations (including nonprofits, community service organizations, and faith-based organizations) and academics. In the early 1990s, the key organizations promoting HRE in the United States included Amnesty International-USA and their Human Rights Educators Network, the People's Decade for Human Rights Education, the Human Rights Center of the University of Minnesota, Minnesota Advocates for Human Rights, and Street Law, Inc. These organizations began to develop materials and organize trainings, formalizing a partnership in 1992 as a result of a national meeting organized by Shulamith Koenig, the executive director of the People's Decade for HRE, at Columbia University in New York City.

The North America Partners in Human Rights Education continued to network and share practices through the late 1990s, and their collaboration resulted in a Ford Foundation-supported grant to support HRE in the United States, called Human Rights USA. Through the efforts of the four key partners at Amnesty, the University of Minnesota HR Center, Street Law, and the newly founded National Center for HRE (supported by the People's Decade), four US cities participated in an intensive HRE program that included efforts in both the schooling system and community-based organizations. Between 1997 and 1999, numerous HRE activities took place in Atlanta, Georgia, Minneapolis, Minnesota, St. Louis, Missouri, and San Antonio, Texas, which strengthened the strategic planning efforts of the partner organizations.

In the late 1990s and early 2000s, new HRE actors emerged in the United States. Human Rights Education Associates (HREA), which had originally been established in the Netherlands, set up offices in the United States and linked up with existing North American HRE actors in the development of teaching and learning materials for US schools and the use of information and communication technologies for promoting HRE. The Global Human Rights Education listserv was launched by HREA in collaboration with the Human Rights Center of the University of Minnesota in 1999, followed soon after by the North American HRE listserv. Partly as a result of a national workshop organized for community-based organizations through the Human Rights US project, a new network was launched in 2003—US Human Rights Network. This network offers human rights education and training in the nonformal education sector as one strategy in promoting US accountability to international human rights standards.

Additional HRE actors began to emerge and organize within higher education. Following a 1999 HRE conference at the University of Dayton (Ohio), Professor Ted Orlin of Utica College established the International Human Rights Education Consortium. Originally organized to link up faculty members engaged in undergraduate or graduate level teaching of human rights, this consortium has since been expanded to include nonacademics interested in human rights education and research.

Since 2000, the concept of human rights has continued to spread as a way to analyze social issues and problems in the United States. Though not yet having a strong presence in state curriculum frameworks or teacher training institutions, an increasing number of educators and organizations associated with teaching for peace, social justice, global education, and citizenship education are linking up their efforts with human rights concepts and values. Nonprofits such as Facing History and Ourselves and World Savvy, among many others, are now incorporating human rights language within their efforts.

In September 2011, a landmark strategic planning event for HRE in the United States, similar to the one that took place in 1992 in New York City, was organized by HREA in conjunction with Harvard University in Cambridge, Massachusetts. The "Building a Strategy for HRE in U.S. Schools" conference attracted over 70 participants, including key nonprofits, academics from half a dozen universities (with a cohort from the University of San Francisco), and representatives from both teacher unions and teachers and students. The outcome was a draft national strategy and the establishment of the US Human Rights Educators Network (HRE USA), with nearly 500 individual and institutional members at the time this chapter was written. HRE USA is the next iteration of the HRE movement in the United States, forged out of a shared mission to promote the knowledge, understanding, and protection of human rights in the United States and abroad. HRE USA is engaged in a review and advocacy of the inclusion of HRE within state curriculum standards and the development of an online resource center to facilitate the identification of exemplary curriculum. In September 2014, HRE USA submitted a stakeholder report to the UN Office of the High Commissioner for Human Rights on the status of HRE in US schools, based on an online survey and series of civil society consultative meetings. This report can be found on the HRE USA website: www.hreausa.net. Such a network is only as strong as its members, and this book—which illustrates so well the efforts to craft HRE for US learners—will undoubtedly lend itself to this broader movement.

References

Asia-Pacific Regional Resource Center for Human Rights Education. (2003). What is human rights education? *Human Rights Education Pack*, pp. 22–25. Bangkok: ARRC.

Banks, D. (2001). *What is the state of human rights education in K-12 schools in the United States in 2000? A preliminary look at the national survey of human rights education*. Paper presented at the Annual Meeting of the American Educational Research Association, Seattle, WA. ERIC Document ED 454 134.

OSCE Office for Democratic Institutions and Human Rights (ODIHR). (2012). *Guidelines for human rights education in secondary schools*. Warsaw, Poland: OSCE Office for Democratic Institutions and Human Rights (ODIHR).

Stone, A. (2002). Human rights education and public policy in the United States. Mapping the road ahead. *Human Rights Quarterly* 24(2): 537–557.

UNESCO. (November 19, 1974). *UNESCO recommendation concerning education for international understanding, co-operation and peace and education related to human rights and fundamental freedoms*. Paris: United Nations.

UNICEF and UNESCO. (2007). *A human rights-base approach to education for all*. New York and Paris: UNICEF and UNESCO.

United Nations General Assembly. (November 20, 1989). *Convention on the Rights of the Child*. GA 44/25. Geneva: United Nations.

United Nations General Assembly. (December 23, 1994). *United Nations Decade for Human Rights Education*. GA 49/184. Geneva: United Nations.

United Nations General Assembly. (December 19, 2011). *United Nations Declaration on Human Rights Education and Training*. GA 66/127, Art. 2, para 1. Geneva: United Nations.

United Nations Office of the High Commissioner for Human Rights. (2005). *World Programme for Human Rights Education*. Geneva: United Nations.

United Nations Office of the High Commissioner for Human Rights. (1997). *International Plan of Action for the Decade for Human Rights Education*. New York and Geneva: United Nations.

CHAPTER 2

The Challenges and Triumphs of Teaching for Human Rights in US Schools

Susan Roberta Katz and Andrea McEvoy Spero

Critical Need for Human Rights Education (HRE) in the United States

Hamer Academy in East Oakland, California, was located only a few blocks from where Oscar Grant, a young unarmed man, was shot and killed by a local rapid transit police officer on January 1, 2009. For many youth, Grant's death represented the police profiling and abuse of power they witness every day. In the year preceding Grant's murder, 124 homicides were recorded, mostly in the area surrounding their school. At the same time, community resources were being depleted; for example, the school district cut its budget at the unprecedented amount of $100 million (Dolan, 2009). Like most young people of color from under-resourced communities in the US, East Oakland students face daily human rights violations, and yet exhibit sustained activism, hope, and resiliency. This spirit was evident at Hamer Academy in 2010 when students and teachers participated in a human rights education (HRE) project that culminated in a powerful three-hour school-wide performance on December 10, International Human Rights Day.

Through original poetry, spoken word, visual arts, music, and theater, the youth spoke truthfully of both the beauty and the pain of their lives, exposing human rights issues as close to home, not in far-away places. Scenes of violence were reenacted and photos of loved ones lost flashed by on the screen as the audience sat in absolute silence. Naja Hearron, a student performer, described her motivation, "I want them to know that this is every day, like it is stuff that is going on every day and people don't know that they have their rights" (Spero, 2012, p. 92). Naja's dedication echoed that of her fellow students who spoke about their pride in building awareness and sharing a message of hope. Through their performance, these young public intellectuals envisioned a future where their right to freedom, equality, dignity, and safety would be honored and protected.

Earlier that year in August, three social justice-oriented Hamer teachers—John Nepomuceno, Deborah Juarez, and Anita Gillian-Smiley—attended a three-day professional development workshop with The World As It Could Be (TWAICB) in partnership with the University of San Francisco (USF). TWAICB is a HRE program that supports Bay Area teachers and students in using performance arts to deepen understanding of the Universal Declaration of Human Rights (UDHR) (United Nations, 1948) and to become engaged in their communities to manifest the document's written principles (Rex Foundation, 2009). After their participation, the teachers committed to integrating human rights content using the performing arts during the academic year. During the summer institute, Andrea McEvoy Spero (2012), co-editor of this book, presented a historical reframing of human rights and civil rights in the United States. Afterward she decided to document the subsequent process at Hamer for her doctoral dissertation.

During the 2010 fall semester, Spero (2012) conducted her study through classroom observations and interviews with teachers and students. The study captured the transformative impact of connecting the UDHR, performing and visual arts, and classroom content. The lead teacher of the project, John, concluded his students had a stronger grasp of the seriousness and complexity of human rights because they could relate to the content on a personal level. He noted, "As a human being it enriched my understanding of what it is to be human" (Spero, 2012, p. 96). Another participating teacher, Deborah, claimed that knowing the 30 articles of the UDHR led to empowerment:

> It really does mean something for you to be told that you have Human Rights and that no one can take those rights away from you and especially if you are coming up in this community where people are getting killed right and left. (Spero, 2012, p. 104)

For the students, the UDHR provided a frame by which to examine injustice, and the performing arts offered a medium by which to develop and elevate their voices. The public performance became a moving testimonial of their experiences, knowledge, and message about how to create a community of human dignity.

However, the enthusiasm for the project did not negate the difficulties of implementing human rights content within institutional constraints. All three teachers reworked their curriculum to align the UDHR with California State Content Standards. For example, John's American Literature course required the reading of certain events of the twentieth century, including Apartheid and the Holocaust. He found entry points within the standards to highlight the UDHR and connect with students' lives. Like John, Deborah did not radically change her course content, but instead crafted human rights lessons around her existing goal of building literacy skills through social justice themes. Although teachers aligned the human rights project with the state standards, that same content was not included on the California High School Exit Exam (CAHSEE). Unfortunately, since Hamer Academy was under threat of consolidation due to low test scores, administrators tended to emphasize only the content included in the mandated test.

Within a few days of the human rights performance, a debrief meeting was called by Hamer Academy's principal. The meeting began with the principal requesting photos for a local newspaper article about the performance, followed by a lively discussion of its positive impact. The principal then interrupted the discussion by stating, "My feeling on this is that things have to stop this year because there is so much other academic things that need to happen...I do have to concern myself with the testing which will allow us to sink or swim and we are already sinking" (Spero, 2012, p. 77). The principal encouraged John to abandon the human rights project to focus on "CAHSEE boot camp." In an ironic twist, John's students ultimately scored higher on the CAHSEE than in the three previous years, which he deemed directly connected to student engagement in the human rights project. Despite increased scores, Hamer Academy was closed the following summer due to budget cuts.

The journey to Hamer Academy's culminating performance represents both the triumphs and hurdles of integrating HRE in US schools. Initially, the Hamer teachers admittedly knew little of the UDHR, human rights treaties, or HRE. Like many, they generally viewed human rights violations as outside the United States, despite first-hand experiences with poverty, violence, and discrimination. Once introduced to HRE, the teachers identified unique ways to engage their students by connecting human rights with the experiences of their lives. While the pressures of mandated curriculum, high stakes testing, and defunding of public schools create increasingly narrow moments to fully embody HRE, the endeavor is worthy of the struggle.

As Grace Lee Boggs (2011) affirms, our youth deserve and urgently need a different kind of education:

> Instead of trying to bully young people to remain in classrooms isolated from the community and structured to prepare them to become cogs in the existing economic system, we need to recognize that the reason why so many young people drop out from inner-city schools is because they are voting with their feet against an educational system that sorts, tracks, tests and rejects or certifies them like products of a factory because it was created for the age of industrialization. They are crying out for another kind of education that gives them opportunities to exercise their creative energies because it values them as whole human beings. (p. 49)

Like the Hamer Academy teachers, the contributors to this book share with honesty and passion their difficulties and moments of joy in bringing human rights to their classrooms. All authors of the pedagogical chapters are K-16 instructors who became motivated to teach for human rights while learning about HRE as graduate students at USF. Through courage and creativity, these educators put their students' lived experiences of human rights at the front and center of their pedagogy. In this way, they provide unique and exemplary models that can serve to overcome some of the challenges that too often block HRE in US schools.

Challenges to HRE in the United States

US Exceptionalism

Despite the potentially empowering force of HRE, the US government has been slow to support its integration into the educational system and lags behind its fellow UN members in developing and promoting HRE across formal schooling sectors. As described in the previous chapter, the United Nations adopted the Declaration on Human Rights Education and Training in 2011, after many years of grassroots efforts to ensure that people all over the world have access to HRE. This Declaration was further validation of the message originally given in the landmark Universal Declaration of Human Rights (1948), which recognized that teaching and learning were essential processes for promoting "respect for...rights and freedoms and by progressive measures, national and international, to secure their universal and effective recognition and observance" (Preamble). This means that governments are responsible for developing and carrying out a national plan for HRE. However, as of 2014, no coordinated effort exists in the United States at the state or federal level to implement such a pedagogical approach. The reasons behind this reluctance of the United States to support HRE are twofold: US "exceptionalism" and a neoliberal, market-economy approach to education.

US "exceptionalism" implies that human rights violations take place in other countries but never here in our own backyard. As Ignatieff (2006) describes,

> Americans don't see it this way, but the country with the most puzzling human rights record in the world is their own. The global ascendancy of human rights would not have happened without American leadership, yet the United States refuses to comply with important international covenants. Even as it criticizes the human rights records of dozens of countries, the United States resists when its own human rights performance—on capital punishment, for example—is called into question. (p. 383)

Ignatieff (2006) discusses a number of ways in which the United States refuses to be held accountable to international human rights standards, such as never signing international treaties like the Mine Ban Treaty and the US Senate not ratifying major agreements like the International Covenant on Economic, Social & Cultural Rights, the Convention on the Elimination of All Forms of Discrimination Against Women, and the Convention on the Rights of the Child (CRC)—the most widely ratified treaty in the UN system. In fact, the only country in the world that has *not* ratified the CRC is the United States, which does not have an officially recognized government.

Jenkins and Cox (2005) discuss the deep contradiction inherent in the central role the United States played, under the leadership of Eleanor Roosevelt, in the adoption of the UDHR in 1948. Ever since then the United States has used human rights principles more to criticize other governments rather than looking inward and applying them to its own practices. "One concern was the possibility that the Declaration's recognition of economic and social rights—the right to a job, education, adequate food, shelter and health care—could be used to expose the large holes in the US social safety net" (p. 25). Indeed addressing human rights issues at home would challenge the notion of US superiority that lies at the core of national identity, and in turn, leads to inequitable policies. The public's reluctance to accept international human rights treaties stems from a perceived sense of superiority based on the assumption that the United States has nothing to learn from the rest of the world (Cox and Thomas, 2007).

This phenomenon of "US exceptionalism" underlies the fact that very few people in the United States are familiar with the UDHR, let alone international human rights law, and that teachers are rarely trained in HRE, despite its popularity in other parts of the world (Bajaj, 2011; Ramirez, Suárez, and Meyer, 2007).

Neoliberal, Market-Economy Approach to Education

US exceptionalism in general and resistance to HRE in particular have a profound impact on education policy at all levels. Indeed, education (like health care) is increasingly regarded not as a right, but as a commodity to be bought and sold on the marketplace. As a result, the United States does not see itself as bound to safeguard or guarantee economic, social, and cultural rights, such as education, housing, and health care. Instead, it sees those as "aspirational goals," to which individuals are left on their own to achieve.

This view can be traced back to Cold War ideological disputes between primarily the United States and the Soviet Union that led to the creation of two international human rights treaties—the International Covenant of Civil and Political Rights (ICCPR) (1966), on the one hand, and the International Covenant on Economic, Social and Cultural Rights (ICESCR) (1966), on the other. Those who advocated for economic and cultural rights, such as the National Association for the Advancement of Colored People (NAACP), were under constant threat of being labeled "communist." President Jimmy Carter actually supported economic, social, and cultural rights, leading him to sign the ICESCR in 1978, but failed to gain support in the Senate for ratification. Yet when Ronald Reagan was elected president two years later, his administration actively opposed international treaties requiring US compliance with human rights, especially economic rights (Alston, 2008). The failure to recognize and embrace economic, social, and cultural rights as foundational to democracy paved the way for a rise of capitalist models imposed on public services like education.

Consequently, US federal policy has adopted a market-driven approach toward education that has led to neoliberal "reforms" such as school choice and accountability measures based solely on standardized test scores. This approach suppresses the right to education (UDHR Article 26) that calls for the "development of the human personality." In fact, over the past decade, US public schools have faced increased pressure to adhere to scripted curriculum and testing under such federal policies as No Child Left Behind and Race to the Top. As of Summer 2014, 44 of 50 states have adopted Common Core State Standards, national standards that identify learning goals and grade-level benchmarks. Districts are required to implement new computer-based assessment tools without the time or resources for professional development and, in many cases, without the adequate technology to administer the tests. Schools in high-poverty, underserved communities will be at greatest risk of low scores, which in turn can lead to severe consequences, such as the school closure of Hamer Academy discussed earlier.

Identifying as a Human Rights Educator

The combination of deeply ingrained US exceptionalism and consequences of neoliberal educational policy has produced significant top-down pressures inhibiting HRE curriculum and practice in US schools. Despite these obstacles, a growing number of teachers are embracing human rights teaching and learning and, as a result, have contributed to an HRE movement from the ground up. Often, those already engaged in social justice, multicultural, and anti-racist educational practices find alignment with the values and vision of HRE. Through critical pedagogy, these teachers engage students in critiquing economic, political, and social inequality and aim to amplify the voices of underrepresented minorities. Grant and Gibson (2013) describe how human rights can be an important sibling to social justice:

> The most fundamental way that social justice movements align with a human rights framework is in their constant demands for the economic and social rights guaranteed in the UDHR: equal pay for equal work, living wages, adequate health care, social support for the impoverished, equitable and meaningful education, and reducing the gap between rich and poor. (p. 91)

Similarly, the editors and contributors of this book discovered that not only did human rights principles align with our teaching philosophy, but also the international human rights legal framework validated the economic and social issues inherent in social justice teaching.

Social justice educators, highly aware of the intersectionality of political, economic, and social inequalities, find that using international human rights laws can provide a codified framework to link local struggles with global movements. Social justice and human rights educators also encounter common ground in the inherent potential of knowledge and skills to transform current conditions through collective action. The ultimate goal of HRE and social justice education is empowerment. Contrary to the common misperception that HRE is the study of human rights violations outside the United States, the fundamental purpose of HRE is to develop the requisite knowledge and skills to create communities of human dignity (Flowers, 2000). In other words, teachers and students learn about human rights history, legal documents, implementation mechanisms, and the interdependence of civil, political, social, cultural, and economic rights with the intention of acting in defense of human dignity. As Article 2 of the UN Declaration of Human Rights Education and Training (United Nations, 2011) states: effective HRE embraces three essential objectives: (1) providing knowledge *about* human rights, (2) learning and teaching *through* human rights in a respectful way for all parties, and (3) educating *for* human rights with the goal of empowerment.

Many teachers, especially those who identify with a social justice philosophy, are highly motivated to include human rights in their curriculum, but unfortunately lack professional development opportunities to deepen their understanding of human rights content and methodology. For example, Gerber (2008) found that secondary teachers in Boston, Massachusetts, integrated human rights content into their classrooms with a great deal of passion. Nevertheless, they struggled with their inadequate knowledge of international human rights history and treaties, unclear understandings of HRE, as well as being constrained by a crowded, state-mandated curriculum. As evident from Gerber's (2008) study and the co-editors' observations, many teachers want to bring human rights into their classrooms but lack professional development and exemplary models of HRE. Similarly, Flowers and Shiman (1997) stress, "The teacher education program itself must stand for human rights principles in an explicit, public way. It needs to encourage students to see themselves as human rights educators and to urge them to act accordingly" (p. 164).

When we combine the lack of coordinated efforts to implement HRE, high-stakes testing, mandated curriculum, and insufficient knowledge of human rights history and legal mechanisms, the road ahead seems fraught with obstacles. However, when we recognize that many educators are eager to build their understanding of HRE and embrace a pedagogy that encourages teaching and learning *about, through,* and *for* human rights, the possibility of transformation emerges (Flowers, 2004). Preparing educators in HRE theory and practice requires schools of education to embrace the challenge—a challenge not without unique rewards and difficulties.

Graduate Studies in HRE at USF

The story of the evolution of the HRE graduate program at USF provides a case study that can offer hope and inspiration to those seeking to implement HRE. This is particularly important since neoliberal pressures have constrained higher education similarly to K-12 schools, causing HRE to be extremely rare in teacher education. USF is a Jesuit Catholic institution with an explicit commitment to social justice, which creates a unique space for developing curriculum and pedagogy based on social justice and human rights. At times this space contains its own internal contradictions in that "social justice" can be interpreted as "doing good for others" rather than working in solidarity with oppressed peoples for the liberation of all. As a private institution, USF charges high tuition yet offers relatively little financial aid, especially for graduate students, since the university is justifiably dedicated to providing access to first-generation undergraduate students. Yet despite these contradictions, the commitment to diversity in hiring and admissions, the public stance against global injustice and poverty, and the strong value placed on ethical actions blend to create an environment conducive to progressive programs.

Within USF are programs with an impressive history of a commitment to social justice teaching. One example is the Department of International & Multicultural Education (IME) in the USF School of Education that was founded in 1974 by faculty like Professor Alma Flor Ada with strong ties to Paulo Freire, father of critical pedagogy. In 2005 IME professor, Susan Katz, participated in a summer seminar on Human Rights Across the Disciplines, taught by two New York University (NYU) international human rights law professors. When Karen Robinson, formerly education director of Amnesty International, spoke on the last day about the need to bring human rights into the field of education, Susan was inspired to explore the possibility of moving toward that direction at USF. Previously, she had always identified as a social justice educator, yet this intensive seminar revealed how a human rights framework could add both depth and breadth to social justice work by linking local and global experiences.

The IME Department was receptive to the idea of piloting courses in HRE and was situated in an unusual position to do so with its foundation in critical pedagogy. Since IME is unique in the School of Education by offering MA and EdD degrees but not credentials, it enjoys the academic freedom of not being bound to state mandates. Also, the department had just created a new position in Global Studies in 2005, which led to hiring Professor Shabnam Koirala-Azad (now associate dean of the School of Education), who brought expertise in transnational research and became instrumental in the development of the HRE program. In 2006 Susan and Shabnam began collaborating with USF faculty cross-campus who were integrating human rights into their curriculum, and in 2007, both were awarded fellowships from the USF Center for Law & Global Justice that supported their respective research studies.

Course in HRE: Pedagogy and Praxis

In Spring 2007, Professor Katz piloted a new course in HRE, based on the premise that learning about human rights is the first step toward respecting, promoting, and defending those rights. Designed to support teachers of kindergarten through college, as well as educators working in nonformal settings such as community organizations, this course aims to facilitate the teaching of human rights through modeling best practices, such as the use of literature, visual and performing arts, interactive curriculum, and community activism (Katz, 2009).

To demonstrate HRE principles, this course has always focused on several different case studies intertwined with racism, discrimination against women and children, and poverty that are analyzed from a human rights perspective. For the Spring 2007 pilot course, the case studies were: (1) "war on terror" and its implications in unlawful practices such as extraordinary renditions and use of torture post 9/11; (2) immigration rights and militarization of the US–Mexico border; (3) injustice against African Americans as manifested in neglect and displacement after Hurricane Katrina; and (4) genocide in Darfur. Each year these issues are modified to respond to changing realities. For example, the most recent course focused on criminal injustice in the United States, indigenous rights and environmental justice, Lesbian Gay Bisexual Transgender Queer (LGBTQ) street youth, and children's rights in Occupied Palestine. For the final project, students are required to select a particular human rights issue, discuss the relevant international human rights agreements, and develop an effective pedagogical tool to train others about that issue.

After the 2007 pilot, Katz was awarded a USF Human Rights Collaborative Research Fellowship to conduct a small research study of the HRE course. She conducted focus group interviews with all 18 enrolled graduate students as well as analyzed class videotapes and written responses to discussion forums. The students' responses were overwhelmingly positive about the value of the course, expressing that their new knowledge of human rights helped them to better understand current events, improve their teaching, reshape their own research studies from a human rights lens, and become more involved in their communities. The students' primary recommendation was to expand the course to two semesters so that the legal framework of international human rights could be addressed and covered in depth. This recommendation was then implemented in Fall 2008 by expanding the HRE course into two distinct courses: International Human Rights Law for Educators and Human Rights Education: Pedagogy and Praxis (Dixon, Katz, and Schiller, 2011; Fuentes, Koirala-Azad, and Katz, 2012).

Development of the Graduate Program in HRE

Based upon this positive affirmation of the impact of HRE and in consultation with USF faculty in the Human Rights Working Group, Professors Katz and Koirala-Azad received a USF Jesuit Foundation pedagogical grant in Spring 2008 to develop an HRE concentration in the MA and doctoral programs of four courses (12 units): Human Rights Education: Pedagogy and Praxis, International Human Rights Law for Educators, Gender and Globalization, and Immigration and Forced Displacement. This opportunity and institutional support was central to IME launching the first graduate concentration in HRE in the United States in Fall 2008.

Since the inception of the HRE concentration in 2008, IME has witnessed a steady increase in the number of total applicants as well as of enrolled students opting for the concentration. The program seems to have tapped into a well of interest in HRE that had been lying dormant. Between 2008 and 2010, the number of master's and doctoral students choosing the HRE concentration increased fivefold. Currently, over half of all IME master's and about 30 percent of doctoral students are enrolled in the HRE concentration. In fact, the response has been so enthusiastic that we have outgrown what we started. All IME faculty have been involved in developing and offering HRE courses, such as Social Movements and Human Rights taught by Professor Emma Fuentes, Human Rights in the Media by Professor Betty Taylor, and Graphic Novels and Human Rights by Professor Stephen Cary. In addition, leading human rights experts, Dr. Charlie Clements of Harvard University and Felisa Tibbitts (author of chapter 1) have served as visiting faculty in teaching Tools for Human Rights Practice.

Given this growth, as of Fall 2013 we have moved from offering a concentration of four courses to a full-fledged MA degree program in HRE under the direction of renowned HRE scholar, Professor Monisha Bajaj, who previously developed a concentration in Peace and Human Rights Education at Teachers College, Columbia University. As of Fall 2014, she is teaching a new foundational course, HRE: History, Philosophy and Current Debates, to complement HRE: Pedagogy and Praxis so that students can explore both theoretical and pedagogical aspects of HRE in more depth than previously possible in only a one-semester course. Furthermore, under the leadership of Dean Kevin Kumashiro, who came to USF in Fall 2013, we have witnessed continuing and deepening support of HRE and look forward to its further evolution. The growth and enthusiasm for the HRE program at USF illustrates the possibilities to develop human rights teachers in the United States despite the ever-present exceptionalism and pressures on teachers in the field.

Introduction to Pedagogical Chapters

From 2007 to 2014, hundreds of USF graduate students have taken the HRE: Pedagogy and Praxis course and many have implemented their final projects in their own classrooms or communities. The projects represent how teachers who once identified as social justice educators found the transformative potential of the HRE framework. The final project for the course has been to develop a research-based pedagogical tool about a particular human rights issue of their choice that students could then share in an interactive way in their own professional setting. After teaching this course for six years, Susan Katz has witnessed many students carry out their projects in powerful ways in their classrooms and communities, motivating her to take the next step toward publication. This book is a compilation of ten examples of final projects that were selected because they have been effectively implemented in a range of classrooms, from primary grades up through university, mostly in urban settings in northern California. Many have made a profound impact on students and fellow teachers, and some have even been adopted on a school- or district-wide level. What these contexts share is that the students are primarily young people of color exposed for the first time to thinking about their own lives and the world through an empowering human rights lens.

In each pedagogical chapter, these educators describe how they guided their students through phases of examining the systems that cause and perpetuate oppression and exploring possible actions to defend human rights. In doing so, students uncovered their own agency to disrupt cycles of oppression and work toward a more just community. These lessons illuminate the recommendations of UN programs and HRE scholars as well as the emerging, dynamic field of HRE in the United States. These are not simply academic exercises. The curriculum and pedagogical methods in this book reveal the transformative potential of HRE in action as part of the struggle for human dignity. The editors hope that these chapters provide models for other educators who are seeking ways to be bold and take a stand for HRE.

References

Alston, P. (2008). Putting economic, social and cultural rights back on the agenda of the United States. In W. F. Schulz (ed.) *The future of human rights: U.S. policy for a new era*, pp. 120–138. Philadelphia, PA: University of Pennsylvania Press.

Bajaj, M. (2011). Human rights education: Ideology, location, and approaches. *Human Rights Quarterly* 33: 481–508.

Boggs, G. L. (2011). *The next American revolution: Sustainable activism for the twenty-first century*. Berkeley, CA: University of California Press.

Cox, L. and Thomas, D. (2007). Yes, we're ready! Human rights advocacy. *Yes!* 41: 46–49.

Dixon, O., Katz, S., and Schiller, J. (2011). Putting the emphasis on human rights in a post-9/11 world: Human rights education at the University of San Francisco. *Faculty Resource Network Online Journal.* http://www.nyu.edu/frn/publications/engaging.students/Dixon.Katz.Schiller.html.

Dolan, M. (2009, March 29). Oakland has been defined by violence, but its true identity is more complicated. *The Los Angeles Times.* Retrieved February 20, 2012, http://articles.latimes.com/2009/mar/29/local/me-oakland29/

Flowers, N. (2000). *The human rights education handbook: Effective practices for learning, action, and change.* Minneapolis, MN. Human Rights USA Resource Center.

Flowers, N. (2004). How to define human rights education?—A complex answer to a simple question. In V. B. Georgi and M. Seberich (eds.) *International perspectives in human rights education*, pp. 105–127. Gutersloh, DE: Bertelsman Foundation Publishers.

Flowers, N. and Shiman, D. (1997). Teacher education and the human rights vision. In G. J. Andreopoulos and R. P. Claude (eds.) *Human rights education for the twenty-first century*, pp. 161–175. Philadelphia, PA: University of Pennsylvania Press.

Fuentes, E. H., Koirala-Azad, S., and Katz, S. R. (2012). Peace profile: Graduate studies in human rights education: Extending the social justice discourse in education. *Peace Review* 24(2): 114–121.

Gerber, P. (2008). *From convention to classroom: The long road to human rights education.* Saarbrucken, Germany: VDM Verlag.

Grant, C. A. and Gibson, M. L. (2013). "The path of social justice:" A human rights history of social justice education. *Equity and Excellence in Education* 46(1): 81–99.

Ignatieff, M. (2006). No exceptions? The United States pick-and-choose approach to human rights. In R. P. Claude and B. Weston (eds.) *Human rights in the world community: Issues and action*, pp. 383–389. Philadelphia, PA: University of Pennsylvania Press.

Jenkins, A. and Cox, L. (2005). Bringing human rights home. *The Nation* June 27, 2005: 27–29.

Katz, S. R. (2009). Human rights education: Concepts and pedagogies. *Human rights education in the school systems of Europe, Central Asia and North America: A compendium of good practice.* Human Rights Education Associates, OSCE/ODIHR, Council of Europe, and UNESCO.

Ramírez, F. O., Suárez, D., and Meyer, J. W. (2007). The worldwide rise of human rights education. In A. Benavot and C. Braslavsky (eds.) *School knowledge in historical and comparative Perspective: Changing curricula in primary and secondary education*, pp. 35–54. Hong Kong: Comparative Education Research Centre and Springer.

Rex Foundation. (2009). *The World as It Could Be Human Rights Education Program and Goals.* San Francisco, CA: Rex Foundation.

Spero, A. M. (2012). *"This is a public record": Teaching human rights through the performing arts*. Unpublished doctoral dissertation, University of San Francisco.

United Nations. (1948). *Universal Declaration of Human Rights*. Retrieved from http://www.un.org/en/documents/udhr/index.shtml.

United Nations. (2011). *United Nations Declaration on Human Rights Education and Training*. Retrieved from http://www.hre202 0.org/UN-Declaration-on-Human-Rights-Education-and-Training.

PART II

Pedagogical Tools

CHAPTER 3

Each One, Teach One: The History and Legacy of the Black Panther Party for an Elementary School Audience

Jessie Blundell

The well-manicured grounds of a Jesuit university are hardly the place you might expect to meet someone accused of murder, unless that person is Richard Brown, a human rights activist and advocate, and unless the charges were lies, carefully crafted to maintain centuries-old systems of oppression. Then again, Jesuits consider themselves contemplatives in action, and can be found around the world wherever the meanest, most severe human rights offenses occur. In that way, perhaps my initial meeting with Mr. Brown makes sense. This chapter begins with the gentleman so accused, a teacher in a graduate school human rights education (HRE) class, and some unexpected common ground. In it you will find a curriculum for teaching about the Black Panther Party (BPP) for Self Defense and a piece of the party's legacy, the Campaign to Free the San Francisco (SF8). This history remains relevant today and is a vital piece of our collective cultural inheritance.

When I first met Richard Brown in 2011, he had been twice wrongly accused of the same murder. The original case had been dismissed more than 30 years before, the judge citing evidence that police officers in New Orleans used torture to secure the defendants' confessions. The Grand Jury had expired on the second case, freeing Mr. Brown from a month in prison for contempt of court; he had refused to testify. We met at the University of San Francisco (USF), where Mr. Brown was presenting a high school HRE curriculum about the Campaign to Free the SF 8. Listening to him speak, I began to reflect on my own formal education and how little of it had included HRE. My thoughts turned to my daughter and to my students. I knew in my heart that Mr. Brown's story and curriculum needed to reach a younger audience. The unit in this chapter is a modified and expanded version of the original curriculum, written for an elementary school audience.

Mr. Brown's life had run such a different trajectory than mine, and prior to meeting we were separated by different and intersecting systems of oppression. Our paths crossed on the common ground of HRE. HRE has the power to create coalition in places of difference and isolation, and it can be used as a proactive and emancipatory response to tragedy. In my life as a teacher and a student, Mr. Brown created a bridge between the theory and practice of HRE. With gratitude and humility, I dedicate this chapter to him.

History and Context

Disempowering and Discrediting Struggles for Human Rights

The United States has a long history of disempowering and discrediting struggles for human rights. This is done in part by focusing intently on one subsection of rights: civil and political rights. The reasons for this are complex and have as much to do with the politics of the Cold War as they do with maintaining systems of oppression here at home. What gets lost in this partition of human rights includes economic, social, and cultural rights. The National Association for the Advancement of Colored People (NAACP) was an early victim of this type of political maneuvering (Anderson, 2003).

At its inception in 1909, the NAACP advocated for human rights as a means of addressing the legacy of slavery and Jim Crow. However, as time went by it became beholden to certain political alliances, such as those with Eleanor Roosevelt and Harry S. Truman. These relationships required the NAACP to jettison its original human rights mission for the narrow band of political and civil rights prescribed by the US government (Anderson, 2003). This capitulation left a hole in the Black Left, into which the BPP proudly stepped.

The year was 1966. Malcolm X had been assassinated less than a year before, and Martin Luther King Jr. would die in two years time. The Vietnam War was nearing its peak, and the race riots in Watts were capturing national attention. It was a time of political unrest, and in Oakland, California, two Merritt College students, Huey Newton and Bobby Seale, were set to write their own chapter on human rights advocacy. I would not be born for another decade, and I would not begin to learn the full history of this time for another 30 years.

The Black Panther Party

A year after its inception, the BPP published the Ten Point Program which called for "Land, Bread, Housing, Education, Clothing, Justice and Peace" (Abu-Jamal, 2004, pp. 97–100). The organization then went about addressing these concerns. To address the issues of peace and justice, the BPP first organized a community police force to document and impede police brutality (Spencer, 2008). A community newspaper followed, "calling on Black men and women on the scene...to step out front and do what is necessary" (Spencer, 2008, p. 93). The necessary work included securing not only civil rights, but also the full range of human rights due to all peoples. To address the "bread" issue, the BPP opened a free breakfast program for African American children in Oakland. This program was the model for the free and reduced-fee food programs that now exist in all public schools. Other community programs included free clothing, shoe, and food programs; the intercommunal news service and youth institute; cooperative housing programs and child development centers; medical, employment and legal clinics; and transportation services for the elderly and those visiting incarcerated family members.

With its practical and potent human rights agenda, well-articulated demands, and growing body of political coalitions, the BPP soon met with violent opposition by the police. In 1968 Oakland Police killed a young unarmed BPP member, Bobby Hutton. By 1969, 28 Black Panthers had been killed by the police, and the Federal Bureau of Investigation's (FBI) Counter Intelligence Program (COINTELPRO) had issued their now infamous "prevent the rise of a messiah" memorandum (Abu-Jamal, 2004). In this memo, the FBI set explicit long-term goals to obstruct "militant black nationalist groups" from forming coalitions, prevent the rise of a messiah, and curtail the BPP's ability to gain respectability and attract young people (Abu-Jamal, 2004, p. 263). Under the auspices of COINTELPRO, the FBI would use violence and infiltration to cause ruinous internal conflict, creating a devastating climate of fear and mistrust throughout the BPP (Berger, 2009). The US government felt this movement was important enough to destroy, and after meeting Richard Brown, I felt compelled to push back against that destruction.

HRE and the Attempts to Refashion Our Collective Memory

When textbooks neglect the full truth of history, entire chapters are left unwritten and unread. This is what has happened with the Civil Rights Era in US history. Flowers (2003) claims that in higher education, the focus of HRE remains on values rather than outcomes. Definitions of HRE from academics tend to reflect the theory and practice of critical pedagogy developed by Freire (2008) and Boal (2000). Though popular education can be transformative, I know from experience that it can also be difficult to translate in the context of an urban public school. Constraints of time and money, and limited or nonexistent access to high-quality HRE curricula—to say nothing of administrative approval—stymie many a would-be human rights educator. To circumvent these stumbling blocks, educators tend to focus on ways to embed HRE within existing curricula. Flowers (2003) criticizes educators and academics for this polarizing of HRE by "erring on the one hand into soaring idealism and on the other into a constrained accommodation to the status quo" (p. 12). To address this critique of the HRE status quo, the unit in this chapter attempts to bridge idealism to practice by focusing on a human rights organization from the time known as the Civil Rights Era.

Since the establishment of the Department of Homeland Security in 2002, the US government has reopened many Civil Rights Era court cases. These include high-profile cases of both white supremacists and members of the Black Power Movement. Berger (2009) argues that this is an attempt by the state to refashion our collective memory of that time by positioning both the Ku Klux Klan and the Black Power Movement as isolated extremist groups. By prosecuting these cases many decades later, the US government has been able to position both white supremacy and the BPP out of context, discarding the human rights history that frames and makes sense of these polar opposites.

Berger (2009) notes several important differences between the cases. In the white supremacy cases, the defendants have been elderly white men and women who have lived their adult lives outside penal institutions. These leaders and ideologues are prosecuted without reference to the economic, political, and social climate that both facilitated and justified their racist words and deeds. The public may then feel vindicated without undue self-reflection on the persistence of race-based systems of inequity and our role in maintaining them. In the case of Black power, the defendants are elderly Black men with a record of incarceration, who in some cases have remained in prison for decades. These activists and community advocates are prosecuted without reference to the economic, political, and social climate that both incited and criminalized their human rights agenda. Berger notes that former members of the Black Power Movement are also more often tried for conspiracy. An accusation of conspiracy requires a lower standard of evidence than other crimes and makes it easier to reach a guilty verdict. In the end, former members of the Black Power Movement tend to receive more and longer sentences for lesser crimes, when compared to the trials and verdicts of white supremacists.

Berger (2009) argues that by trying these cases in the twenty-first century, the US government is reshaping the Civil Rights Era as case closed. This act ignores the government's historical support of white supremacy groups like the KKK, or the institutional racism that gave rise to the Civil Rights Movement, to the leadership of Martin Luther King Jr. and Malcolm X, and to the grassroots activism of groups like the BPP. It portrays the state as both righting past wrongs, and seeking justice on its own behalf, from the criminal activity of extremists on both ends of the spectrum (Berger, 2009). This obscures both the historic role the state played in exonerating the actions of white supremacists and the role it continues to play by oppressing the human rights agenda of community organizations and educators in the United States. As Berger states,

> These high profile cases from a volatile, and recent, time provide the raw material relied on to construct a usable past. Triumph and tragedy present fertile territory for exploring the shaping and significance of collective memory, and digging up old murder cases uses the courts as a way to make triumph out of tragedy. (p. 3)

The SF8 is one such case.

The Campaign to Free the SF8

To understand this history it is important to frame the Free the SF 8 campaign as a human rights campaign. The Universal Declaration of Human Rights (UDHR) (United Nations, 1948) is a human rights document that articulates the injustices suffered by the SF8. Article 2 of the UDHR states that all human beings are born free and equal in dignity and rights. If this right were equally protected in the United States, the BPP would have had no reason to exist. Article 2 states that these rights are guaranteed without regard to race, color, political, or other opinion. Reports from COINTELPRO make it clear that basic human rights for Americans of African descent are neither guaranteed nor encouraged. Article 5 promises that no one shall be subjected to torture, cruel, or inhuman treatment, and Article 6 maintains that no one shall be subjected to arbitrary arrest or detention. The brief history of the SF8 that follows makes it clear that the New Orleans and San Francisco police departments neglected both of these articles. These most basic of human rights, outlined in the UDHR, were the ones violated, repeatedly, in the case of the SF8.

In 1971, New Orleans police arrested nine men known as Black Panthers. Hoping to bring charges against the men for the 1971 murder of a San Francisco police sergeant, John Young, San Francisco Police Department (SFPD) inspectors Frank McCoy and Ed Erdelatz arrived in New Orleans and interrogated three of the men but failed to extract confessions. After refusing to confess, the three men were tortured by members of the New Orleans police force for several days. Using confessions and statements made by the men during their torture, McCoy and Erdelatz indicted the three men in 1974. After exposing the cruel and illegal circumstances under which the confessions were made, the defense in the case motioned to dismiss the indictments. A San Francisco judge granted these motions in 1975 and 1976, and the case lay dormant until 2001 (Andres, Claude, and The Freedom Archives, 2005).

Though retired from the SFPD, after September 11 former inspectors McCoy and Ederlatz were deputized as Homeland Security agents and given a budget with which to reopen the case (Free the SF8, 2008). The two deputies began to visit eight of the men originally arrested in 1971. (Two of the original men, Herman Bell and Jalil Muntaqim, were serving life sentences in the New York State prison system on different charges. One man, Ronald Stanley Bridgeforth, was missing. Another, John Bowman, passed away in 2007.) The deputies also visited the men's neighbors, families, and places of employment, asking probing questions under the guise of investigating "white activists" from the 1960s (Free the SF8, 2008). When these interviews failed to reveal any new evidence, the six men were subpoenaed to federal and state grand juries and forced to submit fingerprints and DNA samples. When they refused to give testimony, the men were jailed in San Francisco for civil contempt (Andres, Claude, and The Freedom Archives, 2005).

After the Grand Jury expired in 2005, six of the SF8 came together to create the Committee for the Defense of Human Rights (CDHR). Richard Brown was part of this committee, and his work on a high school HRE curriculum caught the attention of my USF professor who invited Mr. Brown to speak to our class. From the moment Richard began, I knew his message needed to reach a wider audience of youth.

As an elementary school teacher, I believe the intellectual capacity of young children is often underestimated. In my experience, even children in preschool demonstrate a sophisticated sense of fairness. The curriculum developed by the Free the SF8 campaign is for secondary students and contains graphic material inappropriate for young children. Keeping close to the spirit of the original documents, and including additional materials on the history of the BPP, I created the unit described in the remainder of this chapter.

Conclusion

In our collective national memory of the Civil Rights Era, we carefully enshrine the triumphs and select memories of popular figures such as Rosa Parks and Ruby Bridges. This one-dimensional approach obscures the complexity of the time, the people, and the history. It also leads our students to the conclusion that everything turned out for the better, which as those of us committed to urban education know, is a fallacy. Our public schools are more segregated than before the landmark 1954 *Brown v Board of Education* case that desegregated public education (Orfield, Bachmeier, James, and Eitle, 1997). The life expectancy of African Americans has declined since the Civil Rights Era, and the African American prison population has grown exponentially (Bell, 2006; Wacquant, 2002). As educators, it is imperative to preserve the history of our human rights tragedies and the continued struggle to gain justice. We can do this by expanding our collective memory to include full and accurate histories of individuals and organizations. We can and must challenge the master narrative that divorces the Civil Rights Era from the larger and current struggle for human rights.

The BPP fought fearlessly for human rights. They pushed relentlessly outside the bounds of the more cautious, less comprehensive organizations within the Civil Rights Movement. Because they demanded real and revolutionary—rather than symbolic—change, BPP members became prime targets for government-sponsored retaliation and the movement was eventually destroyed. The history of the United States, and of human rights, is incomplete without giving this tragedy its own chapter.

As an educator in the San Francisco Bay Area, it feels particularly relevant to create curriculum about the BPP. When this unit was conceived in 2009, it also felt incredibly timely to address the legacy of the Black Power, a movement so powerful that its former members were still considered something of a threat, so powerful that two San Francisco police inspectors would come out of retirement to reopen a closed case. By 2011 the charges against all of the SF8 had been dropped. Richard Brown has retired from his work at the Ella Hill Hutch Community Center, and the Common Core has changed the field of public education in California. My hope is that this curriculum, like the history itself, continues to remain relevant.

Pedagogical Tool

The School Site

Implemented in a second-grade classroom at the Harvey Milk Civil Rights Academy (HMCRA), the instructional goal of this unit was to make the history, significance, and legacy of the BPP accessible to young children. HMCRA is a public school in the San Francisco Unified School District. The school lies in the heart of the Castro neighborhood and is named for the tireless activist and first openly gay city supervisor of San Francisco, who was assassinated in 1978. The Castro is home to a large and politically active gay, lesbian, bisexual and trans community. Historically, this community has maintained many human rights-based political coalitions, including one with the BPP. This is illustrated in the following quote from "A Letter from Huey Newton to the Revolutionary Brothers and Sisters about the Women's Liberation and Gay Liberation Movements" (Blasius and Phelan, 1997):

> We must gain security in ourselves and therefore have respect and feelings for all oppressed people,... I know through reading, and through my life experience and observations that homosexuals are not given freedom and liberty by anyone in the society. They might be the most oppressed people in the society. (Newton, as cited in Blasius and Phelan, 1997, p. 405)

This shared history provided a foundation from which to build the unit in this chapter.

The school itself offered something of an incubator for my ideas. While I believe that the history and important legacy of the BPP can and should be taught to youth everywhere, I also recognize that teaching this unit at this particular school was a somewhat insulated exercise. Not only did I have administrative, staff, and parent support, but also I was building on a shared vocabulary of civil rights held by the students. The contexts of other places with different histories or more restrictive political environments will need to be navigated by educators who choose to teach this content.

Classroom Context

At HMCRA there is no set civil rights curriculum, but certain educators at the school do create and teach this type of content. When I developed this unit, I was working at HMCRA as a literacy specialist. My daughter's teacher graciously allowed me a week's worth of hour-long lessons to pilot the unit. She found it a useful addition to her existing civil rights curriculum and appreciated many content areas embedded in the unit. It also felt important to her that the BPP modeled a local example of human rights activism and organizing.

The classroom teacher observed that students in her class were particularly engaged in the unit. This included her focal students: a second-language learner and two students with exceptional needs, one high performing and one who had not yet reached grade-level academic expectations. It also included a girl in whom the teacher noticed a discrepancy between academic potential and engagement. Several factors may have contributed to the increased engagement. The unit included relevant content for students in the class whose families are active in progressive politics in the San Francisco Bay Area. It also included photographs, stories, and history of human rights activists who identify as Black, and therefore shared common cultural ground with many of the students in the class. Finally, the unit included opportunities for movement, collaboration, and creativity, appealing to students with kinesthetic, visual/spatial, and interpersonal strengths. Most likely it was some combination of these factors, as well as a break from the usual routine, that caused increased student engagement during the unit.

Professional Resources

Several professional resources inform my current thinking about teaching and learning, and feel particularly relevant to the teaching of this unit. In the paragraphs below, I offer a brief rationale for using these resources, as well as a few notes on practical application. I would also be remiss if I did not mention the impact of Linda Christensen (2000) on my thinking and practice as an educator. Fifteen years later, *Reading, Writing, and Rising Up* continues to hold court on my bookshelf and never seems to gather dust. I owe a debt of gratitude to her model for teaching difficult moments in human history.

The content of this unit is contested ground. It will require the teacher to carefully negotiate complex meaning with young children. For this reason I recommend the gradual release. The gradual release is a current iteration of the traditional "I do, We do, You do" frame often used in lesson planning. Based on the research of Pearson and Gallagher (1983), and developed by the New Teacher Center of Santa Cruz, California, the gradual release scaffolds lessons in four parts. First, the teacher models a strategy or skill. This is followed by a second teacher-model that includes student participation and input. Next students practice in small groups or with a partner, while the teacher continues to monitor and provide guidance. Finally students engage in independent practice. It might be described as "I do, you observe;

I do, you help; You do together, I observe; You do." During this unit, the gradual release may be used to provide important and extended intellectual and emotional support as students grapple with the complex HRE content.

On interactive read aloud, the reader is referred to Hoyt (2007a, 2007b, 2007c). The lessons in these resources are linked to specific texts and organized under six tabs: comprehension, story elements, vocabulary/literary language, literary elements and devices, genre, and writing traits. The comprehension lessons help students develop the ability to analyze and evaluate texts. I recommend teaching the grade-appropriate lessons on main idea and cause and effect prior to this unit, and continuing to use the lessons as anchors during the unit proper. Being able to distill the main idea and to identify cause and effect will help students navigate the readings in this unit, such as the plain text Ten Point Program and the biography of Richard Brown.

Finally, I would like to recommend a resource that might help align this unit with the Common Core. One shift required by the Common Core is a new emphasis on student talk; students must acquire academic vocabulary and develop the academic oral language styles, skills, and strategies required for college and the workplace. Zwiers and Crawford (2007) offer a practical and compelling guide to fostering authentic, thoughtful, and scholarly dialogue in classrooms. I highly recommend their text, *Academic Conversations*, to all classroom teachers and particularly to those who embed HRE in their curricular design. In this unit there are many opportunities for student talk. Because the content can be contentious and will require careful management, the scaffolds and rationale provided by Zwiers and Crawford are particularly applicable.

The unit plan and lessons are found below. The instructional materials I created, as well as student work samples, are not included but are available at no cost to classroom teachers and other school-site support staff. I can be emailed at jessieblundell@gmail.com to obtain digital copies of any materials listed.

Unit Title: Each One, Teach One: Teaching the BPP and Its Legacy

Unit Introduction: This unit of study is designed to highlight the historical importance of the BPP and the ongoing struggle for human rights among former party members in San Francisco. It is written with an elementary school audience in mind and was taught in a second-grade classroom. The unit is divided into six lessons, intended to run approximately 50 minutes each. For practical reasons, I have reformatted the lesson plans using a structure and language that adhere to expectations found in the Common Core.

The content remains the same. Sharing and discussing photographs of the BPP serve as an introduction to the unit. This provocative visual input provides both a hook and a way to build background knowledge. This is followed by an interactive read aloud on day two, using a teacher-created text on the family Panthera. On day three, students complete a Venn diagram of the BPP and the family Panthera, making connections between the mythical animal and the party who chose it as their symbol. Day four includes theater of the oppressed-style tableaux that illustrate examples of oppression and coalition. An interactive timeline contains the content for day five. The final day includes a read aloud about Richard Brown and the completion of the KLW from Lesson One. This final lesson might also serve as a springboard to introducing an important human rights activist, or struggle, related to your own community.

Unit Objective: Students will learn about the BPP and its legacy through interactive read alouds, by creating tableaux, and by participating in talking timeline.

Lesson One: Introducing the BPP

Essential Question(s): Why is it important for people to organize against and resist oppression? What is freedom and why is it important? What is oppression and why is it important to learn about oppression? Who were the members of the BPP? What was the Black Panther Party Ten Point Program and what did it demand? What is the legacy of the BPP?

Objectives:

1. Students will participate in an interactive read aloud.
2. Using interactive writing and a KWL chart, students will demonstrate and organize prior and new knowledge about the BPP. The sections of a KWL chart include K for know (background knowledge that can be subdivided into two categories: know for sure and need to verify), W for want to learn (prereading activity), and L for learned (new knowledge).

Time: 50 minutes.

Materials Needed: KWL chart, plain language BPP Ten Point Program, photographs of the BPP.

Introductory Activity: Students view photographs of the BPP and discuss the prompt with a partner. Prompt: "These are photographs of the Black Panther Party (BPP). What do you know about the BPP and what do you notice in these photographs? Turn and talk to your partner."

Steps:

1. Interactive read aloud of plain text BPP Ten Point Program
2. KWL interactive writing
3. Share: Discuss answers to the essential questions.

Assessment: Teacher may record anecdotal evidence by noting the accurate and appropriate use of lesson-related vocabulary as well as by noting student talk and thinking during the lesson.

Lesson Two: Introducing Panthera

Essential Question(s): What are symbols, and why are they used to represent groups? What is a Black Panther? Why did the BPP choose the Black Panther to represent their organization?

Objectives:

1. Students will participate in an interactive read aloud.
2. Using interactive writing and a Venn diagram, students will demonstrate and organize prior and new knowledge about the BPP and the family Panthera.

Time: 50 minutes.
Materials Needed: Venn diagram, Panthera read aloud.
Introductory Activity: Connector: Prompt: Turn and talk to your neighbor about the thing you are most excited about learning during this unit.
Steps:

1. Interactive read aloud of Panthera
2. Venn Diagram Interactive Writing: Compare and contrast characteristics and traits of the BPP with those of the mythical Black Panther
3. Share: Discuss the essential questions.

Assessment: Teacher may record anecdotal evidence by noting the accurate and appropriate use of lesson-related vocabulary, as well as by noting student talk and thinking during the lesson.

Lesson Three: Coalition Tableaux

Essential Question(s): What is coalition and what does it look like?
Objectives: Using six chairs, students will create a visual representation of coalition (shared power).

Time: 50 minutes.

Materials Needed: Six classroom (stacking) chairs.

Introductory Activity: Connector: Prompt: Turn and talk to your neighbor about a time that you solved a difficult problem by working together with a friend or a group of friends.

Steps:

1. Teacher model: Arrange the chairs in a circle to look like a community circle.
2. Partners discuss models of coalition and share with the whole group.
3. Small groups build representations of coalition using a set of six chairs.
4. Share: Discuss the essential questions.

Assessment: Teacher may record anecdotal evidence by noting the accurate and appropriate use of lesson-related vocabulary, as well as by noting student talk and thinking during the lesson.

Lesson Four: Oppression Tableaux

Essential Question(s): What is oppression and what does it look like?

Objective: Using six chairs, students will create a visual representation of oppression (inequitable distribution of power).

Time: 50 minutes.

Materials Needed: Six classroom (stacking) chairs.

Introductory Activity: Connector: Prompt: Turn and talk to your neighbor about the model of coalition you helped to build yesterday. Explain why you chose to arrange the chairs the way you did.

Steps:

1. Teacher model: Arrange the chairs in rows with one chair in the front. This is a model of oppression because it represents one person being in charge.
2. Partners discuss models of coalition and share with the whole group.
3. Small groups build representations of oppression by using a set of six chairs.
4. Share: Discuss the essential questions.

Assessment: Teacher may record anecdotal evidence by noting the accurate and appropriate use of lesson-related vocabulary, as well as by noting student talk and thinking during the lesson.

Lesson Five: Talking Timeline

Essential Question(s): What is a timeline? Why do we use timelines to organize historical events? What are the important events in the life of the BPP? Which events show evidence of coalition building? Which of these events show evidence of oppression?

Objectives:

1. Students will participate in an interactive timeline of important events in the life of the BPP.
2. Students will decide if the events in the timeline show evidence of coalition building or of oppression.

Time: 50 minutes.

Materials Needed: Timeline events printed on individual slips of paper, a large timeline (can be made using painter's tape inside, or chalk outside).

Introductory Activity: Connector: Prompt: Turn and talk to your neighbor about coalition and oppression. One partner gives a definition of coalition and the other a definition of oppression.

Steps:

1. Teacher models the activity.
2. Partners read their timeline events aloud and decide which events represent coalition and which oppression.
3. Whole group: Students line up on the timeline and step forward to speak when it is their turn.
4. Share: Discuss the essential questions.

Assessment: Teacher may record anecdotal evidence by noting the accurate and appropriate use of lesson-related vocabulary, as well as by noting the student talk and thinking during the lesson.

Lesson Six: Richard Brown

Essential Question(s): What is biography? Can individual people influence history? Who is Richard Brown? Who are the SF8? Why is it important for us to know about Richard Brown's life?

Objective: Students will participate in an interactive read aloud of a biography of Richard Brown.

Time: 50 minutes.

Materials Needed: Biography of Richard Brown created based upon resources from Free The SF8 website (http://www.freethesf8.org/)

Introductory Activity: Connector: Prompt: Turn and talk to your neighbor about the BPP. Imagine what it would be like to be a BPP member.
Steps:

1. Interactive read aloud of Richard Brown biography.
2. Share: Discuss the essential questions.

Assessment: Teacher may record anecdotal evidence by noting the accurate and appropriate use of lesson-related vocabulary, as well as by noting student talk and thinking during the lesson.

Conclusion

Originally, this read aloud was followed by a second unit in which students designed a service-learning project related to the SF 8. At the time, the Free the SF8 campaign was still active. After the case was dismissed in 2011, I adapted the unit to include a lesson in which students crafted letters to send to Richard Brown. What I learned from making these changes is that this unit can serve as a springboard for any number of HRE units. Many of the essential questions that frame this unit are applicable to other human rights issues. The fearlessness, loyalty, and global perspective of the BPP continue to inform and inspire my life as an educator. By sharing this unit and the thinking behind it, I hope to contribute, in some small way, to preserving their legacy of resistance and coalition.

Note: For access to any of the materials in this unit, or to collaborate on embedding this unit in your own classroom, I can be contacted at: jessieblundell@gmail.com.

References

Abu-Jamal, M. (2004). *We want freedom: A life in the Black Panther Party*. Boston, MA: South End Press.

Anderson, C. (2003). *Eyes off the prize: The United Nations and the African American struggle for human rights*. 1944–1955. New York: Cambridge University Press.

Andres, A., Claude, M., and The Freedom Archives (directors, producers, and editors). (2005). *Legacy of torture: The war against the Black Liberation Movement* [video]. (Available from The Freedom Archives, 522 Valencia Street San Francisco, CA 94110.)

Bell, J. (2006). Correcting the system of unequal justice. In T. Smiley (ed.) *The covenant with Black America*, pp. 49–69. Chicago, IL: Third World Press.

Berger, D. (2009). Rescuing civil rights from black power. Collective memory and saving the state in twenty-first-century prosecutions of 1960s-era cases. *Journal for the Study of Radicalism* 3(1): 1–27.

Blasius, M. and Phelan, S. (eds.). (1997). *We are everywhere: A historical sourcebook of gay and lesbian politics*. London: Routledge.

Boal, A. (2000). *Theater of the oppressed*. London: Pluto.

Christensen, L. (2000). *Reading, writing, and rising up: Teaching about social justice and the power of the written word*. Milwaukee, WI: Rethinking Schools.

Flowers, N. (2003). What is human rights education? *A Survey of Human Rights Education*, pp. 107–118. Gütersloh, DE: Bertelsmann Verlag.

Free the SF8. (2008). *Drop the charges: An open letter to Attorney General Brown* (2008). Retrieved from: http://freethesf8.org/docs/OPEN_LETTER_TorresSFBG.pdf.

Freire, P. (2008). *Teachers as cultural workers: Letters to those who dare teach*. In M. Cochran-Smith, S. Feiman-Nemser, D. J. McIntyre, and K. E. Demers (eds.) *Handbook of research on teacher education: Enduring questions in changing contexts*, pp. 208–213. London: Routledge.

Hoyt, A. R. B. L. (2007a). *Interactive read-alouds: Grade 4–5*. Portsmouth, NH: Heinemann.

Hoyt, A. R. B. L. (2007b). *Interactive read-alouds: Grade 2–3*. Portsmouth, NH: Heinemann.

Hoyt, A. R. B. L. (2007c). *Interactive read-alouds: Grade K-1*. Portsmouth, NH: Heinemann.

Orfield, G., Bachmeier, M. D., James, D. R., and Eitle, T. (1997). Deepening segregation in American public schools: A special report from the Harvard Project on School Desegregation. *Equity and Excellence in Education* 30(2): 5–24.

Pearson, P. D. and Gallagher, M. C. (1983). The instruction of reading comprehension. *Contemporary Educational Psychology* 8(3): 317–344.

Spencer, R. C. (2008). Engendering the Black freedom struggle: Revolutionary Black women and the Black Panther Party in the Bay Area, Caledonia. *Journal of Women's History* 20(1): 90–113.

United Nations. (1948). *Universal Declaration of Human Rights*. Retrieved from: http://www.un.org/en/documents/udhr/.

Wacquant, L. J. D. (2002). From slavery to mass incarceration: Rethinking the "race question" in the US. *New Left Review* 13: 41–60.

Zwiers, J. and Crawford, M. (2011). *Academic conversations: Classroom talk that fosters critical thinking and content understandings*. Portland, OR: Stenhouse Publishers.

CHAPTER 4

The Right to an Adequate Standard of Living: Human Rights Education in the Elementary Classroom

Erin Brennan

Introduction

Around the world, families living in poverty without access to food, water, housing, and medical care face daily violations of their human rights. These harsh realities are devastating. As an elementary school teacher, I am compelled to bring awareness of social issues to children. While awareness naturally starts with an appreciation for the rights honored in our own lives, I believe it is important to extend that understanding beyond the individual. For a long time as an educator, I did not consider the value of delving deeper into these issues and inspiring activism in young learners. Like many others, I thought that these issues were too complex for young minds to grasp. But after years of listening to my students talk about their own experiences with fairness, I realized the potential of expanding upon what I consider to be children's innate sense of justice.

In continuing my own education at the University of San Francisco, I came to learn about the Universal Declaration of Human Rights (UDHR) (United Nations, 1948) and struggled to consider how to make the content relevant to young learners. I sought to make the connection between human rights in theory and practice by examining the community in which we live. My classroom is a first-grade class in a diverse community of San Francisco, California, where the majority of students identify as Latino/a. We are a school with a mission dedicated to social justice and service to others, so creating a unit based on human rights fit well into the curriculum. My goal was to begin with the most basic human rights. Using Article 25 of the UDHR, which outlines the need for an adequate standard of living, seemed an appropriate place to start with young children.

By the age of two, children have the capacity to show empathy to others and react with prosocial behaviors (Thompson and Gullone, 2003). It is natural to begin making connections to human rights in early childhood, as children already experience these rights in their daily lives. Children recognize what is fair and unfair. It is our role as educators to ensure that they realize our individual responsibility to work toward fairness in our world. An idea succinctly stated by Hugh Starkey in 1994 is that "Human rights are only rights when people know about them and can therefore exercise them" (as cited in Schmidt, et al., 2000, p. 8).

With this point in mind, I decided to explore with my students the impact of poverty in the United States, as the right to the most basic human needs is something every child can relate to. Additionally, hunger is a very real problem in our community. "In San Francisco and Marin, 1 in 4 people faces the threat of hunger on any given day" (San Francisco Food Bank, 2014). It only makes sense to start educating children at a young age about their rights and responsibilities to ensure that they grow into empathetic adults who effect change, honor rights, and empower themselves and others throughout their lives.

In this chapter, I explore a human's right to an adequate standard of living as stated in the UDHR, Article 25, including food, water, housing, and medical care. I reference additional human rights documents specifically focused on women and children. Further, I strive to explain how human rights are interrelated, the strong impact of one violation on another, and how certain organizations are working to make change. Lastly, I explore the importance of human rights education in the elementary classroom as it relates to an adequate standard of living for all. My goal is to help students understand that they can put their sense of justice into practice through education and activism within their own school and community.

The Right to an Adequate Standard of Living

If the UDHR were honored, no one in the United States would go hungry but instead would be able to meet his or her most basic human needs.

Article 25 states that:

Everyone has the right to a standard of living adequate for the health and well-being of himself and of his family, including food, clothing, housing and medical care and necessary social services, and the right to security in the event of unemployment, sickness, disability, widowhood, old age or other lack of livelihood in circumstances beyond his control.

Additionally, "Motherhood and childhood are entitled to special care and assistance. All children, whether born in or out of wedlock, shall enjoy the same social protection."

When considering issues of poverty, food security is a main concern since the basic needs of individuals are not being met. Food security is defined as "physical and economic access to sufficient, safe and nutritious food at all times" (Human Rights Education Associates, 2003, p. 1). In many cases, food and water are available in a region but not actually accessible by all members of the community. Some people may live in chronic food insecurity, while for others this situation may be temporary or seasonal. Additionally, an individual's food security can vary depending upon the climate of the household (Mechlem, 2004). Those living in poverty in the United States, disproportionately from low-income and racial and ethnic minority groups, are experiencing the violation of their rights (Chilton et al., 2009). According to Chilton et al. (2009), "30.2% of female-headed households with children in the United States experience food insecurity" and the "right to food" is a serious issue facing women and children. Malnutrition is a cycle that is passed down from mother to child living in poverty (p. 73).

Living in poverty without access to sufficient food and water causes significant health issues, with children under the age of 5 as the most vulnerable to malnutrition. The Convention on the Rights of the Child (CRC) (United Nations, 1989) states that children should enjoy the "highest attainable standard of health" and "adequate nutritious foods and clean drinking-water." With the United States as the only developed nation to have not ratified the CRC, there is no legal ground to stand on in enforcing these international laws. However, Article 25 of the UDHR does address these rights, and as a signatory to the UDHR, the United States holds responsibility to protect and provide access to food and water.

The World Declaration and Plan of Action on Nutrition, adopted by the International Conference on Nutrition at Rome, Italy, in December 1992, declared:

> We recognize that access to nutritionally adequate and safe food is a right of each individual. We recognize that globally there is enough food for all and that inequitable access is the main problem. Bearing in mind the right to an adequate standard of living, including food, contained in the Universal Declaration of Human Rights, we pledge to act in solidarity to ensure that freedom from hunger becomes a reality. (p. 3)

The declaration acknowledges the apathetic and discriminatory policies of many countries and recommends research and surveillance to rectify the discrepancies. Additionally, the declaration states that food and water, as the most basic needs for a person, represent the first step in the development of a society (Human Rights Education Associates, 2003).

Poverty and Health

While poverty is often addressed as an issue of food and housing, there is a growing recognition of the relationship between social conditions such as poverty, housing, and education as correlated to physical, mental, and emotional health (Braveman, 2010). Researchers have expanded the definition of basic social conditions to include "quality of housing, homelessness, educational attainment and quality, unemployment, wage levels, lack of control over the organization of work, racial residential segregation, and other forms of discrimination" and their effects on an individual's health (Braveman, 2010, p. 32). These social conditions are interrelated and connected to early brain development in children, affecting school readiness and performance, which then affect a student's future financial success (Braveman, 2010). The International Covenant on Economic, Social and Cultural Rights (ICESCR) (United Nations, 1966), Article 12, references "the right of everyone to the enjoyment of the highest attainable standard of physical and mental health" (p. 4). The right to health is often referred to as the right to health care and medicine without paying attention to the underlying issues that initially cause poor health conditions for people. Yet the link between poverty and poor health is unmistakable (Meier and Fox, 2008).

Food stability and overall health are inextricably linked as malnutrition causes weaker immune systems, leaving individuals more likely to contract diseases at the same time that having a disease likely leads to poor nutrition (Mechlem, 2004). Access or availability of food is not the only defining factor for nutrition and good health. The food must be of high quality to positively affect health, leading researchers to determine that the term "food security" should be changed to "nutrition security" (Mechlem, 2004, p. 636). What must be taken into account is the availability of resources, access to food, environment, and policy, among other factors. Recognizing the high cost of fruits and vegetables, which makes healthy meals out of reach for low-income families, is one clear connection (Finney Rutten et al., 2010). Furthermore, those living in poverty are inevitably experiencing higher levels of stress, a condition that has been linked to poor health (Braveman, 2010).

The US government must provide opportunity for quality health and, to do so, must recognize the relationship between social conditions and health. "The reductions in infectious diseases at the beginning of the twentieth century, though often mistakenly attributed solely to advancements in medical technologies, resulted largely from broad improvements in economic development, higher standards of living, and the creation of social welfare programs" (Meier and Fox, 2008, p. 263). If changes are made to improve the conditions of those living in poverty, health benefits will inevitably follow (Meier and Fox, 2008).

Creating Change

While the research and statistics paint a grave picture of the human rights violations taking place, many organizations offer hope in their efforts to empower people living in poverty to create change. In an effort to expand students' understanding of human rights violations, it is critical to explore organizations and groups of people dedicated to working toward justice. For example, Witness to Hunger, a program supporting women in documenting their experiences through photography, bears witness to hunger in the United States. Taking place in Philadelphia, the program recognizes the social, economic, and cultural rights currently not being granted to low-income mothers and children (Chilton et al., 2009). The participatory nature of the program recognizes the importance of hearing from those experiencing the violation of rights firsthand. Witness to Hunger is the first of its kind to document human rights violations in the United States using "photovoice," which gives power to those who are often unheard and ignored. Photovoice is a method that gives participants cameras to document their lived experience as a way of sharing knowledge that goes beyond the written word. The visual aspect of the project provides an opportunity for those who are not literate in written language to voice their feelings and experiences.

The women participating in the Witness to Hunger photovoice project have used the power of their vision to connect within the community and advocate for change. This largely disenfranchised group is consistently left out of the political sphere and decisions that directly affect them. Members of the Witness to Hunger project were able to participate in a Senate Committee meeting and speak about important issues related to health care, low-income housing, poverty, and hunger (Chilton et al. 2009). Clearly, the issue of women's rights is connected to food rights as well as access to an adequate standard of living. Witness to Hunger portrayed violations against not only the provisions of the UDHR but also those inscribed in the CRC, the ICESCR, and the Convention on the Elimination of All Forms of Discrimination against Women (CEDAW) (United Nations, 1979). CEDAW recognizes women and children's rights as being interconnected and that the health of the child is related to adequate food supply.

Several other organizations are attempting to address the issues of child poverty as interrelated and multidimensional. For example, Making Connections, with sites across the United States, seeks to eradicate poverty by increasing family income and assets, providing child and family support, improving family access to health care, and promoting school readiness. This organization is active in largely low-income neighborhoods and recognizes the value of supporting families within a caring environment (Anthony, King, and Austin, 2011).

The Children's Services Council is an additional program that addresses the issues of poverty beyond food security. Children's Services Council focuses on the very early years of life with attention to healthy births, reduced child abuse, and neglect as well as school readiness. An interesting aspect of this program is its commitment to provide support and make connections across services that already exist in an area rather than attempting to create new ones (Anthony, King, and Austin, 2011). This type of plan empowers community members already involved in creating change and builds support for the movement to eradicate poverty at all levels. As a result of this program, researchers determined an increase in "informal and community support" as well as improvements in "parenting skills and practices" (Anthony, King and Austin, 2011, p. 2005).

Food banks across the country are often essential organizations dedicated to supporting those who experience hunger or food scarcity. The San Francisco Food Bank has seen an increase in need due to the economic recession that impacts not just homeless individuals but those who work every day, often in low-wage positions, and struggle to afford healthy food for their children and families. Donations, volunteers, and collections from supermarkets all support the food bank and ensure that "more than 105,000 meals each day" are distributed (San Francisco Food Bank, 2014, p. 2).

These programs recognize the value, and undoubtedly the difficulties, of addressing the range of effects that poverty has on individuals, particularly on children. With 2.8 billion people in the world living on less than $2 per day, the ramifications are severe, with many living without proper sanitation, clean drinking water, or a stable food source. Living in this environment can lead to disease and malnutrition, undeniably linked to poor health. The violation of rights is interrelated as poverty or lack of education can lead to poor health, limited ability to function socially or to defend one's rights (Braveman, 2010). To create change, a wider net must be cast in order to achieve a greater understanding of the dimensions of poverty. It is clear that human rights are indivisible; recognizing this fact is to realize that where one human right is violated, none are honored.

Human Rights Education in Elementary School

The role of the educator goes beyond teaching basic reading and writing skills and extends to promoting and instilling a sense of responsibility and membership to society. Should we hope for students to grow into adults that create change in the world, we must instill a value in the principles of citizenship and a "sense of belonging" (United Nations Committee on the Rights of the Child, 2006, p. 91). As educators, we honor students' rights and educate about human rights by teaching through differentiating instruction to meet their needs. We can go further to educate young children about human rights by calling attention to the violation of those rights around the world and within our own communities.

Many people feel that early childhood is too young to address issues of human rights. However, in reality, human rights are an everyday part of the life of a child. According to Amnesty International USA's (2000) *Our World, Our Rights*, the recommendation of the Council of Europe Committee of Ministers of Education in 1985 stated, "Concepts associated with human rights can and should, be acquired at an early stage. For example, the nonviolent resolution of conflict and respect for other people can already be experienced [within] the life of a preschool or primary class" (Schmidt et al., 2000, p. 7). Tapping into a child's innate sense of justice and calling attention to human rights issues while building community is a natural, powerful step for making change in society.

For elementary school students, the opportunity to discuss real issues that affect other children like them and to make connections to these issues through literature provides a powerful and effective tool for human rights education. As natural egocentrics, children often have difficulty seeing outside of themselves and their own lives. While they recognize the concept of fairness as related to themselves, we can expand upon this to help them realize what a violation of rights would mean in their own everyday lives. Calling attention to the similarities in children everywhere allows students to begin building a foundation for understanding the connectedness of our world, including their responsibility in the honoring of each individual's rights (Schmidt, et al., 2000). On a basic level, children at a very young age have the capacity to understand what it means to have basic human needs met. In fact, this is often their primary concern. Opening up the dialogue to allow students to engage in conversation around issues of adequate living standards is natural for children who eat food, drink water, and come to school each day. The classroom as a community is a natural place to start raising awareness of these issues.

With an understanding of community as a social studies content standard, children already engage in an exploration of this topic in many primary classrooms in the United States. Therefore, an extended discussion of the essentials of a community can occur quite smoothly. If students can determine what is essential and recognize true "wants" and "needs," they can then explore what could happen if these essentials were to disappear. Using literature with easily relatable characters allows children to take their understanding to the next level as they make connections to their own lives, other stories they have read, and the greater world around them. Building community is truly the first step not only for a positive classroom environment but also for an understanding of human rights. In order to honor children's rights, it is the responsibility of teachers and adults to create positive learning spaces that allow students to engage, participate, and communicate about their rights and issues affecting their lives (United Nations Committee on the Rights of the Child, 2006). Human connection, empathy, and understanding can be achieved within a classroom if effective teaching takes place.

Classroom Realities

While considering the process of teaching about human rights in my first-grade classroom, I first thought about my students and their own experiences. Many families in my school face financial struggles and some have experience with food insecurity or homelessness as well as injustice in many forms. This unit invites students to expand their understanding of human rights violations in a safe and encouraging environment. It offers an opportunity to maximize the potential that already exists within each child to genuinely care about the rights of others.

My students sincerely enjoyed these activities and were often rightfully outraged to learn that many in the world and in our community live without having their basic needs met. I found that they were often curious and critical in a way many do not expect from young minds. Students suggested that items like a computer or a cell phone should be considered a "need." Instead of arguing that one could live without such things, I asked questions and delved deeper to explore why they felt that way. I asked students to convince me, and when a child explained that the computer helps them learn, it seemed wrong to argue otherwise.

Students shared stories of their own encounters with homeless individuals on the street and reflected upon why they were there and how these experiences made them feel. It was important for me to create a space where that type of conversation was encouraged and students felt that they would not be judged. I wanted to make sure that they did not receive stock answers about how sad homelessness and hunger are, but rather admit that these complicated issues are connected and that learning and sharing our thoughts is the first step toward finding solutions. Having these conversations with young children can be quite difficult at times; realizing that you, as the educator, do not have all the answers may seem frustrating to you and surprising to your students, but I found that being honest was by far the most fulfilling way to enter into this unit of study.

Personally, teaching this unit was heartwarming and encouraging. It simply solidified my belief that children innately hold a sense of justice that often over time society teaches them to lose. If we can halt the process of jading young children and instead motivate them to action, perhaps more students will feel that despite the unfairness in the world, there is something they can do.

Final Reflections

It can be easy to get frustrated about the state of our country and the world when we look closely at statistics and realities of human rights violations. I find it especially unnerving when the most basic needs of food, water, housing, and medicine are denied to members of our human community, even more so when these violations affect children who are the most vulnerable among us. Despite these frustrations, I realize the value and power that come with knowledge. Understanding these realities can lead toward change. It is important to explore the international laws that we have in place and to be educated on the role the United States is playing in breaking those laws.

Furthermore, we can learn a great deal by exploring the cause and effect of these violations as well as those recognizing individuals and groups who are taking great strides to make change. Researching successful programs around the country and the world is an important step in understanding human rights. Having that understanding as an educator allows me to effectively translate the information in a developmentally appropriate way for children. With the knowledge that children are capable of making connections from their own life to the real world, human rights education in the elementary classroom is invaluable. Children are tomorrow's change-makers; therefore, human rights education in the elementary classroom is essential.

Pedagogical Tool

Unit Title: The Right to an Adequate Standard of Living: Human Rights in Elementary School

Unit Introduction: This unit is a multidisciplinary project aimed at teaching human rights to elementary grade students. These lessons were specifically designed for a first-grade classroom but could be easily modified for preschool through fourth grade. The lessons are based in California History-Social Science and English Language Arts Content Standards and incorporate many dimensions of mathematics, science, and classroom community building. The goal is for students to complete this unit with a foundational understanding of human rights and a desire to take action within their community and their world.

Lesson One: Wants and Needs

Objectives: To understand the difference between a "want" and a "need," and to apply to items in everyday life.

Time: 45 minutes.

Materials Needed: Vocabulary cards with pictures (food, water, toys, books, ball, candy, etc.), poster paper, markers, magazines, scissors, glue, *Those Shoes* by Maribeth Boelts (2007).

Introductory Activity: As a class read *Those Shoes* by Maribeth Boelts (2007) and discuss the story of a young boy who wants a new pair of shoes to be like his classmates. When his grandma references their household as a "needs" not a "wants home," begin a dialogue with students. Ask, "What do you think Grandma means when she says this?" "What do you think a 'needs home' is?" "What do you think a 'wants home' is?" Hold a class discussion about the events in the story. Ask students to make connections between the book and their own lives, "When have you wanted something that you could not have?"

Steps:

1. Write the words "want" and "need" on the board. Ask the class what they think these words mean and to give examples. Discuss with students how they determine the difference between a "want" and a "need."
2. Pass out flash cards with various photos on them (clothes, camera, food, water, car, family, candy, ball, etc.). Ask students to engage in a think-pair-share discussion. Ask students to discuss with their partners the following questions: "What item is in the photo? How is the item used? Is the item a want or a need?" Rotate the photos so that each group discusses at least three examples.
3. Ask students to share out what their partner said. This is a great way to determine which students are truly listening to their partners, demonstrating the interconnectedness of the class.
4. Ask each student to hold a card and to choose one side of the room: the "wants" to one side and the "needs" to the other side. As a class

discuss what students see on each side. If people are standing on a side that does not seem appropriate, open up the discussion to the class. For example, one student with a card that has a wagon on it stands on the "needs" side. Prompt the class by asking, "Raise your hand if you have a wagon" and "Can you imagine life without a wagon?" "If not everyone has one here, can we determine that it is a 'want' or a 'need'?" Allow the class to decide.

Independent Practice:

1. Explain that the students will create their own chart using magazines. Provide students with magazines and ask them to cut out pictures to show what they consider to be "wants" and "needs." Provide a premade worksheet with a labeled chart to sort into the two groups. Ask students to share completed work with a friend.
2. Transferring of knowledge: Briefly look at the community posters that the students have previously made with pictures of people, places, and things in a community and point out some "wants" and "needs." As a class discuss their observations.

Lesson Two: Human Rights and Education

Objectives: To understand our "rights" and the importance of education. To explore education as a human need.

Time: 1 hour or two 30-minute lessons.

Materials Needed: Beanbag or small toy, whiteboard or chart paper, markers, writing paper, pencils, *Listen to the Wind* by Greg Mortenson (2009).

Introductory Activity: Have students sit in a circle with a beanbag or small toy. Remind them of the previous lesson on "wants" and "needs." Ask students to pass the beanbag around and share one "need" that was met for them today. Students may answer "I ate a banana this morning" or "I brushed my teeth with water," "I took a shower," or "I slept in a warm bed" and so on. Next pass the beanbag and share one thing you really want. Students may say anything that comes to their mind. Complete the activity by pointing out the differences in what they mentioned that they needed and the things that they wanted.

Steps:

1. Create a word web with the word "human" and the word "right" in a circle with lines extending out of it. Ask the students to say what they think of when they hear the word "human." Write down all ideas.

The word "right" is a bit more challenging, so write down words and prompt them with sayings, such as "What do you think of when I say that you have the right to go to recess?" Allow students to share anything that comes to their mind. Eventually, guide students to an understanding of the word "right" as something they can and should be able to do in order to meet basic needs. You can introduce it as new vocabulary and explain that we use this word in different ways and today we will talk about "right" as something you deserve or are supposed to have. "A right is a need that every person must have." Facilitate a basic understanding of a human right as something that every person is entitled to simply because they are human.

2. Next write the word "adequate" on the board. Have students repeat and explain what it means. Lead to an understanding of the word as meaning "enough." Use the word in a sentence and ask students to pair-share a sentence using the word.
3. Review the discussion of "wants" and "needs" and discuss the importance of school and education. Have a brief discussion about school, why it is important, and why it might be considered a "right." Ask, "Why do we go to school?" "What is important about school?" "Why do we need school?" "What might happen if we thought of school as a 'want'?" Read *Listen to the Wind* by Greg Mortenson (2009) and talk about how the community worked together to build a school. Ask: "Why might they have done that?" "How is this similar or different from your experience with school?"

Independent Practice: Choose one of the following writing activities for the class.

1. Complete a Venn diagram that shows similarities and differences between the school in the story and our school.
2. Write descriptive sentences that explain what happened in the story, including how the school is similar and different from ours.
3. Create your own story and drawing that explain a series of events, including information that is similar to or different from our school. When the writing assignment is complete, have students pair-share ideas and then report out their partner's work to the whole class.

Lesson Three: Human Rights Group Project

Objectives: Students will delve deeper into understanding just one "need" and further be able to explain their need as a human right. Students will make connections to their own life and to the importance of having their needs fulfilled.

Time: One hour.

Materials: Children's literature about food, housing, school and water, index cards, tape, vocabulary cards with pictures (food, water, toys, books, ball, candy, etc.), premade handouts with prompt questions, pencils, crayons, markers.

Introductory Activity: Based on the previous activities, students should have an understanding of the needs we have as human beings. Take the vocabulary cards that were previously determined to be "needs" and put them together on the board or in a pocket chart. Create a new title of "Human Rights" over the cards and state that we have a "right" to these "needs." Explain that we have many human rights but we are focusing on these essential rights that we need to survive. Tape a card in four separate corners of the room that are labeled "food," "water," "home," and "school." Ask students to walk to the corner of the room in which they are most interested. Instruct students in the following way: "Stop and talk to someone in that corner about why this is a human right or how you use this right every day. Move to another corner. Spend only about 5–7 minutes on this part."

Steps:

1. Gather students together and explain that the class will be working in groups to further explore these rights, why they are important, how we use them, and what might happen if we did not have them. This exploration will take place through a basic literature circle and group research project.
2. Break children up into three groups with a sticker nametag for each. Group 1 becomes the "readers" who are responsible for going over the book/s, reading important information, and explaining the story. Group 2 is the "recorders" who have the worksheets with discussion questions and are expected to prompt discussion and write down the answers of their group mates. Group 3 consists of "reporters" who are in charge of listening carefully to group discussion, reading the written answers, and being prepared to answer questions from the class. Have groups talk to each other about their responsibilities. Take questions and clarify if necessary.
3. Groups are then formed with one student of each role in every group so the "food" group will have a reader, recorder, and reporter. (If necessary, give one group two recorders or create a new role as "discussion leader" separate from recorder.) Each group finds a quiet, safe place in the classroom to work. Students must complete a worksheet with

questions including, "How do you and your family use this right? How do the books show others using it? Why do you need it? What might happen if you didn't have it?" Prepare this worksheet beforehand with space for drawing and writing answers. Be sure to move around the room to support groups as necessary.
4. When the group work is near completion, give a warning and reminders to the reporters that they need to be prepared to share. Gather the class together and have each reporter give a synopsis of the group's report. After each group's presentation, ask the class if we can agree that this is a human right. Why or why not?
5. Facilitate a group discussion reflecting on group work and how the groups worked together. Without pointing out other students or naming names, ask for explanations of struggles that groups might have had in completing work. Talk about why it is important to work together. Ask students to think about how the project might have gone if a group member had been absent. Make reference to when a student had to leave the classroom for a break or otherwise, and ask, "What did your group do to make up for that loss?" (You may even intentionally pull a student away from a group to ensure this experience takes place and determine how the groups respond). Make connections between this experience and the work of a community. When we have members of a community, everyone has their role. What can happen if a member is missing and his/her job does not get completed?

Assessment: Teacher observation of student engagement and anecdotal records along with completed handouts will be used as assessment. Make notes of quotes and comments that students make along with observations. You can create an "exit ticket" in which each student writes one sentence reflection on their experience working in the group. "What did you learn?" "How did it go?" "What do you know about rights or needs?"

Lesson Four: Building Together

Objectives: To engage in team building and to understand the importance of community. Students will recognize basic needs as human rights and empathize with those whose needs are violated.

Time: One hour.

Materials Needed: Building blocks, unifix cubes, stickers.

Introductory Activity: Reengage students and remind them of previous activities that have been completed. You may want to read some quotes or comments that you wrote down in previous lessons or sentences that students had written to catch their interest.

Steps: Explain to students that they will again be working in groups. Remind them of the importance of working together and of each person taking responsibility for his/her role.

1. The goal of the project is to build a structure. Give each group four blocks that they must use in their structure. The remaining blocks can be a combination of any materials set out on the table (a mix of unifix cubes, three-dimensional shapes, Legos, or other objects). Each of the four blocks has a word on them: "food," "water," "home," and "school." All four of those blocks must be used in the structure. The group has a 2-minute time period to build their structure and all group members must work together.
2. Place the four blocks on the group table, but the remaining blocks on a separate table. Explain that only one person may retrieve blocks from the separate table at a time. Explain that this will be challenging. Ask: "How are you, as a group, going to decide who retrieves blocks?"
3. Start the clock and let the students get to work. Observe how they determine who retrieves blocks, the time it takes to decide, what roles students take, and what leaders emerge. Make notes of observations or record groups with a video camera. Stop the clock. Ask students to freeze and observe their structures. Allow students to move around the room to look at other groups' work.
4. Frustrations and conflict are likely to emerge as students decide who is in charge of what or who is allowed to get blocks. Have a discussion about what works and what doesn't. Point out groups or individuals that appropriately chose people (took turns, did rock/paper/scissors to decide, or let others go before them). Make reference to the completion of the structures as being connected to the time spent on building versus the time spent on conflict. Talk about how students felt during the process and if students were controlling or left out. Again, be careful to discuss feelings and not point out individual students; recognize this as a learning experience.
5. Make reference to the four building blocks of "food," "water," "home," and "school" as being critical to the foundation of the building. Now give students a second chance. They will have two minutes to once again build a new structure based on the knowledge from the previous experience. When time is up, call all the students away from their buildings. Recognize the four building blocks and ask what might happen if just one of those were taken away. Ask a student

to remove one of the four building blocks from the structure and observe what happens. Talk about how it feels to have one of your buildings knocked down.
6. Make the connection between the building and the word on the block. "If the food is taken away, what happens?" "How does it make you feel?" "How can you tell what others are feeling?"

Assessment: Gather together in a circle on the carpet. Use a talking stick or toy to demonstrate that only one person may talk at a time. Ask the following questions: "When we were building our structures, many of you got frustrated when one block was taken away, why did that happen?" "Now imagine that the block I took away was your actual food, how do you think that would feel?" "Try to consider someone, not taking your blocks, but taking your home, what would you do?" "If we have food, water, a home and a school, why should we care if others do or do not?" Allow the discussion to flow naturally as students will likely have many thoughts, comments, questions, and concerns. You may want to allow quiet writing reflection time as well.

Lesson Five: Activate

Objectives: To understand the value of activism and our role and responsibility to take action to create change.

Time: 45 minutes, possibility of extension beyond to multiple lessons.

Introductory Activity: Revisit one piece of literature that was especially meaningful for your students. As you read, ask questions about things they might not have noticed the first time around. Talk about how we feel about human rights.

Steps:

1. Explain they will have an opportunity to express what they have learned about human rights and how they feel. Students will use a variety of art materials to depict one important way they use human rights in their lives using paint, clay, paper, markers, and other three-dimensional materials. Give students time to create and provide choices to express themselves.
2. With photos of their artwork, put together a class photo book similar to *A Cool Drink of Water* by Barbara Kerley (2006). Discuss connections to the book. Consider with whom the book could be shared. Perhaps they could take turns reading the book to younger grade students or to families on Parent Night where multiple copies are made and distributed.

3. Review the rights the class previously discussed and clarify that these are only some of our human rights. Briefly introduce other rights such as voting, movement, or rest and leisure. (Look to the UDHR for a full list.) Discuss how these rights are honored in our lives.
4. As a class, brainstorm ideas for ways students can honor human rights. Review a basic activity that the class or school may do each year such as food drives at Thanksgiving, socks for the homeless in November, and toiletries at Christmas. Talk about how these are merely the first steps we can take to honor the rights of others.
5. Introduce your students to a community organization working to eradicate poverty and/or hunger. Look through the organization's website together and talk about children just like them who are living without their needs met. Ask what this means for them, and brainstorm how the whole class could get involved. Perhaps take students on a field trip to a food bank where they can contribute by serving or donating food. Maybe students can produce a class photo book to sell as a way to support a nearby organization. Students may want to visit the organization and bring the money raised. Try to make a connection with a neighboring school to simultaneously complete the unit of study and bring them together to plan the next steps. Students will get a sense of community building beyond the walls of the classroom and learn even more from the experiences of others. Continue encouraging students to consider ways they can get involved.

References

Amnesty International USA. (2000). *Our world, our rights: Teaching about rights and responsibilities in the elementary school.* New York: Amnesty International USA.

Anthony, E., King, B., and Austin, M. (2011). Reducing child poverty while promoting child well-being: Identify best practices in a time of great need. *Children and Youth Services Review* 33: 1999–2009.

Boelts, M. (2007). *Those shoes.* Somerville, MA: Candlewick Press.

Braveman, P. (2010). Social conditions, health equity and human rights. *Health and Human Rights* 12: 33–48.

Chilton, M., Rabinowic, J., and Council, C. (2009). Witnesses to hunger: Participation through photovoice to ensure the right to food. *Health and Human Rights* 11: 73–85.

Finney Rutten, L., Yaroah, A., Colon-Ramos, U., Johnson-Askew, W. and Story, M. (2010). Poverty, food insecurity and obesity: A conceptual framework for research, practice and policy. *Journal of Hunger and Environmental Nutrition* 5: 403–415.

Human Rights Education Associates. (2003). *Food and water*. Retrieved from www.hrea.org/index.php?doc_id=404.

Kerley, B. (2006). *A cool drink of water*. Washington, DC: National Geographic Society.

Mechlem, K. (2004). Food security and the right to food in the discourse of the United Nations. *European Law Journal* 10: 631–648.

Meier, B. M. and Fox, A. M. (2008). Development as health: Employing the collective right to development to achieve the goals of the individual right to health. *Human Rights Quarterly* 30: 259–355.

Mortenson, G. (2009). *Listen to the wind: The story of Dr. Greg and three cups of tea*. New York: The Penguin Group.

San Francisco Food Bank. (2014). Retrieved from http://www.sfmfoodbank.org/.

Schmidt, J. C., Manson, P. A., and Windschitl, T. A. (eds.). (2000). *Our world our rights: Teaching about rights and responsibilities in the elementary schools*. New York: Amnesty International USA. Retrieved from: http://www.amnesty.org/en/human-rights-education/resource-centre/download/SEC01%2C001%2C2000/en/pdf.

Thompson, K. and Gullone, E. (2003). Promotion of empathy and prosocial behavior in children through humane education. *Australian Psychologist* 36: 175–182.

United Nations. (1948). *Universal Declaration of Human Rights*. Retrieved from http://www.un.org/en/documents/udhr/.

United Nations. (1966). *International Covenant on Economic, Social and Cultural Rights*. Retrieved from http://www.ohchr.org/EN/ProfessionalInterest/Pages/CESCR.aspx.

United Nations. (1979). *Convention on the Elimination of All Forms of Discrimination against Women*. Retrieved from http://www.un.org/womenwatch/daw/cedaw/.

United Nations. (1989). *Convention on the Rights of the Child*. Retrieved from http://www.ohchr.org/en/professionalinterest/pages/crc.aspx.

United Nations Committee on the Rights of the Child, United Nations Children's Fund, Bernard van Leer Foundation. (2006). *A guide to general comment 7: 'Implementing child rights in early childhood'*. The Hague, Netherlands. Bernard van Leer Foundation.

World Declaration and Plan of Action on Nutrition. (1992). Retrieved from http://whqlibdoc.who.int/hq/1992/a34303.pdf. 1–50.

CHAPTER 5

Bringing to Life Human Rights Education in the Science Classroom

Annie S. Adamian

Introduction

If teachers working toward social justice are serious about bringing to life the spirit of democracy, exploring the ways in which human rights education (HRE) inspires critical consciousness and agency toward the development of beloved communities is crucial (hooks, 1994; King, 1957). Creating and sustaining classroom practices that reflect the principles of human rights requires "recognition of the inherent dignity and of the equal and inalienable rights of all members of the human family [as] the foundation of freedom, justice and peace in the world," which honors the intentions of the United Nation's human rights declarations and treaties (UDHR, 1948, p. 1). Indeed, HRE is a humanizing epistemology that acknowledges teaching and learning as acts of love.

In this chapter, I argue that HRE is a crucial component of creating and sustaining equitable classrooms, schools, and communities, with a particular focus on the science classroom. I start by sharing the ways in which HRE can be practiced in the classroom, leading to a discussion about the challenges faced by public school teachers implementing HRE while teaching state-mandated standards. More specifically, I utilize a case study analysis to share how HRE transforms teaching and learning in the classroom into humanizing educational experiences. Finally, I conclude with the ways in which HRE inspires student and teacher agency, fosters anti-oppressive education (Kumashiro, 2009), and generates spaces of healing and transformation.

HRE provides the hope for justice and the practice toward freedom that we feel in our hearts and imagine in our minds. In public schools, HRE has the potential to foster both the academic and democratic skills necessary for the full development of our youth and their teachers and the dismantling of inequitable practices and unjust policies. In the pages ahead, I demonstrate how HRE works to transform schooling into democratic sites where social justice is at the core of classroom practices. Using the language of human rights remolds dehumanizing static spaces from which the oppressed need a break into fluid transformative spaces that honor students' identities (Tatum, 1997). For example, Julio (all names are pseudonyms), a seventh-grade student, shared his insight about the ways in which HRE is experienced in our science classroom:

> This experience was pretty emotional for me because I've never been talked about like this. I've only been talked about like this with my family. I have never seen a teacher actually go out and actually talk to a kid about school and the class and how we feel about the system. It brings up sadness and happiness.... First I was sad because when we talked about like the system and how I used to think that white people were better and now I am happy because I know that only my thinking had got the better of me. I feel better now and I know I'm just as smart.

Julio's analysis reflects how HRE in a science classroom respects students' lived experiences, identities, and knowledge. Through action and reflection, students and teachers consistently agitate dehumanizing social constructs that have been normalized, value their own and others' identities, and work toward dismantling oppressive practices in their classroom, school, and community.

HRE in a Science Classroom

In 1994 the United Nations asserted that the following ten years would be the Decade of Human Rights Education, but the work toward the implementation of HRE mainly focused on the humanities, law, and social sciences. Absent was the capacity to include the sciences during the promotion of HRE (Claude, 2002). Today, "questions of how, when, and where to integrate HRE into the [science] curriculum represent some of the main areas of current discussion" (Suarez, 2007, p. 52). Thus, sharing how HRE has been and is currently being implemented within the field of science and science education is essential. Therefore, gaining insight into the ways in which students and teachers practice HRE in the classroom generates a powerful space for new forms of knowledge to develop, both in community with each other, and in response to the United Nations' call for HRE in public schools.

Human Rights Treaties and Science

The United Nations Educational Scientific and Cultural Organization (UNESCO) and the International Covenant on Economic, Social and Cultural Rights (ICESCR) (1966) play a crucial role in promoting and upholding the principles of the UDHR in order to recognize the moral, ethical, and legal responsibilities in the field of science. For example, UNESCO promotes the responsibilities and practices of bioethics through the development, implementation, and recognition of the: (1) Universal Declaration on the Human Genome and Human Rights (1999), (2) International Declaration on Human Genetic Data (2003), and (3) Universal Declaration on Bioethics and Human Rights (2005). These declarations seek "to balance the freedom of scientists to pursue their work with the need to safeguard human rights and protect humanity from potential abuses" (Claude, 2002, p. 50).

HRE promotes science-based declarations, which align with Article 15 of the ICESCR, an international treaty intended to legally uphold human rights violations, and can serve as a human rights framework in the classroom. For example, human rights language and legal instruments are negotiated with California State Science Standards while teaching and learning standards-based units on Cells, Genetics, and Evolution. Within these unit topics are legacies of human rights violations and commonsense assumptions in relationship to scientific practices that go unquestioned. For example, one of the lessons shared later in this chapter illustrates how students learn about the dehumanizing and unjust practices of Monsanto and Genetically Modified Organisms (GMOs). With these lessons in mind, the next section puts into context how to create and sustain a science classroom culture that reflects the principles of critical pedagogy, human rights, and teacher/student agency.

Our Classroom and School as a Case-Study Example

Our school is located in northern California in a town with a population of about 85,000. Its junior high school student population includes a little over 600 youth. On average, about 55 percent of our students qualify for free or reduced priced lunch, and about 45 percent of our students are youth of color. I have been teaching science for 13 years; traditionally, I teach

Life Science five periods a day with classroom sizes ranging from 30 to 40 students.

Within this context, I share the ways in which my students and I experienced teaching and learning the state and federally mandated science standards in an equitable environment that consistently transformed through action and reflection. HRE and standards-based science content were experienced through multiple layers of democratic practice which included: (a) the understanding and practice of human rights declarations and treaties; (b) collaboration through equitable group projects; (c) production of an inclusive student run, school-wide science newspaper rooted in human rights and anti-oppression; (d) standards-based content using a critical lens; (e) lessons on equity, diversity, and racism; (f) students' journal reflections; (g) student presentations; and (h) counter-action, wherein my students and I worked toward dismantling the inequities and unjust practices we recognized within our own lives, classroom, school, and communities through the process of participatory action research. These approaches dignified the principles of the UDHR, while teaching and learning the California State Science Standards in our seventh-grade science classroom.

HRE provides students and teachers a legal framework from which to build, through action and reflection—praxis (Freire, 1970, 1998). With the intention of disrupting oppressive practices, implementing HRE in a science classroom while simultaneously teaching and learning the California State Science Standards in anti-oppressive ways dismantles schooling conditions that attempt to reproduce the unjust status quo. In this sense, while learning standards-based science concepts, students and teachers critically think about the ways in which state-adopted standards and textbooks normalize oppressive practices. For example, during a lesson on genetics, my students critically examined the social constructions of race and gender, and through dialogue generated insight about the ways in which scientific research historically and currently is used to falsely justify oppressive practices. In response to the ongoing lessons on racism, Monica shared that:

> Now I know that race is in small things and there are things we, and people like us need to change things. Like I can walk out knowing the things I wanted to say for a while now, like I can let them out. It feels good and I feel free.

Through experience, I recognize that HRE can occur in a science classroom while simultaneously teaching the state-mandated standards. For example, HRE became a fluid part of our everyday science lessons and did not take away time from teaching and learning the state standards. The negotiation of science standards and HRE in the classroom generates liberating classroom practices that are reflected in Julio's response:

> Like science because most of the time we do experiments and learn more about things that are little like cells and things that we process in our heads. And we think about things that most people don't think about. In science we go beyond to a whole world that we didn't even know existed. I guess like, you don't get to experienced crazy mind things in other places. In the other classes they teach you differently. With science you are able to figure out a whole different world beyond.

As Julio's quote demonstrates, HRE does not take away from learning standards-based science concepts. Negotiating with the state standards carves out spaces in the classroom wherein critical consciousness, reflection, and purpose are a "normal" part of teaching and learning. My students see themselves as part of the curriculum and therefore are engaged, valued, and inspired. They actively participate in generating new forms of knowledge rooted in acts of love and collaboration, while disrupting the dominant culture's discourse with intention and care. For example, in regard to the dominant culture's discourse and practices, Victor shared that:

> In history class we are studying about the Aztecs and Mayans and I feel like my people are left out and we aren't being represented accurately. In my history class they only talk about who conquered us and what they found. Also, they don't give more information about people of color. The textbooks just seem to focus on the white race and they aren't giving people of color credit for what they have created.

Several months later, as we continued to teach and learn in anti-oppressive ways, Victor shared the ways in which his knowledge was honored and how he continued to build on his experiences through action and reflection:

> Today, I am more aware of what I do and say. I came into this class with knowledge that my family taught me about how I should be treated with respect and so should others. After talking in class about race, I got the courage to stand up for others. People think it's okay to be racist, but truly people haven't learned about it so they think it's okay to be racist. All in all I wish we could all unite together and end racism.

In this sense, HRE in the classroom not only transforms the ways in which we teach and learn in our classroom, but also transcends beyond our classroom, in that students carry liberating practices with them and begin to challenge systems of oppression in different spaces through action and reflection.

Negotiating HRE in Public Schools

In stark contrast to HRE, US public schools often embody sites of punishment and failure, rather than sites of sustenance and hope. Misguided policies place the blame on teachers and students for the pitfalls of our system. Dehumanizing policies and practices including, but not limited to, California's Propositions 187 (which severely restricted the rights of undocumented immigrants) and 227 (which prohibited bilingual instruction), No Child Left Behind (NCLB), tracking, inequitable funding for schools, and "the war on drugs" (Leonardo, 2009) reflect the violent attack on communities of color, and the looting of resources to which young people and communities of color have a right. These actions confirm, promote, and perpetuate the unjust status quo in regard to the inequities they produce in prepackaged lyrics framed as "common sense" (Gramsci, 1971; Kumashiro, 2008).

When students and teachers working in public schools carve out spaces for HRE to come alive, classrooms transform into spaces where teachers and students work toward "the full development of the human personality and to the strengthening of respect for human rights and fundamental freedoms" (UDHR, 1948, p.1). In our classroom, I observed students reclaiming their sense of belonging and resisting oppressive practices, while I worked to do the same. Students began to intentionally participate in classroom practices that before attempted to silence their voices.

Below, Javier provides meaningful insight about how a classroom culture rooted in the principles of HRE honored his voice and self worth:

> I feel really comfortable in class and I wouldn't change a thing. You and the students and getting to know everybody else makes me feel good in here. Like when someone reads a word wrong the person sitting next to them helps them out. I like all the participation and how nobody is laughing when someone gets it wrong. I feel more confident since I've been in here. Like ever since like first grade all the way to sixth grade, I never wanted to raise my hand and read and participate and all that because I thought kids would want to laugh at me. And from here, when I have, nobody has ever laughed.

US policies rooted in hegemonic practices continue to suffocate the democratic ideals that schools and communities have a right to experience (Giroux, 2004; Gramsci, 1971; Kumashiro, 2009, 2012). In the discipline of science, students typically learn about the white male scientists and their contributions to science, yet are rarely exposed to stories about the contributions by people of color, females, or the Lesbian Gay Bisexual Transgender (LGBT) community. Specifically, students and teachers need to ask the questions: "What is missing from the curriculum? Who is missing, and why?" Then, the legacies of injustice that continue today are recognized (Kumashiro, 2009). In this way, students learn how to critically reflect on the dominant culture's discourse and practices and work toward dismantling dehumanizing rhetoric. In turn, the narratives in the classroom shift toward anti-oppressive practices rooted in human rights and fundamental freedoms, as Monica expressed:

> The reason I wanted to be in your class was because my brother and sister said that when you explain things you don't just do it on one race and that you make sure everybody is comfortable in your class. I feel very comfortable and it's my favorite class. I feel like I can be myself... In this class I like it because if you say something there are like no stares and stuff, like here, my mom says I'm creative and stuff, and in here you let me be creative. And people in class are okay with my comments and questions and it used to be like they thought I was weird or a crazy person and now they don't. And in my other classes I'm quiet and serious because I'm not as comfortable. And just that we respect one another and they understand that people have their differences.

Student testimonies reflect how the attack on public schools requires that teachers and students work together and consistently seek ways to problematize the rigid and unjust practices imposed and sustained through sanctions and incentives based on standardized test scores (Fuller, 2003; Oakes, 2005; Kumashiro, 2012; Sleeter, 2005). Students deserve to teach and learn in spaces that foster their full development academically, socially, and emotionally.

In the classroom, my students and I work toward creating and sustaining anti-oppressive spaces that inspire the realization of our fundamental freedoms and human rights with dignity in mind. In relationship to building beloved communities, Mary described how the class inspired her and her peers to create a crew named Courageous Youth Agency (C'YA). They started presenting at a local university to preservice teachers and more recently at a statewide teacher conference. She described her experience with C'YA:

> The more I got into it, it was extremely intense! I was confused but at the same time I had a little understanding. But since I went through science class things have gotten clearer and C'YA is better than I expected... My

life changed because the way my mind thought changed. It's changed the way I see the world and classroom. Everything is much different now. Just walking through the halls and listening to everyone it's different. Since I have awareness I can catch people and tell them it's not okay. My friends and family kind of get the idea but they don't fully understand it so it's hard to talk about it. I want C'YA to go worldwide telling kids stories.

Mary's response represents how my students work alongside one another, in order to "challenge, resist, and change the root cause of their suffering [which] is at the core of any democratic process" (Ginwright and James, 2002, p. 31). In this way, "knowledge emerges only through invention and re-invention, through the restless, impatient continuing, hopeful inquiry human beings pursue in the world, with the world, and with each other" (Freire, 1970/1993, p. 72). Sheila, a parent, reflected on how HRE in the classroom inspired her son:

I want (John) to stay a part of C'YA. He was getting into a lot of trouble at school and ever since you started working with him, I have noticed his grades go up and he loves going to school now. I think all kids should be a part of C'YA. I was really excited to see (John) speak in front of adults. Then I started to hear all the kids and their compassion for racism, I really felt bad for what's going on. (John) has really become passionate about racism. He has matured a lot over the year. I am so thankful for you and what you have done. Listening to the kids has made me really think about what kids go through.

Sheila's insight was part of the reason I developed the Teacher and Student Participatory Action Research (TSPAR) project in our science classroom. She supported me and recognized that what members of C'YA were experiencing outside of the classroom was a process that needed to occur as a "normal" part of our curriculum. Indeed, TSPAR was inspired by a parent's reflection and shaped by gaining meaningful insight about Youth Participatory Action Research (YPAR) and Participatory Action Research (PAR) from youth who participated in these methodologies alongside educators to create change in their communities (e.g., Akom, Cammarota, and Ginwright, 2008; Cammarota, 2011a, 2011b; Cammarota and Romero, 2009, 2010; Ginwright and James, 2002; Mirra and Morrell, 2011; Stovall, Calderon, Carrera, and King, 2009). Hence, the pressure to "cover" the standards leaves many teachers feeling like PAR is something that needs to be done outside of the classroom, during the summer, or through grant-funded electives.

TSPAR challenges educational policies that normalize oppressive practices in classrooms by developing ways to practice PAR in the classroom while still having the curriculum align with state-mandated standards. For example, the scientific method is a required part of the curriculum. In addition, California State Standards 7(a–e) requires students to "develop their own questions and perform their own investigations." In this sense, by using the language from the state standards, and flipping the script on the scientific method, TSPAR became a part of our curriculum wherein students took action to create changes in their own lives, classrooms, schools, and communities (see Lesson Six for details).

The practice of TSPAR in public schools supports students and teachers who take collective action toward dismantling unjust schooling practices rooted in economic, racial, gender, and youth disparities. Indeed, "it is essential to be able to transform individual values into collective ones, identifying elements of convergence and solidarity with others sharing the same values," ultimately providing the healing space for the development of a collective identity (Della Porta & Diani, 2009, p. 72). TSPAR generates a movement toward justice, with the players most central in the ongoing struggle for equitable schools rooted in racial, class, youth, and gender justice. TSPAR aims to provide students the equitable and anti-oppressive education they deserve and teachers the autonomy to work alongside their students in building beloved communities. TSPAR carves out a space for teachers and students to navigate "between lived experiences of oppression and the empowered realization that things do not have to be this way; that change is indeed possible" (Negrón-Gonzales, 2009, p. 2). In this way, students and teachers begin "creating cultural works that enable communities to envision what's possible with collective action, personal self transformation, and will" (Kelly, 2002, p. 7). For example, all five of my class periods participated in TSPAR in 2013, wherein each class chose different problems on campus they wanted to change. Simultaneously, I worked alongside them learning from and supporting their process as illustrated in the pedagogical tool below.

Pedagogical Tool

Unit Title: Science, Society, and Human Rights

Unit Introduction: As a public school teacher, creating lessons using a human rights framework provided me with the ability to work alongside my students to co-create and sustain an anti-oppressive classroom. I share the ways in which teaching and learning toward social justice inspired and reflected students': (1) identities, (2) creation of authentic and meaningful work that transcended beyond the classroom walls, (3) self-worth, (4) working together, (5) critical consciousness, (6) agency, (7) understanding and valuing of difference, and (8) disposition toward learning by using HRE as a form of resistance toward oppressive practices. This unit provides a framework for teachers to design programs alongside their students at their own school sites that reflect their schools' and communities' needs, in order to transform the inequities they experience on a daily basis. The lessons highlighted in this unit plan are unique to our particular community, yet they provide a model of movement building for other educators to work with.

Lesson One: Working in Groups—Equity Lesson

Essential Question(s):

- What do we mean, when we say something is "normal?"
- What are the similarities and differences between the phrases being *tolerant of folks* and *treating folks with dignity*? Which one of these phrases do the tenets of the UDHR reflect?
- In what ways can your differences help your group to be successful while learning science?
- In what ways can your similarities help your group to be successful while learning science?
- What is the difference between *equity* and *equality*?

Time: Three days, with 50-minute class periods.

Materials Needed: Gregorc Activity copies (http://gregorc.com), construction paper, and markers.

Introductory Activity: Write on the board (left side), "What are some ways that working in groups have not worked well for you in the past?" Write on the board (right side), "What can we do to create groups that work together in ways that are fair, meaningful, and supportive?" Have students share out their previous experiences of working in groups. For Question 2, provide students the space to share examples of meaningful and equitable group work practices.

Steps: At the core of democratic practice is working together toward a common goal. During the first week of school, students learn the expectations, structure, and function of their life science class with three days dedicated to the Gregorc activity. At the top of a sheet of poster paper, students write down their chosen group name, construct a t-chart directly below it, and write down similarities and differences based on the Gregorc activity.

At the bottom of the poster paper, students write one to two sentences responding to the questions, "In what ways can your differences help your group be successful while learning science?" "In what ways can your similarities help your group be successful while learning science?"

Assessment: Observations of students' relationships with each other; Group Poster.

Lesson Two: Cell Model Project:
Using HRE to Work toward a Common Goal

Objectives: To attain the standards listed below, students work in groups playing the role of a Science Model Company to create a three-dimensional plant cell model to scale and a commercial with a jingle, slogan, and message about the importance of using their cell model as a learning tool. It is essential that students learn how to work together toward a common goal through practice and reflection, think critically/question media and advertisements, and teach and learn seventh-grade science standards. Using the UDHR as a framework, students as a whole class construct a human rights teamwork rubric before working in groups. The rubric is then used as the foundation for creating and sustaining an equitable classroom rooted in dignity, respect, and cooperation.

California Science Standards:

1(a–f). All living organisms are composed of cells, from just one to many trillions, whose details usually are visible only through a microscope.

7(a–e). Scientific progress is made by asking meaningful questions and conducting careful investigations. As a basis for understanding this concept and addressing the content in the other three strands, students should develop their own questions and perform investigations.

Time: Six days, with 50-minute class periods.

Materials Needed: Blank Student Rubric, Teacher Made Rubric, Cell Model Jobs, Cell Model to Scale Worksheet, video camera, and supplies for building a cell model (Styrofoam measuring 20 cm × 30 cm, assorted objects for organelles).

Introductory Activity: Introduction to the Universal Declaration of Human Rights (UDHR), Cooperative Team Building—Working Together Toward A Common Goal.

Before an introduction to the UDHR, students spend a few minutes responding to the question, "What are human rights?" Students then place their paper with their written responses faced down on their tables.

Next students are introduced to the creation and purpose of the UDHR. Articles 1, 2, 3, 5, 19, and 26 (http://www.un.org/en/documents/udhr/) and the preamble are shared via a projector on to the whiteboard and handouts. After reading each article, students define and record unfamiliar words in the margins of their handouts. Students and teachers share how UDHR articles could be enacted in the classroom. Students are encouraged to share their thoughts about each article.

After the introduction to the UDHR, students spend a few minutes answering the questions, "What do you know about human rights?" and "In what ways have your rights been honored or violated?" on the backside of the paper with their initial response. Students are then asked to record a list of words to use as categories for the Human Rights—Teamwork Rubric. The rubric is a matrix consisting of 25 blank squares.

As a class, students share 10–14 words for categories, such as "encouragement," "determination," "cooperation," and "patience," which are written on the whiteboard. Students then vote on five words they want to use for the class rubric, which can be used during any group activity. For this lesson, the rubric was used while constructing a cell model and writing a script for a commercial that was video-recorded and shared with all my science classes.

During the project, students are reminded to refer to their rubrics and to reflect on ways to create and sustain equitable group practices. Several times during and after the project is complete, students are asked to assess themselves as a group using their Teamwork Rubric.

Steps: While working in groups, students use their individual Handout 1: Sizing Up a Cell (see Table 5.1) to construct a cell model together. Students select a job title, choose their supplies, construct a cell model, and create a commercial.

Time: The duration of this project is six days, with 50 minutes per class period. The sixth day of the project involves student presentations and assessment.

Assessment: Peer grading of student presentations and cell models. Teacher grading of student presentations and cell model. Grades reflect the total feedback from students and teacher. Teamwork is also assessed using Teamwork Rubric.

Lesson Three: Dignity and Bioethics

Objectives: Students are introduced to the UNESCO and several principles of bioethics including the: (1) Universal Declaration on the Human Genome and Human Rights, (2) International Declaration on Human Genetic Data, (3) Universal Declaration on Bioethics and Human Rights, and (4) ICESR. As students begin to recognize the moral, ethical, and legal tools for promoting human rights within the field of science, they grapple with standards-based genetics concepts using a critical lens rooted in human rights. Real world lessons provide students with meaningful curricula to promote lifelong learning dispositions and greater understanding of core science concepts.

California Science Standards:

- 1(a–f). All living organisms are composed of cells, from just one to many trillions, whose details usually are visible only through a microscope.
- 2(a–e). A typical cell of any organism contains genetic instructions that specify its traits. Those traits may be modified by environmental influences.

Time: Two days, with 50-minute class periods.

Materials Needed: Handout of UDHR Articles, Handout of Human Genome, Bioethics, and ICESCR Articles (Articles 1–9), Documentary link to *The Way of All Flesh* (Curtis, 1997), and Handout of Margonelli's (2010) Book Review.

Introductory Activity: Brief introduction and review of UDHR Articles 12, 19, 26, 27, and 29. In-depth introduction to the ICESCR Article 15 (http://www.ohchr.org/EN/ProfessionalInterest/Pages/CESCR.aspx) and the Universal Declaration on the Human Genome and Human Rights Articles 1–9 (http://www.unesco.org/new/en/cairo/social-and-human-sciences/bioethics/bioethics-education/). Students then watch the last 15 minutes (start @ 38 minute mark) of the documentary, *The Way of All Flesh* (Curtis, 1997). Note: Students at this point have used microscopes to view their own cheek cells and are able to identify and describe the structure and function of animal cells.

Procedure: Students take turns reading aloud a book review by Margonelli (2010) in response to Skloot's (2010) book, *The Immortal Life of Henrietta Lacks* (http://www.nytimes.com/2010/02/07/books/review/Margonelli-t.html?pagewanted=all&_r=0). During the reading, students discuss issues of race, poverty, and human rights as well as unfamiliar words. Students place a check mark next to the UDHR articles violated in Henrietta Lacks's story (Curtis, 1997).

Students then respond individually to the question written on the whiteboard, "Choose one article you checked off as a violation and explain why." After completing their responses, students get into their groups and share their answers. One member from each group reports the group's responses to the class. This story will be revisited later with critical and complex questions once students have had the opportunity to build on their understanding of race, mitosis, heredity, and bioethics during the genetics unit. In addition, students will learn distinctions among UN international agreements, conventions, and declarations.

Assessment: Students' written and verbal responses to Henrietta Lacks's story.

Lesson Four: Lesson—Understanding Race as a Social Construct

Objectives: During the genetics unit, five days are dedicated to understanding race as a social construct. The purpose of this lesson is for students to reflect on their hidden biases and assumptions, to understand white privilege, and to recognize their full human potential essential in working toward the practice of freedom. The invention of race was initially justified with "scientific data," and students learn to recognize that race is a social construct without scientific validity. During the five days, students: (1) take pre- and post-surveys in regards to race, (2) complete a Public Broadcasting Service (PBS) online activity about race, (3) reexamine the story of Henrietta Lacks after reading hook's (2013) critique, and (4) participate in a class discussion about race. These lessons intertwine with understanding standards-based genetics concepts such as heredity, phenotypes, genes, alleles, and DNA.

California State Standards:

1(a–f). All living organisms are composed of cells, from just one to many trillions, whose details usually are visible only through a microscope.
2(a–e). A typical cell of any organism contains genetic instructions that specify its traits. Those traits may be modified by environmental influences.

Time: Five days, with 50-minute periods.
Materials Needed: Printed copies of hooks (2013) *Writing Beyond Race: Living Theory*, pp. 81–91, Link to *RACE—The Power of An Illusion* website (http://www.pbs.org/race/000_General/000_00-Home.htm), Handout 2: Race—The Power of An Illusion (see Table 5.2) and Handout 2, Part 2: Race (see Table 5.3).
Steps: During the first two days, students work in pairs and complete a guided worksheet while they navigate an online companion website for the documentary, *RACE—The Power of an Illusion* on PBS.org (California Newsreel, 2003).

On the third day, students respond to two of the following questions in their personal journals (throughout the year students write entries in their reflection journal):

1. What is race?
2. What was your hypothesis before you began the online activity? Based on what you have learned from the online activity, was your hypothesis correct? Please explain.
3. What is institutional racism? Give an example of a form of institutional racism that exists today.
4. How does institutional racism impact social and economic rights? Please use at least one article from the UDHR or ICESCR to support your response.

On day four and five students participate in a class discussion on race and write a personal narrative related to racism.
Assessment: Students' responses on Handout 2: Race—The Power of Illusion (see Table 5.2) and Handout 2, Part 2: Race (see Table 5.3) classroom conversations about race, and students' personal narratives.

Lesson Five: Inclusive Science Newspaper Rooted in Human Rights

Objectives: This project provides students with the opportunity to recognize that their work can transcend beyond the walls of their classroom. Students are given the opportunity to: (1) share their work school wide, (2) research a standards-based topic they are interested in, (3) learn about contributions to science beyond the dominant culture's discourse, (4) develop their understanding of race as a social construct, (5) use technology to research, share, and collaborate, (6) improve their literacy skills as related to technology, research, writing, and critical thinking, (7) incorporate the UDHR, ICESCR, and principles of bioethics in their work, and (8) produce authentic, collaborative, and meaningful work.
California State Standards:

7(a–e). Scientific progress is made by asking meaningful questions and conducting careful investigations. As a basis for understanding this concept and addressing the content in the other three strands, students should develop their own questions and perform investigations.

Time: Three days, with 50-minute class periods.
Materials Needed: Handout 3: Genetics Research Article (see Table 5.4).

Steps: In groups, students choose a genetics topic in order to write an article for the school's science newsletter. All students are encouraged to use a critical lens rooted in human rights which they have learned in their life science class.

Assessment: Final Submission of Research Article.

Lesson Six: Teacher and Student Participatory Action Research (TSPAR)

Objectives: Students move beyond California State Content Standards and flip the script on the scientific method by using the principles of participatory action research to create change at their school site.

California State Standards:

> 7(a–e). Scientific progress is made by asking meaningful questions and conducting careful investigations. As a basis for understanding this concept and addressing the content in the other three strands, students should develop their own questions and perform investigations.

Time: Two months: The first three days are dedicated entirely to TSPAR. The following 40 days for 20 minutes per class period are dedicated to TSPAR while students start their unit on Evolution. At times, students will work on TSPAR-related assignments, while other group members work on assignments related to evolution. TSPAR can occur during any unit, since students have different responsibilities at different times (literature review, outside of class collecting data, designing data collection instruments, etc.). Having both processes taking place simultaneously during the TSPAR process provides students with a more meaningful and engaging environment.

Materials: Varies (e.g., digital cameras w/ video recording, audio recorders, supplies for building think boxes, and access to internet and computers).

Steps: Each class period, students work to: (1) identify a problem at their school that they want to change, (2) develop their research question(s), (3) choose literature to read, (4) develop the design of the investigation, (5) generate qualitative data collection instruments, (6) collect data, (7) analyze the data, and (8) take action toward creating better conditions at their school.

On day one, students share out problems identified at their school site and then write responses on the whiteboard. The class then votes on the problem they want to explore further. For example, during the 2013–2014 school year, one period chose "cafeteria food" and came up with the problem statement: "Our school cafeteria has unhealthy food that doesn't fit the needs for students to have balanced meals for breakfast and lunch because the food is processed, fattening, expired, and undercooked." Next students develop their research question, such as "How can we change the processed, fattening, undercooked and expired food that is served in the cafeteria to create healthy and balanced meals?"

On day two, students in groups of four decide which data collection instrument they want to use (such as surveys, interviews, think boxes, pictures, and grease graphs). Each group either chooses a different instrument or proposes using the same instrument in different ways. Students then create their instruments and begin collecting data. During this process, students research articles and create literature reviews to address their research problem. After analyzing the data, each group shares results with the class. Finally, the class as a whole explores ways to take action in order to create change on campus.

Assessment: Students' design of the investigation, literature review, creation of data instrument, results, and analysis.

Table 5.1 Handout 1: Sizing up a Cell

Name_____

Date_____

Period_____

Sizing Up a Cell

Cell Structure	Actual Size	$1\,\mu m : 1\,mm$
Plant Cell (Cell Wall)	$150\,\mu m \times 100\,\mu m$	___mm = ___cm ___mm = ___cm
Nucleus (1) Round	$8\,\mu m$	___mm = ___cm
Vacuole (1) Blob	$130\,\mu m$	___mm = ___cm
Chloroplast (3) Oval / Green	$7\,\mu m$	___mm = ___cm
Ribosome (Many) Dots	$.020\,\mu m$	___mm = ___cm
Golgi Bodies (3) Spiral	$3\,\mu m$	___mm = ___cm
Lysosomes (3) Round	$1\,\mu m$	___mm = ___cm

$1\,\mu m = 1/1,000,000$ of a millimeter.

Table 5.2 Handout 2: Race—The Power of Illusion

Name_____

Date_____

Period_____

Race—The Power of An Illusion

Based on prior experience, define the meaning of race to the best of your ability.

_____

_____

_____

As a class, let's define race. What is our current definition of race?

_____

_____

_____

_____

Problem: *Is race a social construct or scientific fact? Write a hypothesis.*

_____

_____

_____

_____

Using the website below investigate your hypothesis.

Website: www.pbs.org/race/

Table 5.3 Handout 2 Part 2: Race—The Power of Illusion

What is Race?

Sorting People – What was the purpose of this activity? What did you learn from this activity?

Race Timeline – Share one or two thoughts based on this activity.

Human Diversity – Share one or two concepts you learned from this activity?

Me, My Race, and I–Please share any thoughts you have about this portion of the activity?

Where Race Lives – Do you feel this activity is true? Why or why not?

Write down three questions you have now that you have finished the online activity.

1.
2.
3.

Is there anything you disagree with from the online activity? Explain.

Share at least one thing that you think differently about now that you have completed this activity and explain.

Was your hypothesis correct? Why or why not?

Table 5.4 Handout 3: Genetics Research Article

Group name_____   Name:_____
                                Date:_____
                                Period:_____

Genetics Research Article

Project Description (50 Points)

Your group will write a research article on a topic related to genetics. The article should be informative in these ways: include interesting information, be written from a critical lens, include critique, and cite references. This should be your best work. It is suggested you prepare note cards, construct an outline, write a rough draft and follow the instructions listed below.

Possible Project Ideas

People: Barbara McClintock, George Washington Carver, Harriet Baldwin Creighton, Rosalind Franklin, Severo Ochoa de Albornoz, Watson and Crick, Henrietta Lacks, Susumu Tonegawa, Gregor Mendel, Aprille Ericsson

Modern Genetics: Cloning, Genetic Engineering, DNA Fingerprinting, The Human Genome Project, Bioethics, Monsanto

Understanding through Genetics: Diversity, Race, Racism, School, Race and Genes, Gender, Society, Race, and Genes

All articles must reference at least one article from the UDHR or ICESCR. Groups writing about modern genetics need to reference the principles discussed in the Universal Declaration on the Human Genome and Human Rights, the International Declaration on Human Genetic Data and/or the Universal Declaration on Bioethics and Human Rights.

Project Format

The paper will include the following sections:

1. Cover page with the title of your paper, your names, the date, and class period
2. Body of paper should be five paragraphs in length, double space typed, and 12 font
3. Grammar, spelling, and punctuation should be correct
4. Reference page

Due Date:_____

Extra Credit (10 points) – This is upon completion of your group's five-paragraph essay. Create a genetics and or human rights related crossword puzzle, comic strip, or diagram that can be included in our science newspaper.

References

Akom, A. A., Cammarota, J., and Ginwright, S. (2008). Youthtopias: Towards a new paradigm of critical youth studies. *Youth Media Reporter* 2(1–6): 108–129.

California Newsreel. (2003). *RACE—The power of an illusion*. Retrieved from http:www.pbs. org/race/.

Cammarota, J. (2011a). From hopelessness to hope: Social justice pedagogy in urban education and youth development. *Urban Education* 46(4): 828–844.

Cammarota, J. (2011b). The value of a multicultural and critical pedagogy: Learning democracy through diversity and dissent. *Multicultural Perspectives* 13(2): 62–69.

Cammarota, J. and Romero, A. (2010). Participatory action research for high school students: Transforming policy, practice, and the personal with social justice education. *Educational Policy* 25(3): 488–506.

Cammarota, J. and Romero, A. F. (2009). A social justice epistemology and pedagogy for Latina/o students: Transforming public education with participatory action research. *New Directions for Youth Development* 2009(123): 53–65.

Claude, R. P. (2002). *Science in the service of human rights*. Philadelphia, PA: University of Pennsylvania Press. *The way of all flesh* (1997). Dir. Adam Curtis. Perf. Documentary. BBC. Videocassette.

Della Porta, D. and Diani, M. (2009). *Social movements: An introduction*. Malden, MA: Blackwell.

Freire, P. (1970/1993). *Pedagogy of the oppressed*, Rev. edn. New York: The Continuum International Publishing Group.

Freire, P. (1998). *Pedagogy of freedom*. Lanham, MD: Rowman and Littlefield Publishers.

Fuller, B. (2003). Education policy under cultural pluralism. *Educational Researcher* 32(9): 15–24.

Ginwright, S. and James, T. (2002). From assets to agents of change: Social justice, organizing, and youth development. *New Directions for Youth Development* 2002(96): 27–46.

Giroux, H. (2004). *Neoliberalism and the demise of democracy: Resurrecting hope in dark times*. Retrieved from http://dissidentvoice.org /Aug04/ Giroux 0807.html.

Gramsci, A. (1971). *Selections from the prison notebooks*. New York: International Publishers.

hooks, b. (1994). *Teaching to transgress: Education as the practice of freedom*. New York: Routledge.

hooks, b. (2013). *Writing beyond race: Living theory and practice*. New York: Routledge.

Kelly, R. D. G. (2002). *Freedom dreams: The black radical imagination*. Boston, MA: Beacon Press.

King Jr., Martin L. "The Birth of a New Nation." Sermon at Dexter Avenue Baptist Church, April 7, 1957. *MLK Online*, Web. June 12, 2012.

Kumashiro, K. (2008). *The seduction of common sense: How the right has framed the debate on America's schools.* New York: Teachers College Press.

Kumashiro, K. (2009). *Against common sense: Teaching and learning toward social justice.* New York: Routledge.

Kumashiro, K. (2012). *Bad teacher: How blaming teachers distorts the bigger picture.* New York: Teachers College Press.

Leonardo, Z. (2009). *Race, whiteness, and education.* New York: Routledge.

Margonelli, L. (2010). *Eternal life.* Retrieved from http://www.nytimes.com/2010/02/07/books/review/Margonelli-t.html?pagewanted=all&_r=0.

Mirra, N. and Morrell, E. (2011). Teachers as civic agents: Toward a critical democratic theory of urban teacher development. *Journal of Teacher Education* 62(4): 408–420.

Negrón-Gonzales, G. (2009). *Hegemony, ideology and oppositional consciousness: Undocumented youth and the personal-political struggle for educational justice.* Berkeley, CA: Institute for the Study of Societal Issues.

Oakes, J. (2005). *Keeping track: How schools structure inequality.* New Haven, CT: Yale University Press.

Skloot, R. (2010). *The immortal life of Henrietta Lacks.* New York: Crown Publishing Group.

Sleeter, C. (2005). *Un-standardizing curriculum: Multicultural teaching in the standards-based classroom.* New York: Teachers College Press.

Stovall, D., Calderon, A., Carrera, L., and King, S. (2009). Youth, media, and justice: Lessons from the Chicago doc your bloc project. *Radical Teacher* 86: 50–58.

Suarez, D. (2007). Education professionals and the construction of human rights education. *Comparative Education Review* 51(1): 48–79.

Tatum, B. (1997). *Why are all the black kids sitting together in the cafeteria?* New York: Basic Books.

United Nations. (1948). *Universal Declaration of Human Rights.* Retrieved from http://www.un.org/en/documents/udhr/index.shtml.

United Nations. (1966). *International Convention on Economic, Social and Cultural Rights.* Retrieved from http://www2.ohchr.org/english/law/.

CHAPTER 6

Challenging Islamophobia in the Middle School Classroom: Using Critical Media Literacy to Teach Human Rights

Kelly Delaney

Introduction

I teach seventh and eighth grade in a public middle school on the San Francisco peninsula situated within a community that is culturally, linguistically, ethnically, racially, and socioeconomically diverse. We have six public elementary schools, one middle school, and one high school. My students are native speakers of dozens of languages with families from a variety of countries. Some students have parents in jail and are being raised by extended family members, while others are from households with two college-educated parents and attenuating class privilege. In the same classroom, I have students classified as gifted along with students who carry a diagnosis of emotional disturbance.

In addition to social studies courses, I teach an elective course called Advancement Via Individual Determination (AVID), a college preparatory study skills class for students in the academic middle with potential to be the first generation in their family to attend college. The program aims to support students of color and/or low socioeconomic status to succeed in advanced academic classes in order to increase their enrollment in four-year universities. The curriculum focuses on building process skills, like note taking, metacognition and time management, as well as leadership and team building. The program's goal is to explicitly teach inside school those skills that privileged students often acquire outside of school, while avoiding the dumbing down of the curriculum often associated with teaching process skills.

Within these broad outlines, I have considerable freedom as to the curricular content and pedagogy of the AVID course. Given this, I chose the general framework of human rights and specifically the Universal Declaration of Human Rights (UDHR) (United Nations, 1948) as a vehicle for examining oppression in society. We began by reading the UDHR and developing the students' knowledge of specific articles while adding a new lens through which to view the world. During the early portion of the year, the UDHR helped to build a classroom community with a common working language and collectively established norms. I created a unit that examined the issue of Islamophobia in US popular culture, primarily with a critical analysis of the Walt Disney movie *Aladdin* (Clements, 1992) through the framework of human rights. Throughout this unit, students learned how to critically analyze media by examining Islamophobia as a specific type of oppression and to connect this issue with specific human rights inscribed in the UDHR.

During this unit, my students and I used van Driel's (2004) definition of Islamophobia as a "term to refer to an irrational distrust, fear or rejection of the Muslim religion and those who are (perceived as) Muslims" (p. x). Islamophobic behavior and practices often target not only Muslims, but also anyone who looks or acts vaguely similar, including Arabs, Sikhs, and Persians who may or may not be Muslim. Islamophobia in popular culture has two defining features. The first is the reinforcement of negative stereotypes of Arabs and Muslims as wholly different people who should be feared and distrusted (Luyendijk, 2009; Said, 1978; Sensoy and Stonebanks, 2009; Shaheen, 2001). The second is a corresponding lack of positive counter-narratives depicting Muslims going about their daily lives like everyone else (Gottschalk and Greenberg, 2008; Malek, 2011; Said, 1997; Sensoy and Stonebanks, 2009; Shaheen, 2008; van Driel, 2004).

Rationale for Unit

For several reasons, I believe that a focus on Islamophobia in a middle school classroom is imperative. The experiences of my own students provide a strong motivating factor in my decision to focus on this issue. To begin, I estimate that about 10 percent of my students are targets of Islamophobia, because they either are Muslim or are perceived to be. Ever present in the United States and exacerbated by the 9/11 events, Islamophobia became a renewed concern of mine after the killing of Osama bin Laden in May 2011 as incidents at my school increased. Epithets of "terrorist" were launched with increasing impunity, and the school administration and many teachers responded inadequately. I felt the need not only to advocate for those students who were—and continue to be—under attack, but also to help the other 90 percent of students to understand their role in contributing to a climate of hostility. Youth need to understand the interconnectedness of the various forms of oppression that reinforce cultural hegemony. They also need to hear from a non-Muslim adult like me who finds Islamophobia unacceptable. Part of my responsibility as a white teacher is to acknowledge and leverage my privilege in the service of human rights.

In addition to my concern as an educator, this topic is of critical importance to me on a personal level. First, I grew up in this community, which is my home. I have an inherent stake in ensuring that my neighbors and friends are able to live in dignity. My partner is a Palestinian American Muslim, and it is infuriating for me to witness how differently he is treated. Even though he is a US citizen, owner of a local business for over 20 years, and prototypically American in many ways, he is often viewed with suspicion and fear in the most ordinary of situations. I was raised within the Catholic tradition by women who emphasized responsibility for others above all else. "Am I my brother's keeper?" (Holy Bible, 1982, Genesis, 4:9) was a constant question growing up, as was the exhortation that "to whom much is given, much is required" (Holy Bible, 1982; Luke, 12:48). Growing up I was expected to appreciate my blessings and to understand the responsibility I had to work for social justice in solidarity with others. I still take this message very seriously in both my professional and personal life.

Examining Islamophobia

An examination of any type of oppression must begin with an overview of the pedagogical lens through which to view this oppression. Freire's (1970) concepts of *conscientization* and *praxis* as a means to transform education and society are essential to effective teaching practice. Equally important are the ideas of more contemporary educators who have adapted Freire's work to current realities. For example, Darder (2002) expresses that critical pedagogy is an act of love, and bell hooks (1994) describes a pedagogy that empowers students and fosters social justice. Lorde (1984) and Duncan-Andrade and Morrell (2008) call for systemic change in the dismantling of oppression. In addition, Valenzuela (1999) and Delpit (2006) write about the importance of community and the practice of "othering" that happens to children of color in the US educational system.

The work of these primarily female educators constitutes an important framework through which to analyze Islamophobia. The process of "othering" that Delpit (2006) and hooks (2010) discuss is the same as the false dichotomy between "us" and "them" that is propounded by supporters of Islamophobia. Said (1978) first wrote about this false dichotomy pitting the Occident (us) against the Orient (them) in art and literature in the nineteenth century. Later in *Covering Islam* (1997), Said expanded his analysis to include politics and mass media, as did Luyendijk (2009) in *People Like Us*. Said's (1978) groundbreaking work in *Orientalism* served as a foundation for scholars studying Islam and the Arab world. His main thesis contends that essentialism has reduced the Arab and Islamic world to one narrowly defined stereotype in opposition to the Western traditions of Europe and the United States. As Said (1978) describes, essentialism states that all Muslims are crazed, oil-rich, and lazy terrorists bent on seducing white women and forcing the West to accept a worldwide caliphate. In contrast, Westerners are enlightened purveyors of freedom and democracy. The mass media omits any evidence that dispels the myth of the violent Muslim yet treats Westerners as complex individuals with great diversity inside the group.

In his later work, Said (1997) adds that this false dichotomy of "us versus them" lies in the stubborn refusal of the West to acknowledge that knowledge is subjective. Luyendijk (2009) echoes Said's (1997) sentiment, arguing that the problem lies in the biased language used to describe a purportedly objective situation:

> Muslims who based their political orientation on their faith were "fundamentalists," whereas, in most Western media reports, an American presidential candidate with the same religious convictions would be labeled "evangelical" or "deeply religious." If that American won the election, almost nobody would say that Christianity was marching forwards; but when Muslims who were inspired in their politics by the Koran came out on top many a Western commentator would say that Islam was on the march. If an Arab leader clashed with a Western government, he was "anti-Western"; Western governments were never "anti-Arab." (p. 140)

The words chosen to describe the world can influence how others view that world. Therefore, journalists and producers of media need to be cognizant of their responsibility to avoid the double standard often applied to Arabs and Muslims.

Shaheen (2008) has written extensively about the targeting of Arabs and Muslims in popular films and television in the United States. In *Guilty: Hollywood's Verdict on Arabs After 9/11*, Shaheen (2008) states that Arabs and Muslims comprise one of the last groups of people who are still acceptable targets for stereotyping and slander, a perspective echoed by others (Khan, 2009; Said, 1997; Sensoy and Stonebanks, 2009). The negative stereotypes of Arabs and Muslims are so often repeated in US movies and television, excluding any contrary evidence, that these negative images become the reality for most Americans. Shaheen connects the very real negative consequences of a xenophobic worldview, reminding readers of the World War II Japanese American internment camps, the extermination of millions during the Holocaust, and the denial of human rights to African Americans throughout US history. As he warns, "This is what happens when people are dehumanized" (Shaheen, 2001, p. 4).

Shaheen's (2001) work describes the specific stereotypes of Arabs and Muslims in Hollywood films and television; while not all Arabs are Muslim and not all Muslims are Arabs, Hollywood treats the two as if they were one and the same. Shaheen discusses the lack of representation of everyday Arabs and Muslims in films and television. He argues that when the only depiction of a group of people shows them as "other," they can be more easily demonized. Yet showing Arabs and Muslims engaged in normal everyday activities would serve to humanize them, helping people to see Arabs and Muslims as a diverse people.

As Ali Khan (2009) writes in *On Being Us and Them*, "complexity is not a friend of prejudice... Nuances and differentiations appear to be the luxury of power-holders, ('we' get to have many different faces), whereas the lines of Muslim identity are crudely drawn, ('they' are all the same)" (p. 154). She describes what appears to be an "irreconcilable gulf between *them* and *us*" (p. 155) that only exacerbates instances of Islamophobia. She comments on the paucity of representations of everyday Muslims in popular culture in the West, which others have attributed to the persistent negative stereotype of the bloodthirsty Muslim terrorist. Stonebanks (2009) also argues that the absence of Muslim images debunking the common stereotype is significant. He mentions news reports of Muslim girls in Canada who were denied the right to play various sports because they wore hijab. Despite the fact that these girls' activities did not fit the stereotype of sheltered, submissive Muslim women, the coverage focused on the hijab itself as a symbol of oppression (Stonebanks, 2009).

van Driel (2004) discusses the problem of Islamophobia as well as the responsibility that purveyors of popular culture, politicians, educators, and the mass media have to end it. The majority in the West have "also never bothered to inform itself about this major world religion or the teachings of the Qur'an. For this reason, the popular media, politicians and other agenda setters can have a disproportionate influence on public opinion" (p. x). In the absence of accurate knowledge, most people tend to believe the images they see in popular culture and mass media.

Islamophobia is by no means the only problem in US society, but is part of the overall phenomenon of dehumanization. Each type of oppression is interconnected, reinforcing one another and leading to harmful divisions among people. According to the UDHR, all rights and freedoms are inextricably linked. Racism, sexism, heterosexism, xenophobia, Islamophobia— each form of oppression keeps us from becoming united as one human family composed of unique individuals and gloriously diverse cultures and traditions.

Violations of the UDHR and CRC

In all of its forms, Islamophobia is a violation of multiple articles in both the UDHR and the Convention on the Rights of the Child (CRC) (1989). Islamophobia reflects violations of UDHR Articles 1, 2, 5, 7, 9,18, 26, and 27, and Articles 14, 28, and 29 of the CRC, which extends human rights particularly enshrined to children. Moreover, the climate created by a country awash in Islamophobia leads to actions within our legal, penal, and educational system that have a far-reaching impact beyond violating specific articles in human rights agreements.

Articles 1 and 2 of the UDHR state that all people are born free and equal, and that human rights apply to everyone regardless of race, color, sex, language, religion, national origin, and political affiliation. Article 7 is similar to the equal protection clause in the 14th Amendment to the US Constitution. These three articles require one set of laws and rules for everyone. While treating people differently because of their identity, nationality or religion is a violation of these rights; this is precisely what happens with Islamophobia. Racial profiling of Arabs and Muslims at airports is a common practice that violates UDHR Articles 1, 2, and 7. This is also an example of a violation of Article 9 that guarantees people the right to be free from arbitrary arrest or detainment. Examples abound of Arabs and Muslims who are detained and arrested in airports simply based upon their identity as Arabs or Muslims (Malek, 2011; van Driel, 2004).

Article 18 of the UDHR and Article 14 of the CRC deal with the freedom to practice one's religion. However, the climate of Islamophobia in the United States has produced a society where the most typical and innocuous outward signs of Islamic practice, including prayer, are seen as something to be feared (Abo-Zena, Sahili, and Tobais-Nahi, 2009). Likewise, Article 27 of the UDHR, which guarantees the right to participate in the cultural life of the community, is violated by this same climate of fear directed at Muslims. If a Muslim cannot pray in public without being labeled a suspected terrorist, how can it be said that their human rights are being honored?

Article 26 of the UDHR and Articles 28 and 29 of the CRC concern the right to a free and fair education. The CRC articles go further and describe children's right to an education that develops all of their talents and abilities to their fullest potential, and which builds respect for human rights, students' parents and cultural heritage, as well as the heritage of others and the natural world. Yet the realities contrast with these principles: popular culture still condones Islamophobia, Muslim students are still open targets, Muslim girls have their hijabs ripped from their heads, and Muslim boys are branded as terrorists with little consequence. The rights of many children of color are violated every day in schools all across the United States, placing Arab and Muslim students especially in jeopardy in the current political climate.

Pedagogical Tool

While many of my students of color are certainly aware of various forms of oppression, many of my white students are not, particularly those coming from positions of privilege (class, gender, sexual orientation, gender identity, etc.). My school's student body is extremely heterogeneous, and students come into my classroom with a multitude of life experiences. Nevertheless, very few are able to situate the circumstances of their lives within a larger context of systemic and institutionalized oppression, much less able to utilize the academic vocabulary necessary to discuss these issues. Gaining access to this language is a critical first step in being able to "read the world," as Freire (1970) states. As a result, I developed the following unit to begin a yearlong focus on creating critical consciousness and contextualizing the world of my students as experienced through the educational system and mass media.

I intentionally selected the film, *Aladdin*, as the centerpiece of the unit for several reasons. First, my audience is made up of youth aged 11–14 with a fairly wide range of abilities and experiences. In addition, many middle school students try to pretend they are all grown up, but in actuality get really excited by cartoons. Finally, and perhaps most pertinently, *Aladdin* embodies many of the problems regarding Islamophobia as outlined by the authors cited above. Arabs are portrayed with exaggerated physical features as evil, violent, and backward, while Anglicized characters are the heroes. Notably absent are three-dimensional female characters as well as positive characters who are demonstrably Muslim, or almost any mention of Islam at all—odd for a tale set in medieval Iraq. The film also serves as an example of issues of race, class, gender, and heterosexism, with a strong bias in favor of capitalism. I asked students to take note of those examples so that they could understand the intersectionality of oppression. In general, I want my students to know how different systems of oppression work together to reinforce divisions between people and keep them from working together for change.

The unit began by defining vocabulary and modeling the process of media deconstruction. I emphasized think/pair/share activities before the culminating project in which students deconstructed a particular piece of media (a song, television show, or internet video) and problematized the underlying dominant narrative(s). Subsequent lessons focused on challenging these dominant narratives as well as proposing solutions. Examples of these actions ranged from posting counter-narratives online to developing an anti-bullying campaign at school.

The earliest lessons in this unit included an explanation of critical media literacy, as well as definitions of forms of oppression such as racism and classism. Next, I defined "dominant narrative" and "counter-narrative" by using the framework of critical race theory outlined by Ladson-Billings and Tate (1995). After teaching this unit over the years, I have expanded this section to include students' own counter-narratives, poems, and iMovies as personal *testimonios* in the tradition of Moraga and Anzaldúa (1970). Once we established a common language, I modeled the media deconstruction process through showing specific examples of advertisements. (A plethora of images and video is easily searchable online.) After I modeled the process of deconstruction, students engaged in pair/share activities using additional samples. Eventually, they worked together in pairs or triads to brainstorm examples to share with the whole class.

Next students began to deconstruct Disney's *The Little Mermaid* (Clements, 1989) and *Aladdin* (Clements, 1992), using a simple three-column graphic organizer. In the first column students identified the type of oppression found and then described the specific offensive image or words in the second column. The third column asked students to identify the dominant narrative supported by the example.

The first time I taught this lesson, the third column asked students to identify the hidden message because I had been using the analogy of students being detectives having to uncover hidden messages since often oppression is subtle. Unfortunately, when students encountered a particularly obvious offense, they did not realize they knew the answer since it was too easy. Therefore, I decided it was preferable to teach students to use the more precise language of "dominant narrative." I also added a fourth column for students to provide a counter-narrative for each example. Students used this graphic organizer for the deconstruction of two different movies as well as to help with their final projects. Over time, I refined the unit to better support students by adding in-class work time, providing more explanation, and modeling how to evaluate and cite sources. We worked together as a class to decide what specific issues we would like to address to narrow the focus, and I supported each pair in problem-solving skills.

This unit is easily adaptable to other classrooms and contexts. My class focused on Disney animation films, but modifications for elementary students could easily be made in a number of ways, such as limiting the number of concepts covered. Alternatively, these same concepts could be taught using advertising that targets children, such as gendered toy packaging. Conversely, the unit could be adjusted for high school or college students by using more sophisticated media content and adding more complex concepts and language (such as "hegemony"). The most important guidance I give to pre-service teachers is to always adapt a lesson they like for the particular group of students they are teaching. First and foremost, pay attention to your own students, and then modify the content accordingly.

Reflection

Although I have adapted this unit over time based upon my students' needs and input, the essence and objectives have remained the same. My students' engagement, participation, and ownership during this unit led to outstanding final projects. Just as significantly, many students have learned to understand that the dynamics of oppression in their own lives are very real and do not reside in their imagination. This understanding of oppression represents critical knowledge to be shared and analyzed inside the classroom as well as in the world. As a result of this unit, I witnessed a shift in the level of discourse in the classroom and on campus.

The first time I taught these lessons, I had a student in my class who basically refused to participate in school and was labeled defiant or disrespectful by other teachers. He had always been respectful to me, but I struggled to get him to complete challenging work in class. Early in this unit, students worked in groups discussing personal experiences of discrimination. When I approached his group, he asked if he could take out his phone and share his example. The previous year he had taken photos of signs in the local grocery store for Black History Month advertising special sales on Kool-Aid and watermelon. He asked if this was what I meant by a personal example. When I said, "Yes," he requested that I show his images to the class so he could talk about them. He asked, "Do you mean this is a real thing? I thought it was messed up, but I didn't think it was a real thing." We all crowded around his phone and took turns observing the photos while he explained where he saw them and what he thought about them. He told me later that this was the first time anyone had ever listened to him at school and the first time he had ever known the right answer.

Student feedback like that is what keeps me going as a teacher. Another group of students told me at graduation that they liked my class because they learned about "real life" and "things that mattered." Many students visit after graduation and mention this unit as particularly meaningful. Students have started coming to me or talking to one another when they notice oppressive situations in school, in the neighborhood, or even in the news. They have their eyes open now, and they are excited to share this new awareness with their peers.

I have also learned so much from my students: how to be a better listener, a better learner, and a better teacher. One of the most important gifts that my students have given me is faith. Some days I hear the news and find it so depressing that I just want to give up. But my students have taught me that anything is possible if we work together. They are so amazing, hard working, and passionate, that I have complete faith in their ability to change the world. No question.

Lesson Plans

Days 1–2 (Given one hour periods)
Essential Questions:

- What is the hidden agenda of this video?
- Who is producing this media and what are their motives?
- What are the effects produced on self-image, for example?
- What is critical media literacy?
- How does critical media literacy connect to the UDHR?

Standards:

- AVID—students will learn to take complete and accurate Cornell notes.

- Common Core State Standards (CCSS): English Language Arts (ELA) Literacy Reading History.6–8.2 Determine central ideas.

Objectives:

- Students will take complete and accurate Cornell notes regarding important vocabulary and concepts related to critical media literacy.
- Students will make connections between previous learning about the UDHR, media literacy, and their lived experience during think/pair/share.

Materials Needed:

- Computer and LCD projector or equivalent
- Theory, Language and Framework PowerPoint: Define terms like oppression, racism, sexism.
- Cornell Note paper or binder paper (Cornell notes is the preferred note-taking system at our school).

Hook:

- Play YouTube video "The Distortion of Beauty" (n.d.).
- Discuss the lesson's essential questions and additional questions raised by video.

Steps:

- Present a Critical Media Literacy PowerPoint and ask students to take Cornell notes.
- Review correct procedures for Cornell notes as you present information.
- Stop frequently at slides with questions to do think/pair/share.
- Continue with the PowerPoint until all slides have been presented (two to three days).

Days 3–5
Essential Questions:

- What does critical media analysis look like?
- What is (are) the hidden agenda(s) in this film?
- How does this film perpetuate prejudice?

Standards:

- CCSS: ELA Literacy, Speaking and Listening 7.2: Analyze the main ideas and supporting details presented in diverse media and formats.

Objectives: Students will begin the process of critical media analysis as evidenced by the completion of a graphic organizer with the help of the instructor.

Materials Needed:

- Computer and LCD projector or equivalent
- DVD (or streaming version) of Disney's *The Little Mermaid* (Clements, 1989).
- Critical Media Analysis Graphic Organizer. The four-column worksheet described above helps students deconstruct different types of media. The first column asks students to list the type of oppression (Islamophobia, for example). The second asks them to list the specific example seen or heard. (All of the evil characters have exaggerated and stereotyped physical features.) The third asks students to think about the dominant narrative being expressed by this example. (Arabs are evil.) The fourth column asks students to provide a counter-narrative that answers the dominant narrative. ("My friend Michael is an Arab, and he isn't evil.")

Steps:

- Students and instructor watch together Disney's *The Little Mermaid* (Clements, 1989).
- Instructor stops frequently to model critical media analysis out loud to identify specific examples of oppression in the film.
- Instructor completes the graphic organizer on the document camera along with students.
- After modeling several examples of analysis, instructor asks students to make connections between analysis of this movie and other media, or events in their own lives.

Independent Practice:

- Reflection: Respond to the following prompt at the end of the final day:
  - How does this movie perpetuate prejudice?
  - How does this violate the UDHR?

Challenging Islamophobia in the Middle School Classroom • 99

- Give at least three specific examples of other media that violate the UDHR in similar ways.

Day 6
Essential Questions:

- What is a stereotype?
- How do stereotypes affect what we think we know about people who are different from ourselves?
- What are some problems with stereotypes?
- Can you name/describe a stereotype that you have experienced as a victim?
- Can you name one stereotype that you once believed to be true but no longer think so? What happened to change your view?
- What is Islamophobia?
- What are stereotypes of Arabs and Muslims?

Standards:

- California Social Studies Content Standards 7.7.2: Analyze the geographic, political, economic, religious, and social structures of civilizations of Islam.
- CCSS: ELA Literacy Speaking & Listening.7.1: Engage effectively in a range of collaborative discussions.

Objectives:

- Students will discuss stereotypes and how negative and incomplete images of groups of people contribute to fear and hatred of people who are different.
- Students will discuss how stereotypes about Arabs and Muslims contribute to Islamophobia.

Materials Needed:

- Giant pad of paper
- Students will need binder paper

Hook:

- Watch video of student experience after 9/11 from Facing History and Ourselves (2008), http://www.facinghistory.org/video/student-yasameen-r-becomes-upstander-through.

- Watch from time stamp: 30 seconds to 2:00 minutes about a student's experience after 9/11 and discuss. (The rest of the video will be shown later in a lesson about bystanders.)

Steps:

- Students will do a silent chalk walk with big paper placed around the room. Each paper will contain one of the first six essential questions.
- After students have had a chance to answer, discuss the results as a class ending with the final question.
- If students are having a hard time placing Islamophobia, instructor will give context and examples.
- Students will then work in small groups to identify stereotypes of Arabs and Muslims.
- Results will be shared with the class in dialogue.

Independent Practice: Students will reflect on the following prompt: "Free write about a time when stereotypes caused a problem for you or someone you know."

Note: Ideally, this lesson should take place after significant time has been spent working with students to build a community of respect. It is recommended for teachers to reflect on their own and their students' positionality as well as anticipating how to respond if students are upset by comments or discussions.

Days 7–9
Essential Questions:

- What messages are being sent?
- What is the hidden agenda?
- What is missing that should not be?
- How could different audiences interpret this?

Standards:

- CASS Content Standards 7.7.2: Analyze the geographic, political, economic, religious, and social structures of civilizations of Islam.
- CCSS: ELA Literacy.SL 7.2: Analyze the main ideas and supporting details presented in diverse media and formats.

Objectives: Students will critically analyze Disney's *Aladdin* (1992) for instances of racism, sexism, and other types of oppression with a special focus on Islamophobia as evidenced by the completion of a graphic organizer.

Materials Needed:

- Computer and LCD projector or equivalent
- ELMO document camera
- DVD (or streaming version) of Disney's *Aladdin* (1992)
- Critical Media Analysis Graphic Organizer.

Steps:

- Students watch Disney's *Aladdin* and critically analyze the film in small groups of three or four.
- Students complete a graphic organizer asking them to describe specific examples of oppression.
- Instructor pauses the movie frequently to allow students to discuss and write.
- Instructor reminds students about the previous lessons and provides leading questions if necessary, asking often for questions and clarification.

Independent Practice:

- Identify three examples of Islamophobia in your life (things you or someone you know heard, said or saw). Be prepared to share with the class.

Days 10–14
Essential Questions:

- What are some examples of Islamophobia in popular culture?
- How are these specific examples violations of the UDHR?
- What are the consequences of or problems created by these violations?
- What can you/we do about those problems?

Standards:

- CCSS.ELA Literacy.Writing.7.7: Conduct short research projects to answer a question, drawing on several sources and generating additional related, focused questions for further research and investigation.

- CCSS.ELA-Literacy.Writing.7.8: Gather relevant information from multiple print and digital sources, using search terms effectively; assess the credibility and accuracy of each source; and quote or paraphrase the data and conclusions of others while avoiding plagiarism and following a standard format for citation.
- CCSS.ELA-Literacy.Writing.7.9: Draw evidence from literary or informational texts to support analysis, reflection, and research.

Objectives:

- Students will research different examples of Islamophobia on the Internet.
- Students will connect these examples to specific violations of the UDHR.
- Students will create an iMovie, Prezi, wiki, or PowerPoint presentation to present findings to the class and as evidence of learning.

Materials Needed:

- Access to computers for each pair
- Project directions and rubric handout
- Students will need paper for taking notes.

Hook:

- Dialogue as a class about last night's reflection homework.

Steps:

- Students work in pairs to research specific examples of Islamophobia in popular culture.
- Students discuss with their partners how these examples violate specific articles of the UDHR.
- Students create a media presentation containing a synthesis of their learning.

Independent Practice:

- If incomplete after a week of support and instruction, students may do work at home.

Days 15–17
Essential Questions:

- How is Islamophobia being manifested in our popular culture?
- What are the consequences of this type of prejudice?
- What can we do as individuals or as a class to counter this behavior?

Standards: ELA 7.2.3: Deliver research presentations.

Objectives:

- Students share their examples with peers.
- Students connect their examples with specific violations of the UDHR.
- Students problem-pose in dialogue about possible solutions to some of the problems identified in various presentations.

Materials Needed:

- Computer and LCD projector or equivalent
- Stars and Wishes sheets

Steps:

- Students will present their projects to the class in pairs.
- Students who are listening will complete a stars and wishes section for each presentation aside from their own.
- At the end of each presentation, presenting students will dialogue with the class about possible solutions to some of the problems discussed in the presentation.

References

Abo-Zena, M., Sahili, B., and Tobais-Nahi, C. S. (2009). Testing the courage of their convictions. In O. Sensoy and C. D. Stonebanks (eds.) *Muslim voices in school: Narratives of identity and pluralism*, pp. 3–26. Boston, MA: Sense Publishing.

Clements, R. (Director). (1989). *The little mermaid* [Motion picture]. USA: Buena Vista Pictures.

Clements, R. (Director). (1992). *Aladdin* [Motion picture]. USA: Buena Vista Pictures.

Convention on the Rights of the Child. (1989). *OHCHR homepage*. Retrieved November 24, 2011, from http://www2.ohchr.org/english/law/crc.htm.

Darder, A. (2002). *Reinventing Paulo Freire: A pedagogy of love.* Boulder, CO: Westview Press.

Delpit, L. (2006). *Other people's children: Cultural conflict in the classroom.* New York: The New Press.

Duncan-Andrade, J. M. R. and Morrell, E. (2008). *The art of critical pedagogy: Possibilities for moving from theory to practice in urban schools.* New York: Peter Lang.

Facing History and Ourselves. (2008). Student Yasameen R. becomes an upstander through Facing History. Retrieved November 24, 2011, from https://www.youtube.com/watch?v=8X4_UejCL-w

Freire, P. (1970). *Pedagogy of the oppressed.* New York: Seabury Press.

Gottschalk, P. and Greenberg, G. (2008). *Islamophobia making Muslims the enemy.* Lanham, MD: Rowman and Littlefield.

Holy Bible (Revised standard version edn.). (1982). Nashville, TN: Holman Bible Publishers.

hooks, b. (1994). *Teaching to transgress: Education as the practice of freedom.* New York: Routledge.

hooks, b. (2010). *Teaching critical thinking: Practical wisdom.* New York: Routledge.

Khan, C. A. (2009). On being us *and* them: A voice from the edge. In O. Sensoy and C. D. Stonebanks (eds.) *Muslim voices in school: Narratives of identity and pluralism*, pp. 153–168. Boston, MA: Sense Publishing.

Ladson-Billings, G. and Tate, W. F. (1995). Toward a critical race theory of education. *Teachers College Record* 97(1): 47–68.

leydiilovesmakeup (n.d.). The distortion of beauty – YouTube. *YouTube – Broadcast yourself.* Retrieved November 3, 2011, from http://www.youtube.com/watch?v=8PWdW4BruF4.

Lorde, A. (1984). *Sister outsider: Essays and speeches.* Trumansburg, NY: Crossing Press.

Luyendijk, J. (2009). *People like us: Misrepresenting the Middle East.* New York: Soft Skull Press.

Malek, A. (2011). *Patriot acts: Narratives of post-9/11 injustice.* San Francisco, CA: McSweeney's and Voice of Witness.

Moraga, C. and Anzaldúa, G. (1970). *This bridge called my back: Writings of radical women of color.* New York: Kitchen Table, Women of Color Press.

Said, E. W. (1978). *Orientalism.* New York: Pantheon Books.

Said, E. W. (1997). *Covering Islam: How the media and the experts determine how we see the rest of the world*, Rev. edn. New York: Vintage Books.

Sensoy, O. and Stonebanks, C. D. (2009). *Muslim voices in school: Narratives of identity and pluralism.* Boston, MA: Sense Publishing.

Shaheen, J. G. (2001). *Reel bad Arabs: How Hollywood vilifies a people.* New York: Olive Branch Press.

Shaheen, J. G. (2008). *Guilty: Hollywood's verdict on Arabs after 9/11.* Northampton, MA: Olive Branch Press.

Stonebanks, C. D. (2009). If Nancy Drew wouldn't wear a hijab, would the Hardy Boys wear a kufi? In O. Sensoy and C. D. Stonebanks (eds.) *Muslim voices in school: Narratives of identity and pluralism*, pp. 169–183. Boston, MA: Sense Publishing.

United Nations. (1948). *The Universal Declaration of Human Rights*. Retrieved November 24, 2011, from http://www.un.org/en/documents/udhr/.

Valenzuela, A. (1999). *Subtractive schooling: U.S.–Mexican youth and the politics of schooling*. Albany, NY: SUNY Press.

van Driel, B. (2004). *Confronting Islamophobia in educational practice*. Stoke-on-Trent, UK: Trentham.

CHAPTER 7

Tout moun se moun "Every Person Is a Human Being": Understanding the Struggle for Human Rights in Haiti

Victoria Isabel Durán

*K**ole Zepól*, shoulder to shoulder. This expression demonstrates a sense of unity, compassion, and solidarity, which has impacted me most about the people of Haiti. I first witnessed and experienced the resistance and hope for the future of Haiti as I stepped into a youth community center in Cite Soleil in July of 2010. It was in this Sun City, located in the metropolitan area of Port-au-Prince, that I experienced the radiance of the youth in the community. Having joined the Haiti Action Committee and Haiti Emergency Relief Fund, I participated in a delegation with teachers and students to distribute materials to grassroots programs. At *Fondasyon Kole Zepól Sove Ti Moun* Shoulder to Shoulder Foundation to Save Children program we learned of the photography and journalism programs offered in a small, makeshift space with youth from 3 to 14 years of age. The community welcomed us with songs as well as curiosity toward the contents of the bags carried in by the delegation. As I was distributing the food donations of rice, beans, cooking oil, and other items, I began to wonder how long the contents would last. How far would this bag go toward helping the people of Haiti, when a need exists far beyond the food staples we could provide?

The people that I encountered that day had survived more than just the catastrophic impact of the 7.0 magnitude earthquake that struck on January 12, 2010. They not only had survived the aftermath of the quake, but also prior to that tragedy had managed to survive amid the devastating conditions presented in one of the most impoverished nations in the Western hemisphere. The purpose of this chapter is to evaluate post-earthquake Haiti in an attempt to understand the fight for human rights in the name of democracy as well as to further explore the question of the future for the children of Haiti.

Haiti's history and present-day circumstances demonstrate its endless fight and demand for human rights. Haitians are generating activism as grassroots leaders advocate for true democracy and fight for a system of social equality in securing a basic standard of living and system of public education. The first democratically elected Haitian president, Jean-Bertrand Aristide (2000), stated that true social equality reflects the access to basic human necessities.

> Democracy asks us to put the needs and rights of people at the center of our endeavors. This means investing in people. Investing in people translates to providing them with food, clean water, education and healthcare. These are basic human rights. It is the challenge of any real democracy to guarantee them. (p. 36)

Former president Aristide identified two articles of the Universal Declaration of Human Rights (UDHR) (1948) as instrumental components of a real democracy. Article 25 states that everyone has the right to a:

> standard of living adequate for the health and well being of himself and of his family, including food, clothing, housing, and medical care and necessary social services, and the right to security in the event of unemployment, sickness, disability, widowhood, old age or other lack of livelihood in circumstances beyond his control.

It does not take much time in traveling outside of the Toussaint Louverture International Airport to witness the violations of Article 25 and the substandard living conditions to which the majority of Haitians are subjected. Tarps provided by the United States Agency for International Development (USAID) surely do not serve as adequate living conditions to replace the concrete homes destroyed in the quake.

Also contributing to the inadequacies of Haiti's infrastructure is the education system. As Article 26 of the UDHR explains, everyone has the right to education.

Education shall be free at least in the elementary and fundamental stages. Elementary education shall be compulsory. Technical and professional education shall be made generally available and higher education shall be equally accessible to all on the basis of merit.

According to the World Factbook (2011), only 52 percent of Haitians over the age of 15 are literate; thus, the opportunities that exist through education are afforded to very few. While education is vital to the transformation of the nation, as it currently functions in Haiti, it only benefits the elite class.

Human Rights

The Haiti Justice Alliance (2011) indicates the comparison of two quakes. On February 27 an 8.8 magnitude earthquake struck Chile and caused 279 deaths; in contrast, the earthquake in Haiti on January 12 was a 7.0 magnitude quake responsible for the death of over 230,000 people. When comparing the data, it is apparent that the conditions and infrastructure of Haiti were not able to sustain the impact of the quake, causing the displacement of over 1.5 million people. The combination of inadequate infrastructure, over-population in Port-au-Prince, and extreme poverty in a country where people earn less than $2 a day all attributed to the magnitude of the human catastrophe that struck on that day. Haiti had been subject to such conditions as a lasting legacy of colonization.

In 1825, France's King Charles IV declared Haiti was responsible for paying 90 million gold francs (Haiti Justice Alliance, 2011). In an effort to settle this independence debt, Haiti resorted to efforts of deforestation and exploitation of natural resources; by 1940, Haiti paid $21.7 billion dollars to France. The system of semi-feudal farming served as a means to prevent peasants and farm workers from owning land, therefore sustaining the status of the privileged elite (*Bitter Cane*, 1988). During the course of US occupation from 1915 to 1934, American practices in mass agricultural productivity set the stage for the future relationship with Haiti: the United States would profit while Haitians would work in the textile industries.

Haiti became a vessel for foreign interest. The Caribbean nation was transformed into a target for developed countries, including the United

States, France, and Canada, to exert control as dominant world leaders in a globalized market. The lasting legacies of France, the United States, and the current presence of the United Nations Stabilization Mission in Haiti (MINUSTAH) troops since 2004, have perpetuated the impoverished conditions of Haitians. The substandard conditions that exist in Haiti are attributed to the roles of dominant world powers and their authority, leaving Haiti with poor infrastructure, environmental destruction, and economic systems that only intensified the magnitude of the 2010 earthquake.

Frantz (2011) refers to the foreign interest and presence in Haiti as increased abuses of human rights; "when foreigners are awarded impunity and broad power to maintain security, they gain a remarkably large amount of de facto control over the population, allowing for human rights violations to occur" (para 20). The foreign interest aims to heavily profit from Haiti's "Open for Business" slogan as $124 million in US taxpayer dollars has been invested in a textile factory in northern Haiti (Haiti Grassroots Watch, 2011). The organization found a series of human rights violations in foreign-owned sweatshops where Haitian factory workers are earning less today in 2014 as compared to wages earned under former president Duvalier. In 1982 workers were earning the equivalent of US$3 a day, and the average income in 2011 was US$2.53 a day in 1982 dollars (Haiti Grassroots Watch, 2011). Salaries are not livable wages for Haitians, as half of the daily income is paid toward transportation and food.

In a Haiti Grassroots Watch (2011) interview, factory worker Pierre-Paul explained that even after 25 years of working in the factory industry, she still is not able to afford a house. Prior to the earthquake, Pierre-Paul paid $250 a year in renting two rooms for her and her four children. Since her dwelling was destroyed, she has been residing in a tent. The foreign interest in Haiti does not include prioritizing the establishment of adequate living wages or the recognition of workers' rights.

The peacekeeping function of the MINUSTAH was outlined in the UN Charter. Chapter VII of the agreement indicated that the Security Council "may impose measures on states that have obligatory legal force and therefore need not depend on the consent of the states involved. To do this, the Council must determine that the situation constitutes a threat or breach of the peace" (Frantz, 2011, para 3). Therefore, since 2004 the function of MINUSTAH has been to occupy Haiti, as the assumed violence in the nation poses a threat to the international community. The presence of the United Nations in Haiti is not well received, as MINUSTAH does not prioritize the interests of the Haitian people, especially the poor. For example, in 2005 the United Nations attacked the community of Cite Soleil because the private sector and elite were in fear of the criminals in the area. As many as 1,440 MINUSTAH officials entered Cite Soleil and shot over 22,000 rounds of ammunition to massacre the community under the direction of the head of MINUSTAH, Juan Gabriel Valdés. Doctors without Borders reported at least 26 casualties of adults and children; however, the United Nations reported an official death toll of six (Frantz, 2011). Reports identified that the "poor Haitians [were] being slaughtered not for being violent but for demanding the return of President Aristide who had been captured in a *coup d'état* in 2004" (Frantz, 2011, para 12).

Interviews conducted by journalist Ansel Herz in 2009 indicate that Haitians protested and organized to resist MINUSTAH as, "they were tired of an occupation in their country" (Frantz, 2011, para 3). Haitians also noted that the significant stipend allocated to the United Nations would be better spent on "concrete humanitarian activity that could actually improve education and healthcare" (Frantz, 2011, para 3). Haiti Observer (2011) indicates that under the current presidency of Michele Martelly, $95 million have been allocated to the training of 3,500 soldiers as he aims to reestablish the Haitian military under the supposed agenda to eliminate the MINUSTAH occupation. Reinstating the Haitian military not only counters the longtime efforts of former president Aristide in dismantling the army, but also puts the interest of armed forces above the basic rights of quake survivors.

In addition to the housing threats, Haitians have also experienced the devastating impact of cholera resulting from Nepalese UN soldiers disposing their waste in the Artibonite River. The outbreak of cholera caused increased death tolls, but the United Nations denied any responsibility. Another violation by MINUSTAH was documented in videos of sexual abuse, including the gang rape by Uruguayan UN soldiers of a young Haitian male. Reports also indicate that UN officers have exchanged money and items for sex with young girls (Frantz, 2011). The function of the UN presence in Haiti is heavily rejected due to the atrocities associated with MINUSTAH soldiers.

International Laws

The 1987 Haitian Constitution recognizes the natural human rights outlined in the UDHR (1948). The inconsistencies and failures of the government to enforce laws represent clear violations of the citizens' constitutional protections. Robbins (2010) suggests that human rights must be safeguarded in order for conditions to improve over time. Therefore, human rights should serve as the method to measure the reconstruction efforts, aid distribution, and all attempts to rebuild the nation. While laws are in place purporting to offer such protection, they often lack the level of enforcement necessary to effect serious change. For instance, the Haitian government has not ratified the International Covenant on Economic, Social and Cultural Rights (ICESCR) (1966), so it is not a legally binding convention (Robbins, 2010). The mission of the ICESCR is in affording employment training and assistance in addition to offering support in economic, social, and cultural arenas; however, such practices are not executed or achieved in Haiti (Robbins, 2010). The Haitian government's inability to ratify and implement the ICESR fails to serve the economic, social, and cultural advancement of the nation. Instead, it only strengthens the dependency on foreign investment in textile industries, serving as economic opportunities that fail to support the majority in Haiti.

While the United Nations Convention on the Rights of the Child (CRC) (1989) has been signed and ratified by Haiti, it has yet to be implemented effectively to honor and advocate for the rights of children (Robbins, 2010). In 1804, Haiti proclaimed its independence from France and a termination to the institutionalized system of slavery, but the lasting legacies of slavery persist in the form of domestic servitude (Aristide, 2000). For example, *restavèk*s are young children from the countryside who have been sent to the city to work, live with a family, and hopefully attend school. *Restavèk*s serve as domestic servants to Haitian families, and while most are girls, young girls and boys are in danger of emotional, mental, physical, and sexual abuse (Flynn and Roth, 2005). Child trafficking, incarceration, the *restavèk* system, and poor education are all examples of the Haitian government's failure to implement and guard the human rights of children.

The economic conditions in Haiti serve as a driving force behind the system where families seek hope in sending their children to the cities to have access to education; however, *restavèk*s are not afforded such opportunities. Efforts supporting the covenant of children's rights were successful under the *Lavalas* (flashflood) Movement of 1991 (Flynn and Roth, 2005). The movement included actively engaged Haitians organizing and fighting for democracy through politics and education. Flynn and Roth (2005) indicate that educational programs and scholarships were established to support the over 400,000 *restavèk* population, while legislation eliminated the use of physical punishment in 2001. In 2003, Haiti annulled former laws endorsing child domestic servitude and made the practice illegal, prompting dispute and controversy in a US State Department 2003 Trafficking in Persons Report (Flynn and Roth, 2005). The United States did not recognize the programs Haiti had enacted, criticized the nation, and recognized the same efforts in identical initiatives. Through the efforts of the *Lavalas* Movement and the Aristide Foundation, Haiti has attempted to hold the interests of children as a priority and enacted gains in the protection of children's rights.

Education

According to Farmer (2011), "a child who is not educated has no tools for the future and is not important in the society" (p. 267). In Haiti, the value of education is clear, yet the means to access the system is not attainable for everyone. From 1994 to 2000, Haiti's *Lavalas* grassroots organization built 195 primary schools and 104 high schools; more schools were developed in this 6-year period than created in the 100 years between 1804 and 1994 (Flynn and Roth, 2005). *Lavalas* also granted hundreds of thousands of scholarships to provide access for children to attend private schools. However, the financial responsibility has been a burden for many families, as substandard wages do not support children's desire for education. As a result, former president Aristide and his foundation tried to offset the weight on Haitian families. Aristide (2000) proclaimed that schoolbooks should be free of charge in accordance with Article 32.1 of the Haitian Constitution, which grants free access to education for all Haitian children. The Haitian children and youth are actively engaged in action to generate change in their country. The process in educating children and providing them a space to use their voice is empowering, representing a movement toward civic participation and democracy. For example, the youth radio program, *Radyon Timoun*, provides space for young Haitians to be heard throughout the country and to value youth voices in national issues.

Although substantial gains had been achieved, the realities of Haiti after the kidnapping of President Aristide in 2004 made access to education more difficult. Farmer (2011) describes the impact on education 5 years after the coup d'état, "the Ministry of Education estimated that half of all school-age children were not in school, and that many of those who were in school attended what the Haitians call *lekol bole* lottery schools, so-called because pedagogically, you take your chances there" (p. 43). Factors that contributed to the number of children not in school are attributed to the cost of tuition, school materials and uniforms, and the *restavèk*, child domestic workers. In 2011, the average school fees of US$690 per year were nearly impossible for the average Haitian family to pay (Haiti Grassroots Watch, 2011). Despite the destruction and conditions present after the quake, education is still a priority for the Haitian people. Classes are held outside of the buildings that once stood. Even as they faced the devastation that the earthquake left in its wake, "parents wanted their children and other children who had lost their parents to be able to continue their education" (Roth and Langlois, 2010, p. 8).

Future

Building a better Haiti requires the voice of the youth. A young boy from the Aristide Foundation stated his efforts toward establishing a true democracy in Haiti: "I want you to know that I am right now working so that all children in Haiti will have enough to eat" (as cited in Aristide, 2000, p. 80). Aristide (2000) describes the plight of the working people toward human rights and democracy as a battle against a globalized world. He clarifies that democracy in an affluent developed nation is equal to democracy in an impoverished underdeveloped nation. Robbins (2010) suggests that the methods of rebuilding Haiti must be monitored, "because if Haiti is not rebuilt upon a foundation of human rights, we risk rebuilding the Haiti of January 12th 2010" (para 16). Investment in Haiti should not solely focus on textile factories, hotels, and the formation of the military; first and foremost, it should be placed in the people. To ensure that Haitians have a basic standard of living and education. Farmer (2011) suggests that Haiti should implement by 2020 the strategy of *investor dans l'humain* [investing in people] in order to build a better Haiti. The system will include a free public education system for all and prepare young Haitians to become active in civic engagement. The vision would lead to the demise of the *restavèk* system as all children would benefit from the free schooling, teacher preparation, and educational pedagogy for a literate and educated future in Haiti.

Conclusion

Farmer (2011) states that "when we live in hunger, we will not live in peace; peace will not exist in Haiti until basic needs of food and shelter, education and health care, jobs that promote dignity," are provided for all Haitians (p. 235). Haiti's history and present-day circumstances demonstrate the endless fight and demand for human rights. The fight is for a system of social equality in securing a basic standard of living and system of public education. Haitians continue to carry forth the struggle for human rights as it is deeply rooted in the eighteenth-century slave resistance, opposition to occupation, and the lasting conflict with the United Nations. Rather than enable the country to succumb to poverty and deterioration, it is now time for people everywhere to work in solidarity with Haitians as they rebuild their country to their standards. The Haitian people deserve self-determination to fully attain democracy and a system that secures and respects their basic human rights.

The struggle is to place the people's needs in the future of the nation and stand shoulder to shoulder [*kolezepól*] as an international community to support democracy, especially for the children of Haiti. The youth have survived beyond the catastrophes of the earthquake, and they live daily through the lasting legacies of imperialism and globalization. It is time that they are educated and empowered to find their voice and take part in civic engagement for the future of their nation. The ideology of the fight for equal rights is evident in the *kreyol, tout moun se moun* [every person is a person]. It is time to respect and stand in solidarity with the people of Haiti as they strive for the basic freedoms and securities as human beings.

Pedagogical Tool

> At school my daughter learns to count, to say the alphabet and also she learns hygiene. When I come to walk her back after class she sings to me the songs they sing in school about all the parts of her body, and the days of the week, and months of the year. She is very clever and is learning everything very quickly. The teachers at the schools are caring and love each of the children. They know what are the strengths of each child and they try to help each child. Going to school helps children forget about the earthquake for a short time. (Marjory, as cited in Roth and Langlois, 2010, p. 9)

The powerful narratives of the youth, parents, and grassroots leaders were presented to my 2010 delegation, which prompted my purpose in selecting Haiti as a focus for my tenth-grade human rights unit. As the Haitian youth shared their goals, dreams, and aspirations for the future, it is vital for the world community to hear their voices and recognize the Haitian struggle as a human struggle. Global citizens need to see the common value of life in recognizing the post-earthquake effects of the nation and her people. Since Haiti has demonstrated a legacy of resistance, this teaching unit asks students to explore the impact of slavery and occupation as well as the new influence of global markets within the Caribbean nation. A variety of Haitian proverbs and lyrics demonstrate the history of resistance and the voice of the people (Madhere, as cited in Flynn and Roth, 2005, p. 2).

The following tenth-grade World History lessons aim to build understanding of Haiti and the Haitian people's struggle for human rights. The pedagogical tools include creative writing, films, photo analysis, and an assortment of collaborative learning assignments. Through these selected assignments, students are prompted to reflect upon their personal experiences and educational journey by exploring the historical as well as current methods in which Articles 25 and 26 of the UDHR are both upheld and violated in Haiti. One objective is to explore the overarching questions: How is Haiti rebuilding as a nation after the earthquake? What are examples of human rights violations, violations toward achieving an adequate standard of living, and toward accessing education? How do Haitians advocate for democracy? The second objective of this unit is to uncover the Haitian voice in testimonies of survival stories, photos, resistance songs, humanitarian efforts, and videos documenting the historical and present-day realities presented in Haiti. The final objective is to educate youth in how to navigate and analyze the UDHR as a lifelong skill to empower and educate others.

In teaching Haiti through human rights, UDHR Article 25 is most relevant as the unit focuses on essential needs and nation building for developing nations. This article identifies the security of person and medical care in addition to necessary social services, along with the right to security for all individuals despite their circumstance. All fundamental freedoms and moralities presented in this article have been violated, particularly in the wake of the earthquake. Therefore, Article 25 serves as a solid foundation to understand the struggle for human rights in Haiti.

Teaching a curriculum centered on human rights can facilitate opportunities for academic and student success. Through the use of thought-provoking materials, this teaching unit challenges students to examine current events and reflect on their own personal experiences. Adding a human rights lens promotes the interpretation of the fundamental rights of the human race; it is the purpose and function of human rights education to build students' understanding of their own rights as well as to develop awareness and activism. The transformative experience of human rights education empowers students to take a stand against injustice in the world.

In teaching Haiti through human rights, a global exchange occurs—a sharing of voice, experiences, and histories. This context honors the ideology of standing shoulder to shoulder with Haitians and the pursuit for full democracy. In facilitating lessons and discourse centered on the human rights to education and an adequate standard of living, students from the United States will understand the struggle for education and human rights in Haiti. Haitian voices have been deemed subordinate to the political and economic interests in the United States. As the world becomes more global, it is vital to include the narratives and experiences of those directly affected by the decisions that developed nations, like the United States, impose upon developing nations like Haiti. The transformative process that occurs within the individual through education, empowerment, and activism can serve to increase the critical analysis of the social, political, economic, and cultural systems of the world.

Audience and Pedagogical Philosophy

This unit is constructed for tenth-grade World History students to understand Haiti and the struggle for human rights. The content was adapted for tenth-grade World History and eleventh-grade US History high school courses in San Jose, California. Student demographics represent sophomore and junior students from working and middle class backgrounds. The majority of the participating students include large representations of students of color from Latino and Asian communities in addition to smaller representation of white and black students. The classes included students from a diverse set of academic levels representing students who were making up credits, bilingual students, and students in honors and advance placement courses. In addition, students represented a variety of developmental needs such as Asperger's syndrome, autism, and attention deficit hyperactivity disorder (ADHD). Students who were most engaged with this unit included students who have witnessed or experienced poverty from having visited families in other developing nations or from personal experience growing up in low economic conditions.

The California State Content Standard for tenth-grade World History outlines the following:

> 10.10 Students analyze instances of nation building in the contemporary world in at least two of the following regions or countries: the Middle East, Africa, Mexico and other parts of Latin America and China.

Lessons in this unit can be adapted to accommodate all learners and also can be integrated across disciplines in collaboration with English courses. The unit lasts approximately 2 weeks, with five 90-minute block periods or ten 1-hour class periods.

This unit was commonly well received by students and teachers, as it is interactive, relevant, and personal. Students appreciated the use of music and poetry throughout the lessons and the influence of visual art and videos. Between the 2012 and 2013 school year, students were especially connected to this lesson as two grassroots leaders from Haiti were featured as guest speakers to share the experience of resistance and rebuilding, in addition to the theme of global citizenship. Six students generated enough interest, commitment, and drive that they raised sufficient funds to form their own delegation to Haiti. Students spent 10 days in Haiti and actively engaged with Haitian grassroots leaders, lead activities and lessons at schools, interviewed leaders at the Aristide Foundation, witnessed the movement for self-sufficiency of urban gardens in Cite Soleil, and learned history lessons at the National Museum of Haiti.

As an educator, I created this unit with the goal of honoring the personal stories of the people of Haiti and connecting the experiences of US students in order to develop respect, compassion, and agency through learning the historical past, lived realities of the present and to dream and construct the possibilities of the future. In the course of this teaching unit, students will explore survivor stories in a post-earthquake Haiti, as they participate in a "Survivor Mixer." The objective of this activity is to associate photos and images of Haiti with UDHR articles, create a resistance song, develop personal education stories, and take the call to action in an awareness campaign.

Lesson One: Survivor Mixer

Essential Questions: Who are the survivors? What are their stories? What do their stories reveal?

Objectives: To understand the personal testimonies of survivors and develop an understanding of the impact of the earthquake.

Standards: California World History 10.10: Students analyze instances of nation building in the contemporary world in at least two of the following regions or countries: the Middle East, Africa, Mexico, and other parts of Latin America and China.

Time: 90 minutes (one block period or two 1-hour class periods).

Materials Needed: Survivor Narratives, guided questions, data worksheets, and photos. The data worksheets are from the Disaster Emergency Committee (2010) and the Associated Press (2010).

Modeled after the "Tulsa Race Riot Mixer Activity" (Rethinking Schools, 2014).

Survivor Narratives: Below are links to original news or interview sources. Create a handout for each individual based on excerpts from published articles to provide a testimony of the earthquake.

Rea Dol (Ell, 2010).
Laura Wagner (Wagner, 2010).
Evans Monsignac (Goddard, 2010).
Walter Riley (NBC, 2010).

Introductory Activity: Five-minute journal response: Describe what it means to be a survivor. What is something you have survived in your own life? Discuss student responses for approximately 5 minutes. Show the first 10 minutes of the Al Jazeera Correspondent program, "Haiti: After the Quake" (Walker, 2012). This graphic content of live footage and the aftermath from the earthquake provides a context for the mixer.

Steps for Survivor Mixer:

First, divide students into groups of four and distribute the four different survivor narratives to each group. Students will select one survivor's testimony to present this story as if it were their own narrative, with other classmates. Request that students formally introduce themselves as the survivor, shake hands, make eye contact, and listen attentively to each survivor's story. After students discuss their survivor's story, ask them to respond to the mixer reflection questions and compare survivors' stories. See Questions for the Survivor Mixer. In pairs, students will review data fact sheets from Haiti Earthquake Facts and Figures on the death tolls, statistics, and overall impact of the earthquake (Disaster Emergency Committee, 2010). For additional statistics see Haiti earthquake death toll (Associated Press, 2010). Ask students to develop questions about the impact of the earthquake based on their sources of evidence. Each group will share out one to two questions students developed about the statistics presented. Example questions may include: How did the infrastructure of Haiti contribute to the death toll of the earthquake? Students will continue viewing the video of the Al Jazeera program, *Haiti: After the Quake* (Walker, 2011).

Assessment: Gathering evidence from the video, survivor stories, data, and statistics, develop a one-page reflection of the following question: What does it means to be a survivor of the earthquake in Haiti? Describe the first three things you would do to ensure your safety and the safety of others. Response should be at least three paragraphs. Include a visual piece of art to illustrate your perspective of what it means to survive.

Lesson Two: Gallery Walk

Essential Questions: What have survivors experienced nearly 2 years after the quake? How have manmade tragedies shaped the country?

Objectives: To interpret violations of human rights according to the UDHR based on photos and film of Haiti.

Standards: California World History 10.10: Students analyze instances of nation building in the contemporary world in at least two of the following regions or countries: the Middle East, Africa, Mexico, and other parts of Latin America and China.

Time: 90-minute block period or two 1-hour classes.

Materials Needed: Copy of the Universal Declaration Human Rights (UDHR), Photos of Haiti for Gallery Walk, and Gallery Walk Directions. Note that students will need a general understanding of the UDHR and concepts of the 30 civil, political, social, civil, and cultural rights. For the

Gallery Walk, you may use selected photos of post-earthquake Haiti that reflect human rights themes from online sources, such as Holt's (2013) photos in *The Guardian*.

Introductory Activity: Five-minute journal response: Describe the power of photography. In what ways is photography influential in recording history? Discuss student responses approximately 5–7 minutes.

Steps: Create a gallery of photos in the classroom and ask students to follow the Gallery Walk Directions. Ask students to reflect on the following questions as they analyze the photo: What is occurring in the photo? Does the photo include social, political, economic, or cultural aspects/elements? Is there any violation of human rights in the image?

Assessment: Students will complete the Gallery Walk Directions handout. At the end of the activity, students will participate in a class discussion to share out the examples of photos that resonated most with them. This discussion can also connect back to the introductory questions: Describe the power of photography. In what ways is photography influential in recording history?

Gallery Walk Directions:

- Step 1: Walk around the class and view the series of photos displayed.
- Step 2: Select a photo that connects with you most. This can be an image you like most, or that speaks to your attention.
- Step 3: Individually, you will analyze the photo you chose.
   - What is occurring in the photo?
   - Does the photo include social, political, economic, or cultural aspects/elements?
   - Is there any violation of human rights in the image?
- Step 4: Share the image you selected with your partner and compare.
- Step 5: In partners select one to two Articles of the UDHR that are reflected or suggested in the photos you selected. If the photo could be used as an awareness campaign for a UDHR article, which article would it be?
- Step 6: Using the UDHR articles selected, create captions of the photos in seven words or less.

Lesson Three: Resistance Songs

Essential Question: Where do the problems in Haiti stem from? What is the history of resistance and survival in Haiti?

Objectives: To identify the historical causes of poor economic infrastructure in Haiti at the time of the quake and to interpret the legacy of resistance. Students will read and interpret a Haitian resistance song and analyze the purpose and objective of the song.

Standards: California World History 10.10: Students analyze instances of nation building in the contemporary world in at least two of the following regions or countries: the Middle East, Africa, Mexico, and other parts of Latin America and China.

Time: 110 minutes. Block period or two 1-hour classes.

Materials Needed: "Interactive: Haiti Timeline" (NBC, 2014), Film *Bitter Cane* (1988).

Introductory Activity: Five-minute journal response.

Questions: What is "resistance"? Describe a time when you resisted something. How did you feel? What motivated you to resist? Discuss student responses approximately 5–7 minutes.

Steps: Individually students will read a Haitian resistance song from the film *Bitter Cane* (1988) and discuss the following questions: What is the primary message embedded in the song? What words are most powerful in the lyrics? Why do you think this song was written? Under what conditions would someone sing this song? In groups of three students will share and compare responses. Provide students with a timeline of the history of Haiti and examples of resistance and review definitions of social, economic, political, and cultural factors. Place students in groups to focus on social, economic, political, and cultural aspects of the film *Bitter Cane* (1988). After the film, in groups of three students review the 1987 Haitian Constitution Chapters I–III (Republic of Haiti, 2011). Ask students to underline key expectations from citizens, basic human rights, and protections the government guarantees.

Assessment: Using the document and notes from the film, students develop a resistance song, poem, or rap and perform it to the class. Reference lyrics directly from the film *Bitter Cane* (1988).

Lesson Four: *Restavèks*

Essential Questions: How important is education to the success of a child? Is education accessible for all children in Haiti?

Objectives: To examine the access to education for children of Haiti and explore the consequences of a limited education system.

Standards: California World History 10.10: Students analyze instances of nation building in the contemporary world in at least two of the following regions or countries: the Middle East, Africa, Mexico, and other parts of Latin America and China.

Time: 90 minutes. Block period or two 1-hour classes.

Materials Needed: Copy of the UDHR, *Common Dreams*—a CNN Freedom Project documentary (2011), and the children's book, *Sélavi, That Is Life: A Haitian Story of Hope* (Landowne, 2004).

Introductory Activity: Five-minute journal response.

Questions: How important is education to the success of a child? How hungry are you for an education? Discuss student responses approximately 5–7 minutes.

Steps: Define the experience of *restavèks*. Read *Sélavi, That is Life: A Haitian Story of Hope* (Landowne, 2004) in class and discuss the following questions: What does "*Sélavi*" mean? What circumstances was Sélavi living in before he met TiFrè? What article of the UDHR is violated for Sélavi and his friends? What was the impact of building a tower and radio program to broadcast the voices of the youth? What type of transformation did Sélavi experience?

As a class, view the CNN Freedom Project's 2011 documentary, *Common Dreams*, about the plight of the *restavèks*. Students will be able to identify the significance and transformative power of education and to distinguish the awareness and action of human rights in Haiti.

Discuss the following questions:

- Describe the life of a *restavèk* child?
- Describe the accessibility to education for children in Haiti?
- How important is education to the success of a child?

Assessment: Construct a personal education story. What is your story? How important is education to your personal success? Make reference to Articles 25 and 26 of UDHR and how rights were honored or violated.

Lesson Five: Action Project

Essential Questions: How have students brought awareness and action to human rights in Haiti? In what ways have San Francisco Bay Area students continue to raise awareness?

Objectives: To connect the struggle for human rights and bring it back home. Identify what students in the San Francisco Bay Area are doing to stand in solidarity with Haitians.

Standards: California World History 10.10: Students analyze instances of nation building in the contemporary world in at least two of the following regions or countries: the Middle East, Africa, Mexico, and other parts of Latin America and China.

Time: 90 minutes. Block period or two 1-hour classes.

Materials Needed: "Stand Up for Haiti" music video created by the Peapod Foundation and Adobe Youth Voices (Simplicityx415, 2010).

Introductory Activity: Five-minute journal response.

Questions: What is solidarity? In what ways can youth organize an action project to show solidarity with the people of Haiti? Discuss student responses approximately 10–12 minutes.

Steps: Create with students a human rights awareness action campaign. As you brainstorm ideas, consider your personal education story and your overall knowledge about Haiti from the class lessons. Discuss with students the following questions: How can you use the UDHR as an instrument to educate friends and family about human rights? What have Bay Area high school students done to educate about Haiti?

View as a class "Stand Up for Haiti" music video created by Bay Area students. Explore the purpose of the video and discuss how it serves as a call to action. View the video, *10 Tactics for Turning Information into Action* (Tactical Tech Videos, 2010). As a class brainstorm action ideas to demonstrate solidarity at the local, state, national, and international levels. Research individuals who took the call to action, travel to Haiti or any other country, and have worked in solidarity with the communities. Invite guest speakers to present about their personal experience.

Assessment: Develop an action project where students can educate peers and raise awareness about the UDHR. Ideas include: awareness campaigns about access to education comparing educational attainment levels across different countries, raising attention through political art projects about child slavery, developing a plan for social media to promote democracy, and creating a pamphlet about how people resist dictatorships or oppression around the world. The possibilities are endless in the application of UDHR and developing awareness campaigns to inform local or global communities.

Photos of Haiti for Gallery Walk

Figures 7.1–7.5 show the photos of Haiti for Gallery walk.

Figure 7.1 A Soccer Game in a Tent City.
A soccer game in a tent city outside of Delmas, Haiti 2011. Photo by Victoria Durán.

Figure 7.2 Sunday Afternoon.
Sunday afternoon Port-au-Prince, Haiti 2011, Photo by Victoria Durán.

Figure 7.3 Paving New Roads.
Paving New Roads Cite Soleil, Haiti 2011, Photo by Victoria Durán.

Figure 7.4 What Is Under Construction?
What is under construction? Port-au-Prince, Haiti 2011, Photo by Victoria Durán.

Figure 7.5 Tent City Port-au-Prince One.
Tent City Port-au-Prince, Haiti 2011, Photo by Victoria Durán.

Reflection Questions for the Survivor Mixer

1. Find someone who was at a school when the earthquake struck.
   Who is the person?
   Describe the impact of the earthquake in the community.
   What did this person do for 3 months?
2. Find someone who was conducting research in Haiti.
   Who is the person?
   What is *sòs pwa*? What did this person mistake as *sòs pwa*?
3. Find someone who has a son and daughter who are 4 years old.
   Where was this person when the earthquake struck?
   How long after the earthquake was this person rescued?
4. Find someone who has traveled to Haiti with family.
   What injuries did the family experience?
   Describe what the family did after the earthquake.
5. Identify key facts you learned during this "mixer."
6. What questions do you have about the earthquake in Haiti?

References

Arcelin, J. (1988). *Bitter cane* [Motion picture]. New York: Haiti Films/Crowing Rooster Arts.

Aristide, J.-B. (2002). *Eyes of the heart: Seeking a path for the poor in the age of globalization.* Monroe, ME: Common Courage Press.

Associated Press. (2010). *Haiti earthquake death toll: the devastation in numbers.* Retrieved from http://www.huffingtonpost.com/2010/01/16/haiti-earthquake-death-to_n_425939.html.

Central Intelligence Agency. (2011). *World Factbook.* Retrieved from https://www.cia.gov/library/publications/the-world-factbook/geos/ha.html.

CNN Freedom Project. (2011). *Common dreams.* Retrieved from http://thecnnfreedomproject.blogs.cnn.com/2011/12/01/watch-the-common-dreams-documentary/.

Disaster Emergency Committee. (2010). *Haiti earthquake facts and figures.* Retrieved from http://www.dec.org.uk/haiti-earthquake-facts-and-figures.

Ell, D. (2010). *Education and the cataclysm in Haiti: An interview with Rea Dol. Upside Down World.* Retrieved from http://upsidedownworld.org/main/haiti-archives-51/2682.

Farmer, P. (2005). *The uses of Haiti.* Monroe, ME: Common Courage Press.

Farmer, P. (2011). *Haiti: After the earthquake.* New York: Public Affairs.

Flynn, L. and Roth, R. (2005). *We will not forget! The achievements of Lavalas in Haiti.* Berkeley, CA: Haiti Action Committee.

Frantz, C. (2011). *Haiti's "enforcers": MINUSTAH and the culture of violence in Port-au Prince.* Retrieved from http://www.haitiaction.net/News/COHA/11_29_11/11_29_11.html.

Goddard, J. (2010). *Buried for 27 days: Haiti earthquake survivor's amazing story.* Retrieved from http://www.telegraph.co.uk/news/worldnews/centralamericaandthecaribbean/haiti/7530686/Buried-for-27-days-Haiti-earthquake-survivors-amazing-story.html.

Haiti Action Committee. (2011). *Grassroots groups present counter-perspective on Haiti's human rights record.* Retrieved from http://www.haitiaction.net/News/BAI/3_26_11/3_26_11.html.

Haiti Grassroots Watch. (2011). *Martelly government betting on sweatshops: Haiti: 'Open for business.'* Retrieved from http://www.haiti-liberte.com/archives/volume5-21/Martelly%20government.asp.

Haiti Justice Alliance. (2011). *Haiti: Introducing the justice perspective.* Northfield, MN: Haiti Justice Alliance.

Haiti Observer. (2011). *Michel Martelly plans to restore Haitian military, 3,500 troops to start.* Retrieved from http://www.haitiobserver.com/blog/michel-martelly-plans-to-restore-haitian-military-3-500-troo.html.

Holt, K. (2013). Haiti 2010 earthquake: Then and now—in pictures. *The Guardian.* Retrieved from http://www.theguardian.com/global-development/gallery/2013/feb/19/haiti-2010-earthquake-in-pictures.

Landowne, Y. (2005). *Sélavi, that is life: A Haitian story of hope.* El Paso, TX: Cinco Puntos.

NBC. (2010). Family tells Haiti survivor story. Retrieved from http://www.nbcsandiego.com/news/local/Family-Tells-Haiti-Survivor-Story-81929412.html.

NBC. (2014). Interactive: Haiti timeline. Retrieved from http://www.nbcnews.com/id/34831414/#.VC5M-Of-SIY.

Network of Educators on the Americas (NECA). (1994) *Teaching about Haiti*, 3rd edn. Retrieved from *http://www.teachingforchange.org/books/our-publications/caribbean-connections/teaching-about-haiti-pdf-and-resources.*

Republic of Haiti. (2011). *1987 Constitution of the Republic of Haiti*. Retrieved from http://pdba.georgetown.edu/Constitutions/Haiti/haiti1987.html.

Rethinking Schools. (2014). Tulsa race riots mixer. Retrieved from http://www.rethinkingschools.org/restrict.asp?path=archive/27_01/27_01_christensen.shtml.

Robbins, S. (2010). *Rebuilding and beyond: The role of human rights in post-earthquake Haiti* [Part I]. Retrieved from http://www.thelegality.com/2010/03/02/rebuilding-and-beyond-the-role-ofhuman-rights- in-post-earthquake-haiti-part-i/.

Roth, R. and Langlois, M. (2010). *Haiti Emergency Relief Fund*. Retrieved from http://www.haitiemergencyrelief.org/Haiti_Emergency_Relief_Fund/herf_brochure_front page_files/HERF_brochure.pdf.

Simplicityx415. (2010, May 30). *Stand up for Haiti*. Peapod AYV. Retrieved from https://www.youtube.com/watch?v=kc_z1eSgtko.

Tactical Tech Videos. (2010). *10 tactics for turning information into action*. Retrieved from https://www.youtube.com/watch?v=D9qSYfwKvx8.

United Nations. (1948). *Universal Declaration of Human Rights*. Retrieved from http://www.un.org/en/documents/udhr/index.shtml.

United Nations. (1965). *International Convention on Economic, Social and Cultural Rights*. Retrieved from http://www2.ohchr.org/english/law/.

United Nations. (1989). *International Convention on the Rights of the Child*. http://www.ohchr.org/en/professionalinterest/pages/crc.aspx.

Wagner, L. (2010). *Haiti: A survivor's story*. Retrieved from http://www.salon.com/2010/02/02/haiti_trapped_under_the_rubble/.

Walker, S. (2012). Haiti: After the quake. *Al Jazeera Correspondent*. Retrieved from http://www.aljazeera.com/programmes/aljazeeracorrespondent/2011/09/201196122110280787.html.

CHAPTER 8

Know Your Rights: Understanding the Universal Declaration of Human Rights

Jacqueline Fix and Puja Kumar Clifford

Introduction

Students at San Francisco International High School (SFIHS) come to us from all over the world. They come from the megalopolises of Hong Kong and Mexico City, from the deserts of Yemen and the high steppe of Mongolia. They come speaking the ancient indigenous languages of Central America as well as the cosmopolitan slang of bustling cities. Students come to us alone without parents or family to support them in their new life in the United States. Some come after attending prestigious schools in their home countries, while others enter school for the first time in their lives the day they walk through our doors. SFIHS has served hundreds of immigrant and refugee students over the past five years; even though each brings their own experience from different corners of the world, they have one singular thing in common: they come to us to learn English and to graduate from high school.

As educators at SFIHS, we are tasked with teaching high school content while supporting students' growth in the English language. Additionally, we are keenly aware of our students' social-emotional needs. Our students not only face the normal challenges and obstacles of adolescence but also are adjusting to a new country, culture, and language. Often this transition period is marked with other hardships such as reunification with parents, homelessness, poverty, and working through past trauma. Keeping all of this in mind, we must then design curriculum that meets the vast needs of our unique student population and is relevant to our students' lives (Ladson-Billings, 1992). As a result, we believe that human rights education (HRE) is a uniting factor that can connect us all. HRE can transcend languages, cultures, and experiences, plus offer students the academic language and agency to discuss prior or current injustices they have faced.

Teaching about human rights seems especially critical for our student population, as all of our students are immigrants. The vast majority experienced some hardship before, during, or after their immigration journey. Most have endured one or more traumatic experiences from fleeing war to enduring poverty or being separated from primary caretakers. Many of our students were forced to leave school at a young age in order to work, while others never had the opportunity to go to school at all due to lack of financial resources or access. In our classroom, we use HRE as the lens to allow our students to document and share their stories, to learn and build literacy, to read relevant literature, and to become fluent in the English language.

Too often we find high school English Language Learners (ELLs) engaging in watered-down curriculum in order to learn English. We see high school content compromised in order for students to build their literacy and language skills. Using HRE does the opposite; it validates students' lived experiences and allows them to make connections to each other, to literature, and to the world around them.

Curriculum and Instruction at SFIHS through HRE

SFIHS is different from other newcomer programs or sheltered ELL programs in various ways. One of the school's founding principles is integration of content and language; teachers not only teach their high school subject area such as Biology, Pre-Calculus, American Literature or Economics, but they also teach the language needed within each of these areas. All of our teachers are instructors of language and content. This integration is particularly critical for high school newcomers so that they can simultaneously learn English and rigorous high school subjects in order to have the credits to graduate and then go on to college. Two other essential principles of SFIHS are project-based learning and heterogeneity-based group work. Curriculum is designed around a final project that allows for multiple access points. Teachers at SFIHS have autonomy over their curriculum, and this autonomy combined with the school's essential principles inspired the creation of our unit, *Know Your Rights: Understanding the Universal Declaration of Human Rights (UDHR)*.

HRE dictates that students learn about their basic human rights as well as have the knowledge and the language to engage in the upholding of human rights in their lives and in their communities (United Nations, 1948). We see this notion as especially critical to the population we teach—recently arrived immigrant youth to the United States. In designing this unit, we had several goals in mind: (1) creating space for students to critically engage with and make connections to their own experiences about human rights violations, (2) using the content of human rights education to teach literacy in English, and (3) applying the UDHR to frame a larger unit on human rights and Japanese internment camps during World War II. In selecting a specific human rights violation to focus on in the unit, we chose the Japanese American internment for several reasons. As human rights educators in California, we felt compelled to teach about a violation that occurred on the West Coast, especially one that is rarely discussed within the larger context of World War II. As English teachers of emerging readers, we thought the novel *Farewell to Manzanar* (1995) offered an appropriate mix of challenge and accessibility for our students (and it did not hurt to also have access to a film version of the story).

The unit uses the UDHR as the central pedagogical tool. Students are exposed to the articles of the UDHR in a number of iterations: the original text, student-friendly language, translations in students' native languages artwork, and videos. All activities in this unit are inspired by, stem from, and refer to parts of the UDHR. Students first do various motivating activities that frame the UDHR to prepare them for the main task of becoming experts on two to four of the Declaration's articles to teach to their classmates. Besides the UDHR articles, this unit is supplemented by sources such as videos and age-appropriate interactive websites. Finally, the lessons rely on teacher-created graphic organizers and task cards for newcomer ELLs to support students in interpreting, understanding, discussing, and presenting the UDHR.

Pedagogical Tool

When designing the unit, we asked two essential questions: What are human rights? What are the consequences when people do not have human rights? These questions framed the three weeks in which we delved deeply into the founding document, continued throughout the course of reading the text, *Farewell to Manzanar* (1995), and culminated with writing final persuasive essays. Students had to answer these questions among several others during their research to understand UDHR articles. In order to make sure our newcomer students had access to the content, we did various schema-building activities to prepare them for understanding the primary source document, the UDHR.

The unit consists of three major projects: a jigsaw activity using the UDHR, reading *A Farewell to Manzanar* (1995) through the lens of the UDHR, and writing a final persuasive essay. In its entirety, this unit spans over one semester and contains hundreds of pages. For this chapter, we included six lessons that seemed particularly significant for highlighting not only HRE but also how to use it as a tool to build language and literacy.

As stated in the introduction, all SFIHS teachers simultaneously teach language *and* content. Therefore, it is important to keep in mind that the curriculum was created as a vehicle to teach about not only the UDHR but also literacy to English learners. The unit has been intentionally designed to be an accessible and appropriate literacy-building tool that would most likely require modification for students with native or fluent English proficiency. Lessons One through Four are schema-building activities that give students multiple ways to build understanding, revisit prior knowledge, make connections to their own experiences, and develop their vocabulary and literacy in English. We spent one week developing vocabulary and connecting to prior knowledge before studying the actual document of the UDHR. In terms of adaptation beyond newcomer classrooms, we strongly suggest that educators spend time building schema and allowing students to make personal connections before giving them the UDHR. However, the amount of time would most likely be shorter for non-ELL classrooms.

Lesson One: I see … I wonder … about Human Rights

Objectives: Students will be able to (SWBAT) write descriptive sentences for images that represent human rights and human rights violations. SWBAT write questions and make inferences about human rights.

Standards: Note that all standards included in the unit come from The Common Core State Standards (CCSS) English Language Arts (ELA) grades nine and ten. CCSS.ELA-LITERACY.RI.9–10.1 (Key Ideas and Details) CCSS.ELA-LITERACY.CCRA.R.7 (Integration of Knowledge and Ideas)

Time: The lesson, I see … I wonder … will take newcomers one full 65-minute period.

Materials Needed: An image for each of the students in your class (see the description below on how to find images). "I see/I wonder" document created by the teacher. Classroom desks arranged in a large circle and timer with chime.

Lesson: As this was the first lesson of a semester-long unit, we had students open with a brief journal entry. Making native language connections is an essential part of building our students' skills in English. As a school-wide structure, we use the abbreviation My Language (ML) as a targeted way for students to build vocabulary in English and in their first language (L1). For the opening activity, we had students translate the words "rights," "humans," "human rights," and "violate" into their language. We then asked them to free write for five minutes on the following prompt: What are human rights? What are some examples of human rights?

As this was the first lesson of "Know Your Rights," the purpose was to build schema and allow students the space to make connections to their own life experiences. In order to build schema, we spent the first day of the unit looking at a variety of pictures depicting human rights or human rights violations.

Before class began, we arranged the classroom with the desks in a large circle. We collected a wide range of images in order to visually represent the 30 articles of the UDHR, placing one image at each desk. We found all of these images through online image searches using keywords such as "human rights," "freedom of speech," "right to education," "right to shelter," and "no unfair detainment." We designed a simple handout with two sentence starters for the students (I see...and I wonder...) for engaging with each image. The students were given one minute to look at their image, analyze it, and write two sentences. The first sentence, "I see..." asks students to write descriptions. The second sentence, "I wonder..." elicits questions about the images. We used a timer to signal the end of the minute; students then passed their image to the person to the left and repeated the process with the next image. Each student viewed about 15–20 images. The goal was for students to ask questions about the images and to begin to generate ideas, words, and thoughts in English about what human rights and human rights abuses look like.

Many students in our classrooms were at the beginning stages of learning English and were emergent readers in English. We allowed those students to complete this activity in their native language. We wanted this activity to allow students to practice descriptive writing, but we also recognized that writing a sentence in one minute was not feasible for all our students. Students differentiated for themselves in which language to write. Afterwards, students participated in a dyad, an activity that offered an active listening space to reflect on something they had learned. The dyad gave students time to process orally what they had observed and learned as well as to make and share meaning in English. (An example of a dyad is included in Lesson Six and Lesson Seven handouts.)

Assessment: Lessons One through Four built schema for students, allowed them to make connections to the concept of rights, and gave them the necessary language to read and discuss the UDHR. The purpose of the unit's first week was for students to build, discuss, and share background knowledge around the idea of human rights. While we did not include any summative assessments, we did use several formative assessments throughout each class and the whole week, such as exit tickets and review of I see... I wonder... handout.

Lesson Two: What Are Human Rights? ("The Story of Human Rights" Video and Guide)

Essential Question(s): What are human rights?

Objectives: SWBAT watch and listen to a video in English. SWBAT discuss the video with their classmates. SWBAT respond to questions about human rights. SWBAT understand a brief history of human rights.

Standards: CCSS.ELA-LITERACY.SL.9–10.1 (Comprehension and Collaboration), CCSS.ELA-LITERACY.W.9–10.10 (Range of Writing).

Time: This lesson will take newcomers one full 65-minute period.

Materials Needed: Video and guide, *The Story of Human Rights*, from Youth for Human Rights website: http://www.youthforhumanrights.org/.

Introductory Activity: Since this lesson followed the *I see... I wonder...* lesson, the introductory activity both reinforced that lesson and introduced the new one. The video can be introduced in several ways. Project a few images (screenshots) from the video and ask students to write *I see... I wonder...* sentences for the images. This activity recalls the structure of the previous lesson and connects the concepts of the two lessons. As an extension, students can share their sentences with partners. Another option is to ask students for predictions about the video based on the title. They can describe what they think the "story of human rights" might be and then share predictions with classmates.

Lesson: The video is only nine minutes long, but it took our ELL students an hour to watch. Why? To make watching a video an active and comprehensible process, we always create and give our students "video guides." These guides include snapshots of the video and corresponding questions. When we get to the portion of the video with a snapshot and question, we pause the movie and read the question aloud. Sometimes this leads to partner, group, or full-class discussion. Students then respond to the question, and the teacher circulates to check comprehension and writing.

Assessment: The video guide served as the assessment. As this was a schema-building activity, students were not assessed on their understanding of the UDHR but rather on their specific "language objectives" (Did the student write in complete sentences? Do subjects and verbs agree?), further illustrating the language/content balance in our classes.

Lesson Three: What Is a Human? What Are Rights?

Essential Question(s): What makes a human happy? Why do humans need to be happy? What are human rights?

Objectives: SWBAT collaboratively define human rights. SWBAT collaboratively analyze vocabulary related to human happiness. SWBAT share their ideas in front of the whole class.

Time: The lesson "What is a human? What are rights?" will take newcomers one full 65-minute period. The supplemental "Frayer Model" activity may fit into the period or require more time.

Standards: CCSS.ELA-LITERACY.L.9–10.4 (Vocabulary Acquisition and Use).

Materials Needed: Handouts One and Two (Figures 8.1 and 8.2), Whiteboard and marker. LCD projector or document camera.

Introductory Activity: With some of our students, we conducted silent sustained reading (SSR) to begin this lesson. For others we started with a few short questions and sharing to stimulate thinking about this big concept. Below is an example of some appropriate opening questions:

1. What are three things that make you happy?
2. Why do these things make you happy?
3. What are three ways that humans are different from animals?

Lesson: In this lesson, students were guided toward creating their own definitions of human rights by thinking critically about what humans need to feel happy. We developed this lesson because we wanted to empower students with their own opportunities to define human rights and also to make strong, clear connections between needs and rights. This activity was done in pairs and then as a whole class. First, students were divided into pairs. When pairing students, we usually aim for a skill differential so that an emerging student receives support from a more proficient one. Each student received Handout One (Figure 8.1), "What are humans? What are rights?" This handout has a gingerbread man-type figure with different phrases inside. In pairs, then, the students decided whether they agreed or disagreed with the statement. If they agreed, they circled the phrase. If they disagreed, they crossed it out. During this time, we moved around the room to assist students and encourage discussion. Another option is to provide sentence frames ("I agree with this statement because _____") and, in this case, the teacher should stress that there is no one right answer.

As students finished, we projected the handout on the board and invited pairs to come to the board to cross and/or circle a couple phrases. This could provide a natural time for discussion, as students are likely to disagree about some of the ideas. After our class came to a consensus on the crosses and the circles, we asked the students questions such as, "What do humans need to feel these things and have these things?" Depending on the class, students may brainstorm responses to this question in their pair, individually, or at their table. After a few minutes, we invited students to share their ideas. One at a time, a student came to the board, wrote the "need" they came up with outside the human figure, and connected the need to one or more of the items inside the human figure. For example, a student might write "Education" and draw a line connecting the word to "can read" and "can go to school." This is another good opportunity to encourage organic controversy and discussion.

Finally, to synthesize what they just did, we asked the students in pairs to write their own definition of human rights. During this time, we recommend the teacher circulates and reads students' definitions. A good idea would be to share one exemplary definition and ask all students to copy it down on paper.

Frayer Model: If there is time, or if the teacher wants students to delve deeper into the definition of human rights, the Frayer-style Vocabulary activity is a nice supplemental option. This is another activity that is best done in pairs. Using Handout Two (Figure 8.2), our students started at Box 1 and went counter-clockwise. By the end of the activity, they created a word definition after understanding the word in different contexts. First, students brainstormed facts and characteristics about human rights (Box 1). Next, they listed nonexamples of human rights (Box 2). Third, they wrote examples of human rights (Box 3), and finally, they wrote their own definitions of human rights (Box 4). Although students worked in pairs or groups in order to stimulate conversation, it is a good idea for the teacher to project the handout and periodically bring the whole class together to ensure that students are on the right track.

Assessment: This lesson was very useful in assessing language skills. Another suggestion is to introduce certain sentence stems as language objectives (e.g., I can explain my opinion by saying, "I think ____ because ____"). An exit slip (individual or interview give-one-get-one style) can be an informal assessment after the lesson. Possible questions include:

- What are human rights?
- What are three things all humans need?
- What is an example of a human right?

Lesson Four: Reading Guide and Split Dictation—What Are Human Rights?

Essential Question(s): What are human rights?

Objectives: SWBAT read collaboratively using a reading guide. SWBAT use reading strategies to monitor their understanding of the text. SWBAT practice their fluency and decoding skills in English.

Time: The lesson, Reading Guide and Split Dictation—What are human rights? will take newcomers one full 65-minute period.

Standards: CCSS.ELA-LITERACY.CCRA.R.1 (Key Ideas and Details), CCSS.ELA-LITERACY.CCRA.R.2 (Text Analysis and Summarization)

Materials Needed: Class set of reading guides. Class set of split dictations. We recommend that Partner A is printed in a different color than Partner B to help with student organization and classroom management during the activity.

Introductory Activity: Many times the introductory activity included ten minutes of SSR to build capacity and stamina in independent reading. We often use this structure, which is directed by student choice. Students read any text of their choice in English or in their home language, as long as they are reading. If we were not doing SSR, then we asked students to respond to a journal entry. Here are a few examples of prompts we used to get students thinking about human rights:

- Was there a time that you saw or experienced discrimination? Describe what happened.
- List all of the human rights you think exist. Why do you think these important for people to have? What happens when people do not have them?
- Have you ever seen or experienced bullying? What happened? Do you think bullying is a violation of human rights? Why or why not?

Lesson: Reading guides are a school-wide structure created and used at SFIHS in order to support students in reading collaboratively and to teach the metacognitive process of successful engagement with a text. Reading guides were developed in order to teach active reading strategies, such as making predictions, connections, inferences, checking for understanding, and visualizing. During a reading guide, three to four students collaboratively read texts in small heterogeneous groups. The text of the reading guides is broken into small chunks. After each chunk of text there is a set of questions that the group asks and answers together. Students of varied educational backgrounds work together to engage with the same text. While one student might be reading for comprehension and analysis, another in the same group might be reading for decoding and fluency. The shared nature of the reading guides allows students to support each other wherever they may be in their literacy development. This inclusive practice of shared literacy reinforces the human right to education, as a significant portion of our student population has interrupted or no formal education. For our lesson on human rights, we utilized the reading guide process and asked students to perform the following tasks together:

1. Take turns reading aloud. Groups can decide how to share the reading, but all students take turns reading aloud.
2. Groups read the entire document aloud, stopping to discuss what they read when there is a break in the text.

Although the structure of the reading guide is always the same at SFIHS, the content varies. This specific reading guide discusses the meaning of rights, human rights, violations, and gives a brief history of the UDHR. Examples of questions are: "How is a 'right' different from a privilege?" and "List five examples of human rights." After the reading guide was completed by the group, we used another literacy building structure called "split dictation" to promote oral fluency and decoding in English. A split dictation is a "barrier" or "information gap" activity, which means one partner has information that the other partner needs. This lesson's split dictation is a one-page text explaining human rights, violations, and the UDHR.

This structure generally takes less time than the reading guide and is completed with partners; usually one partner is proficient or advanced while the other's English and school skills are emergent. Students with the handout-marked Partner A began reading, and then Partner B followed along and listened closely to fill in the missing words. We gave the students sentence frames to use such as, "Can you repeat that word/sentence? Can you spell _____ for me? Please read slowly." After Partner B filled in all of the missing words, they switched roles. Depending on the length of the text, split dictation usually takes between 10–20 minutes to complete. As it is merely used to practice fluency, decoding, oral production, and spelling, split dictation should not take up a large portion of the class. One way to go beyond the literacy-building feature of the split dictation is to add comprehension questions at the end of the handout or as a closing activity.

Lesson Five: UDHR Jigsaw and Presentation

Essential Question(s): What are human rights? What are the consequences when people do not have human rights? What has happened in the world to inspire the creation of your UDHR article? How can we fight to protect your UDHR article?

Objectives: SWBAT use the UDHR in both English and their home language to analyze and explain the meaning of each article. SWBAT synthesize the impact their right has on humanity and explain what could happen in the absence of this right. SWBAT collaboratively design a poster for each of their rights to teach their classmates about the articles. SWBAT collaboratively give a presentation teaching the significance of their rights. SWBAT learn about all 30 UDHR articles by listening and taking notes on their classmates' presentations.

Time: The UDHR Jigsaw and Presentation lesson spans over five to seven 65-minute class periods for newcomer students.

Standards: CCSS.ELA-LITERACY.SL.9–10.4 (Presentation of Knowledge and Ideas), CCSS.ELA-LITERACY.W.9–10.2.A (Text Types and Purposes in Writing), CCSS.ELA-LITERACY.W.9–10.2.D (Text Types and Purposes in Writing).

Materials Needed: Printed copies of the UDHR, in both English and students' home languages. Multiple copies of Amnesty International's book, *We Are All Born Free* (2008) to distribute to each group. A laptop computer (or desktop) for each group to stream videos from the website, www.youthforhumanrights.org. Three to four pieces of poster paper per group with art supplies. Access to a printer for students to print images representing their UDHR articles.

Lesson: As this is the culminating project of the unit on human rights, we gave students ample time to delve deeply into the content as well as sufficient time and space to process the information in both English and their native language. We displayed copies of the UDHR in the students' home languages and in student-friendly English in the classroom. This allowed students to gain a great deal of autonomy in using their resources and to access the primary source document throughout the unit and whole semester.

Students worked in groups of four to learn more closely about three to four UDHR articles through a jigsaw activity. A jigsaw is a cooperative learning structure that allows each student to hold an essential "piece" of the puzzle. Just as in a jigsaw puzzle, students need all pieces to come together in order to understand the final product. We split up the UDHR so that each group was responsible for researching and learning about three to four articles. They became experts in their particular articles by watching PSAs on www.youthforhumanrights.org, reading the UDHR article in their home language, and seeing the article illustrated and written in friendly language in the book, *We Are All Born Free* (Amnesty International, 2008).

Students recorded their research for each article on a handout. The handout asked students to draw or describe the video and illustration and to explain how each represented the article. The handout also asked students to answer the essential questions of this lesson. Students answered these questions, as well as created and presented posters about their particular sections of the UDHR. During the presentations, students took notes on a graphic organizer, resulting in a mini-UDHR for each student.

Segmenting the UDHR served multiple purposes. Focusing on only three to four articles allowed the students to become experts in that area of human rights. It also broke down the cognitive load of diving deeply into 30 articles. Finally, group structures like jigsaws created an authentic motivation for learning since students depended on one another to understand the other articles of the UDHR.

Assessment: The jigsaw presentation was the summative assessment for the unit on the UDHR. We used a rubric to assess their group work, presentations, and posters on their articles, along with their participation as audience members.

Lesson Six: Persuasive Essay on Human Rights

Essential Question(s): Who is responsible for protecting human rights? Which rights are universal?

Objectives: SWBAT define human rights. SWBAT write a five-paragraph persuasive essay. SWBAT make connections between the novel, *Farewell to Manzanar* (1995), historical events, and human rights. SWBAT defend a thesis with evidence from the novel, historical events, and the UDHR. SWBAT demonstrate an understanding of three articles from the UDHR. SWBAT make connections between a real-life event and human rights.

Standards: CCSS.ELA-LITERACY.W.9–10.1 (Text Types and Purposes), CCSS.ELA-LITERACY.W.9–10.4 (Production and Distribution of Writing), CCSS.ELA-LITERACY.W.9–10.7 (Research to Build and Present Knowledge).

Time: This culminating project takes one to two weeks.

Materials Needed: The novel *Farewell to Manzanar* (1995) essay prompt, writing and brainstorming tools, UDHR in student-friendly and native language, Handout: Lesson Six, Handout Three (Figure 8.3), Handout: Lesson Six, Challenge (Figure 8.4).

Introductory Activity: Since this project spans at least a week, the introductory activities can vary each day. Suggestions include activities to generate students' thinking about human right violations in the text and to support students' writing skills.

Lesson: This essay was our culminating assessment of the "Know Your Rights" unit and the subsequent unit about Japanese American internment during World War II. The purpose of the essay was for students to make connections between the UDHR and another unit of study. At SFIHS, our students first studied the UDHR and then read the Japanese American internment memoir, *Farewell to Manzanar*. Other teachers may want to focus on a different historical period, current event, or piece of literature depending on their course.

Our culminating project was differentiated into two assignments. The majority of students were asked to write an essay explaining three human rights violations that occurred during the internment of Japanese Americans during World War II at Manzanar, using evidence from *Farewell to Manzanar* to support their claims. Students with more advanced English skills were given a slightly different prompt. We asked them to imagine it was the year 1947 and they were writing a letter to the United Nations. In this letter, they had to advocate for the adoption of the UDHR, specifically explain why the three articles were especially important, and support two of their claims with evidence from *Farewell to Manzanar* and one of their claims with a different historical example.

Although this essay came at the end of the unit, students prepared for their essay throughout their reading of *Farewell to Manzanar*. Every two chapters, students filled out "Evidence Guides," in which they recorded examples of human rights violations in the chapters they had just read. In addition to collecting evidence for their final essay, these evidence guides gave students an opportunity to practice paraphrasing, text analysis, and citation.

Although the concept of evidence collecting for a final essay had been introduced earlier in the unit, we dedicated a full class period to explaining the project immediately before they began writing. We placed students in pairs (making sure each member in the pair received the same assignment) and asked students to read the prompt out loud together and answer the questions. Reading and analyzing the prompt collaboratively gave students a chance to understand the task more deeply and to participate in the process more actively.

The next day, students began writing. SFIHS students are accustomed to end-of-semester portfolios consisting of intensive essay writing; therefore, our 1–2-week writing session went rather smoothly. We displayed on the board all the steps of the two assignments and made a "buffet" of papers at two different tables. These papers included thesis brainstorms, outlines, and editing tools. Since students knew the general steps for the essay writing, they were able to work at their own pace on each handout. Before going on to the next paper, each student checked in with the teacher. This individualized process resulted in students being at different spots and required us to be flexible and willing to push students along or slow them down. Students writing the UN-letter version of the essay needed to conduct Internet research for their final body paragraph. Most students had a strong idea of what they wanted outside topic to be, while a few students needed assistance narrowing down a topic.

Assessment: Students' essays were assessed against the following metrics: responsibility during process, mastery of appropriate English skills, and showing understanding of both human rights and the novel *Farewell to Manzanar*.

These metrics were broken down into a rubric, which included specific objectives (i.e., "I used capital letters and periods in all my sentences" or "I made a strong connection between an event in Manzanar and a human right"). We also assessed students' level of responsibility based on completing deadlines and revisions.

Reflections

At the time this chapter was written, we had just finished teaching the third iteration of the "Know Your Rights" and *Farewell to Manzanar* units. As with the previous two years, we finished the unit feeling triumphant about teaching an important topic and hopeful about the changes we can make to create an even stronger unit for next time. As a guide for teachers, our biggest reflection mirrors the caveat at the beginning of the chapter: This unit was created with English learners in mind and is as much literacy as a human rights unit. We encourage teachers of native or proficient English speakers to expect lessons to take less time and to be prepared to go deeper or to plan for extensions. An element that this unit lacks in the context of a high school classroom is a strong discussion component, which is difficult to accomplish with our population and requires extensive scaffolding like the dyad structure. A Socratic Seminar or Structured Academic Controversy would fit quite nicely into this unit for students with more advanced English language skills.

Our biggest challenges during this unit were time (there is never enough) and the balance between language and content instruction (we cannot focus solely on content). All teachers will have some kind of restraint when teaching a unit, but we have several suggestions for modifying the unit. In the future we hope to incorporate current events. While we were thrilled to expose students to the relatively untold story of Japanese internment, we felt we missed an opportunity to make very real connections by not stopping to learn about and discuss current human rights violations. In addition, we would like to take more advantage of cross-curricular opportunities with the social studies department. Each year we teach this unit, we become a little more aligned with the History classes, and we hope that several years down the road we might be able to create a fully interdisciplinary Humanities unit or mini-project.

One of the most brilliant parts of this unit was the autonomous relationship that students built with the UDHR. Lesson Five, the Jigsaw Lesson, was key in promoting this autonomy. Students became familiar with the UDHR in various formats: child-friendly language, native language, visuals in *We Are All Born Free*, and videos in English and native language. All these versions were available throughout the semester in folders either on the walls or on students' tables. It was amazing to see the independence, ownership, and frequency with which students referenced the document. Many times while reading *Farewell to Manzanar*, students were asked to identify human rights violations and by the end of the unit, almost every student could accomplish this task on their own.

Another success of the unit was evidenced in the deep personal connections that the students made with the UDHR. In the beginning of the unit, many students claimed that human rights violations did not take place in their home countries or San Francisco. However, after being exposed to the language and the details of the UDHR, almost all students could name multiple real-life human rights violations that they had experienced or witnessed. Students seemed grateful for this opportunity to name (in)justices and identified most strongly with Article 26, the Right to Education. Not only did they make this connection because they themselves were students, but also many students named the importance of being educated about human rights. One student, a 16-year-old boy from Bangladesh, shared:

> Right to education (Article #26) is the most important right to me because I think if people go to school or any educational institute then they can be educated, and from my perspective I would say most of the educated people in the world don't violate the right that humans have.

This same student continued, "I think it is important to learn about human rights because if a person doesn't know what are human rights and doesn't practice it, then it will be complicated for him to survive in his/her life."

Students also found ways to apply human rights to their school community. At SFIHS we strive to nurture a positive school culture, and students recognized the natural dovetail of human rights and positive culture. One student, a 17-year-old girl from China, explained how she could use her new knowledge of human rights to create change at school:

> After we studied human rights, the ways that I can create change are making space for others, acting with empathy and trying my best to help others. For example, I will respect other countries' cultures and I won't laugh at others. Also, we can help explain and translate for others who don't understand.

This response shows how an overwhelmingly large concept like human rights can be broken down and applied on a personal level.

Students at SFIHS are all recent immigrants; many have faced human rights violations in their home countries and are susceptible to continue facing them in the United States. While there are miles to go before the UDHR becomes a reality, educating the youth seems to represent a major step forward in pushing toward this reality. After learning about the UDHR, one SFIHS student vowed:

> I will respect human rights. If I see anyone's human rights being violated then I will try my best to make him/her understand that and stop it...I think a person without human rights is a person without a spinal cord.

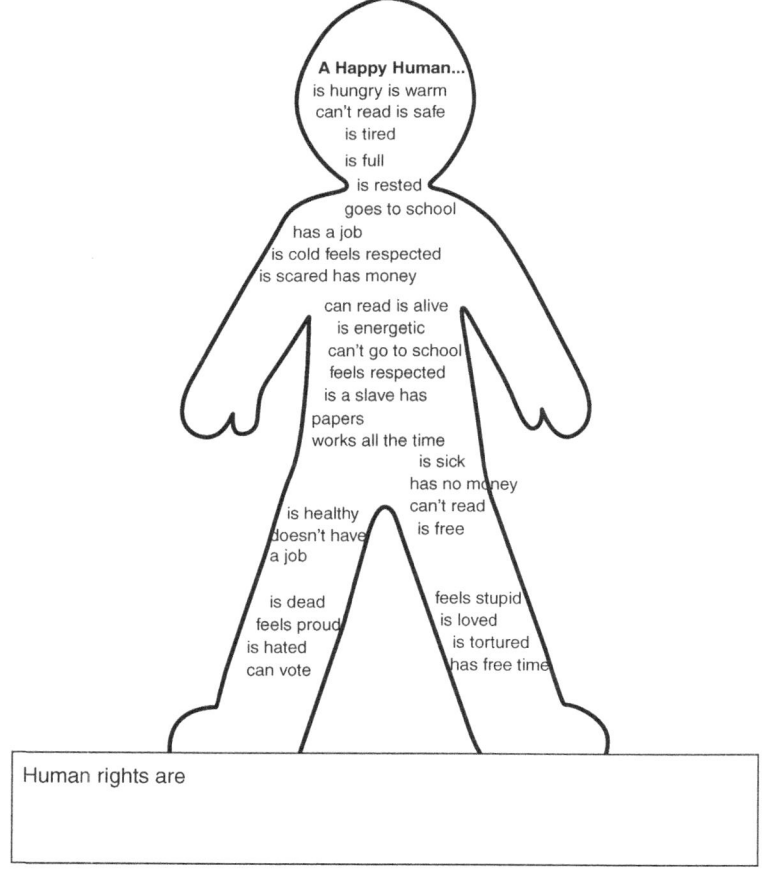

Figure 8.1 Handout: Lesson Three, Handout One: What Is a Human? What Are Human Rights?

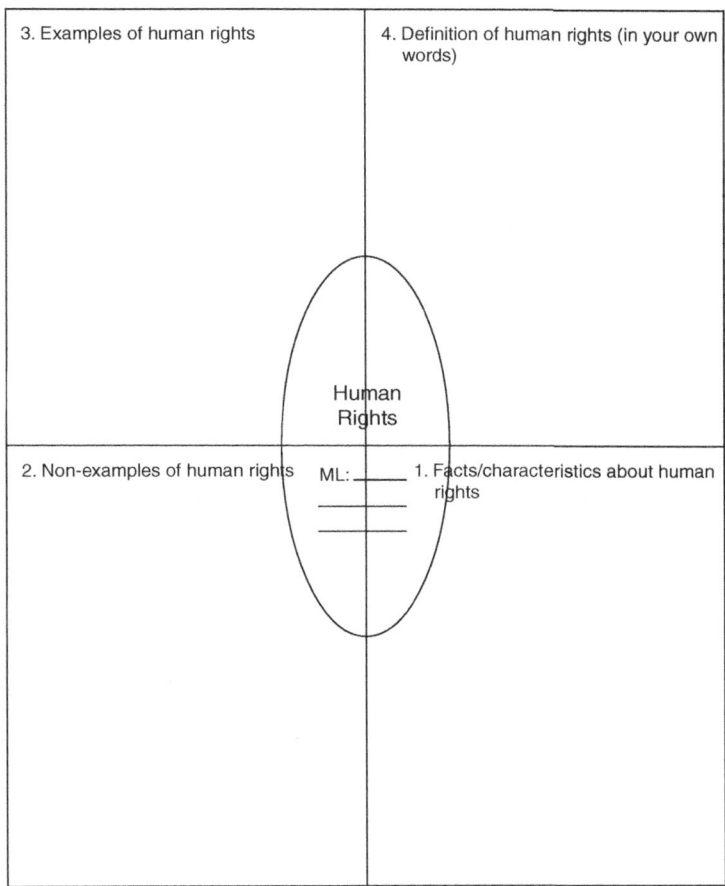

Figure 8.2 Handout: Lesson Three, Handout Two: Frayer-Style Vocabulary.

Figure 8.3 Handout: Lesson Six, Handout Three: Circle Notes (Scaffold).

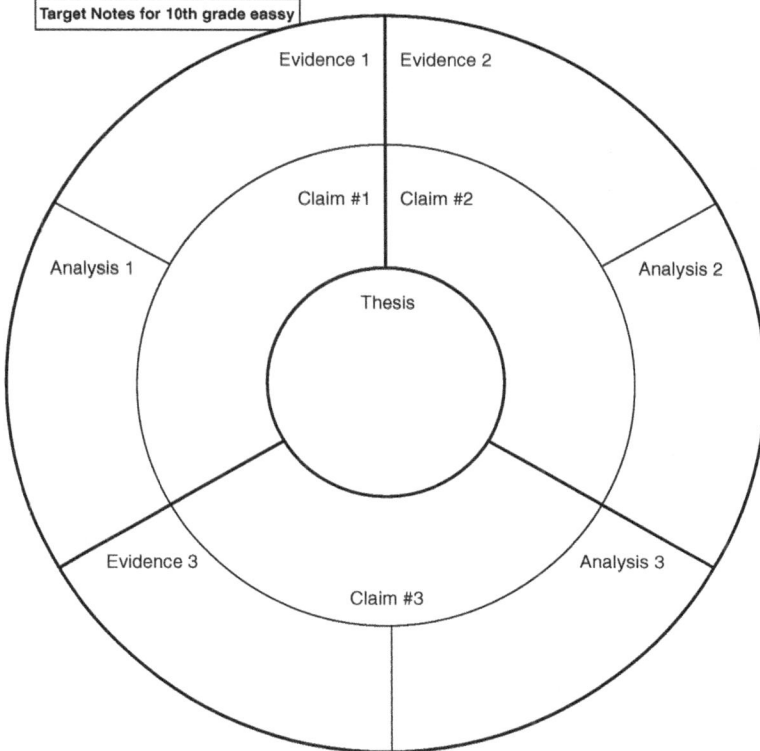

Figure 8.4 Handout: Lesson Six: Circle Notes (Challenge).

References

Amnesty International. (2008). *We are all born free*. London, England: Frances Lincoln Children's Books.

Ladson-Billings, G. (1992). Liberatory consequences of literacy: A case of culturally relevant instruction for African American students. *Journal of Negro Education* 61(3): 378–391.

United for Human Rights. (n.d.). *Youth for human rights*. Retrieved June 22, 2014, from http://www.youthforhumanrights.org/.

United Nations. (1948, December 10). *The Universal Declaration of Human Rights*. Retrieved June 20, 2014, from http://www.un.org/en/documents/udhr/.

Wakatsuki, J. and Houston, J. D. (1995). *Farewell to Manzanar*. New York: Laurel Leaf Books.

CHAPTER 9

Teaching *The Crucible* through Human Rights

Barbara J. Arduini

Introduction

On August 28, 2013, I began my seventh year as an English teacher at a public high school. As many teachers do, I opened my classes with an icebreaker game: Two Truths and a Lie. I chose this game, in which I give the students three "facts" about my life and ask them to guess which statement is false, because it allows me to create an open and trusting environment. In the process of playing this game, I told them about my own experiences with family, with poverty, with education. After playing a few rounds, I then asked the students if they would like to have me guess about them. Many volunteered...and the floodgates opened. One student revealed to me that she had been a prostitute. Another student talked about stabbing her sister's abusive boyfriend with a pair of scissors. And yet another student shared about expecting his first-born child later that year.

In my first few years of teaching, I often feared allowing my students to see me as a person. I thought that personal disclosures would eat away at my authority over them, thus destroying my admittedly fragile grasp on classroom management. Moreover, I often felt unequipped to handle their experiences. I thought that if class discussions became too personal, emotions would derail my lesson plan. Over the years, however, I have discovered that in order to reach them, I *have* to know them. Furthermore, I have found that true learning takes place when curriculum is made relevant to the students' lives. For this reason, I have found that teaching literature through a human rights education (HRE) lens is an essential method to successfully engage the young people in my classroom.

The educational landscape in the United States today, however, is tense. Performance on state-wide (and soon to be nation-wide) exams is becoming the primary focus for many teachers, administrators, curriculum developers, and politicians, while the very nature of standardized testing impedes both student development and creativity. The emphasis on test-taking skills lacks relevance to most students' lives—and this lack of relevance is often reflected in their test scores. Unfortunately, as teachers' salaries and job security are increasingly linked to test performance, low test scores often create more pressure to "teach to the test." This vicious cycle hurts all involved parties—administrators, teachers, and especially students.

Because of the current educational climate, the need for accessible HRE has never been greater. As dropout rates increase—particularly for students of color, English language learners, and students of low economic status—educational models need to change to provide ways to reengage and empower today's youth (Reyes, 2010). By definition, HRE emphasizes "the full development of the human personality and the sense of its dignity" (United Nations, 1996) and is achieved through teaching practices that emphasize the individual's creativity, incorporate relevant curriculum, and produce meaningful outcomes in students' lives.

My first exposure to HRE came to me when I was a student teacher. My master teacher, Dan Reynolds, taught at Mount Diablo High School, a public high school located in Concord, California. Dan, a dedicated activist for student and teacher rights, created the first version of the Human Rights Project for a junior English class. After becoming a full-fledged teacher, I adapted his material for my own students at Concord High School, also located in Concord, California. Since then, this unit has taken hold of the entire English department at my school. It is now used as a common unit for all junior English classes. Each teacher at my school has used the unit in conjunction with a different novel—O'Brien's *The Things They Carried*, Collins's *The Hunger Games*, Camus's *The Stranger*, and so on.

Although the pedagogical unit included in this chapter was initially created for a public high school junior English class, the lessons could be adjusted for older or younger students. The school and district in which I teach are remarkable in its diversity, both religious and ethnic. Because of its diversity, there are sometimes philosophical differences among students. For instance, many of my students oppose gay marriage on religious grounds, whereas other students openly identify as gay, lesbian, bisexual, or transgender. While these differences are obviously not "resolved" through an eight-week unit plan, I have seen many students over the year "agree to respectfully disagree." In this sense, my classroom has been an excellent place to practically apply human rights principles. For example, Article 30 of the Universal Declaration of Human Rights (UDHR) essentially states that no human right should be used to trump another. Because the student body of my school is so diverse, students must learn to speak precisely when discussing their ideas and experiences. Furthermore, this curriculum has also been adopted by every junior English teacher in the school, in hopes that it will not only challenge youth to think critically, but also encourage students to build a more positive school culture.

The Need for HRE

The UDHR states in Article 26 that "Everyone has the right to education. Education shall be free, at least in the elementary and fundamental stages" (United Nations, 1948). Although the United States provides public education at the elementary and secondary levels, the efficacy of the common curriculum models used in schools is debatable. Moreover, the quality of public education varies from district to district; patterns of high school graduation rates, college enrollment rates, and scores on state administered tests clearly indicate that all schools are not created equal. The United States should implement HRE curriculum and teaching methods because HRE is both ethical and effective.

HRE as an Ethical Educational Model

Education is never truly objective. Even in the most careful selection of materials, omissions and commission bespeak an underlying and often unexamined bias. Therefore, decisions about curriculum choices and teaching methods are best viewed through an ethical lens. Throughout history, the lack of such an ethical lens has forged education into a weapon used to further oppress the already oppressed peoples of the world, to broaden the gap between the haves and have-nots, to solidify unfair gender roles and stereotypes, and to stigmatize racial and religious minorities. One needs only to look at Hitler's Germany to see how anti-Semitic propaganda masquerading as education can lead to mass atrocities.

When positively utilized, however, education can provide a context in which vastly different peoples may both listen to and share stories, ultimately inspiring students to make positive contributions to society, to develop their individual identities, and to live their dreams. In this case, public school becomes the ideal arena to foster the understanding and value of human rights. When positively implemented, schools uphold the principles stipulated in the Convention on the Rights of the Child (CRC) (1989), which stipulates in Article 29 that education should focus on elements including:

(a) The development of the child's personality, talents, and mental and physical abilities to their fullest potential;
(b) The development of respect for the child's parents, his or her own cultural identity, language and values, for the national values of the country in which the child is living, the country from which he or she may originate, and for civilizations different from his or her own;
(c) The preparation of the child for responsible life in a free society, in the spirit of understanding, peace, tolerance, equality of sexes, and friendship among all peoples, ethnic, national, and religious groups and persons of indigenous origin. (United Nations, 1989)

Although the United States has not ratified the CRC, the diversity of the country's population calls for educational principles as outlined above, particularly in regard to the development of tolerance between people of different nationalities, ethnicities, religious affiliations, and languages. In order to respect the rights of its citizens, the United States must ensure that curriculum choices are equitable. In my own classroom, I have found that students are far more familiar with civil rights than with the concept of human rights. Once students recognize that these rights are intrinsic to all people (not only to those subject to the US legal system), they are more likely to build solidarity with people around the world.

However, though both the UDHR and the CRC call for inclusive human rights-based education, neither of the documents specifies exactly how the promotion of such values should be taught. One of the difficulties of establishing an equitable public education system in a multicultural nation is the tension between the rights of the individual and the rights of the collective, especially as these sometimes seem to be in contrast with each other (Curren, 2009). For example, sometimes cultural and/or religious norms reinforce oppressive gender roles. How can the rights of all people be honored in a classroom when they are seemingly at odds with each other? HRE's inception was born out of the recognition of just such issues. It not only realizes education's potential for furthering human rights, but also addresses the need to set standards for teaching methods and curriculum use (United Nations, 1996). For that reason, HRE is as pragmatic as it is ethical. Practically speaking, it focuses on three specific aspects of learning:

(a) Knowledge: provision of information about human rights and mechanisms for their protection;
(b) Values, beliefs and attitudes: promotion of a human rights culture through the development of values, beliefs and attitudes which uphold human rights;
(c) Action: encouragement to take action to defend human rights and prevent human rights abuses. (United Nations, 1997)

This teaching model, which can be concisely summarized as "About human rights, through human rights, and for human rights" (United Nations, 2011) allows for pedagogical methods focused around students' individual needs while also educating people on the collective rights of the whole.

HRE as an Effective Educational Model

The failure of public schools in the United States can be likened to the Agatha Christie (1934) novel, *Murder on the Orient Express*. In the novel, a man is murdered by so many different people using so many different weapons, that it is impossible to determine which individual is actually responsible for his death. Similarly, so many disparate problems prevail in low-performing public schools that it is difficult to distinguish which are the most pressing. Students suffer as "socio-economic deprivation and poverty are exacerbated by lack of access to education" (Reyes, 2010, p. 4). This "lack of access" translates into a lack of relevant materials, or sometimes even a lack of basic materials, unprepared teachers, minimal resources, and heightened pressure on students to perform on standardized tests. These issues converge—and consequently murder the motivation and creativity of today's youth. Despite the clearly apparent issues in student achievement, particularly for students of color and students of low socioeconomic status, "the structural inequities that result in the denial of access are not addressed effectively" (Reyes, 2010, p. 4). It is clear that simply understanding and acknowledging a student's right to an equitable education does not solve the problems created by racial and financial inequities in our society (Darby and Levy, 2011).

HRE offers an alternative pedagogical approach to engage students in curriculum, and the method itself allows disenfranchised students the opportunity to learn about and how to advocate for their own rights. In this respect, HRE relies on participative learning, which encourages student self-actualization and organization—and thus requires that teachers reject traditional modes of teaching that have already been shown to be largely ineffective (Print, Ugarte, Naval, and Mihr, 2008).

HRE has already proven effective among high school students in Oakland, California, as evidenced in research conducted by Andrea McEvoy Spero (2013). Because of its participatory nature, students were empowered by the creation and performance of skits depicting human rights issues and the relevance of the UDHR (Spero, 2012). Successes such as this demonstrate that HRE has the potential to transform students' experience with education. Spero (2012) notes that "concrete teaching strategies for HRE are urgently needed in the United States, where many students experience persistent human rights violations in their schools and communities" (p. 29). HRE makes curriculum relevant for students, which engages and inspires them. The benefits of this educational model not only apply to the students, but also to the society for which they learn to advocate.

In my own experience, I have seen the long-lasting effects of HRE in my students' lives. Not only have my students learned from one another, but some have even gone on to pursue human rights activism in college. One of my former students, an Afghani refugee in the United States, now studies human rights law. Another, the daughter of Filipino immigrants, recently earned a scholarship to pursue her passion for international relations in college. These students both found hope in the study of human rights because it contextualized their own experiences of oppression and poverty. They now seek to empower others.

Implementing HRE

Implementing HRE is not always an easy task. In fact, the United Nations Decade for Human Rights Education (UNDHRE), which spanned from 1995 to 2004, was considered by some to be only a marginal success as many countries did not fully embrace HRE or simply did not participate at all (Print et al., 2008). While the students who were exposed to HRE pedagogy responded well, the number of students was too few for HRE to be effective on a broader societal scale. The major reasons for states' reluctance in adopting HRE practices are varied. While some nations promote values contradictory with human rights principles, research actually found that the greater challenge to implementing HRE was financial rather than moral or ethical (Print et al., 2008).

Unfortunately, possible sources of alternative funds for education often come with strings attached. For instance, nongovernmental organizations may "have other limitations beyond their funding, including their idiosyncratic, single-purpose nature...and their all-too-frequent competition with each other for funding and public support" (Print et al., 2008, p. 124). When the educational funding relies on competitive or capitalistic models, the purpose of education may be distorted as materials are geared to meet the particular special interests of specific donor groups. Furthermore, unpredictable funding leads to a lack of cohesiveness in curriculum, for what can be afforded one year may be abandoned the next as donors move on. Without coherency, it is difficult to implement HRE in a meaningful way, for students have no opportunity to build on their skills or to engage with human rights principles on a deep level.

Luckily, HRE can be effectively implemented. If human rights is the lens through which curriculum is taught, then the core curriculum does not necessarily need to be replaced, but only revisioned. In the pedagogical unit, I demonstrate how a commonly taught text such as Arthur Miller's *The Crucible* (1995) can be made relevant to human rights and to students' experiences. It is my belief that almost all English class units can be taught through an HRE lens.

Final Reflections

As a teacher, I know that it is difficult to change curriculum. When this unit was first used by the other teachers at my school, we faced many challenges. How should it be graded? How do we relate personal experiences to the students when we all have different teaching styles? Can we incorporate more informational reading materials to keep with the demands of the new Common Core State Standards?

Thanks to the open mindedness and collaborative effort of my fellow English teachers at Concord High, we were able to overcome these obstacles. Furthermore, the motivation to do so was practical: The curriculum works. Time and again, we found that students generally enjoy discussing and researching human rights. It is my hope that the unit plan outlined below may serve as a guide for any English teacher interested in revisiting traditional texts in a relevant new light, one that engages and empowers youth.

Pedagogical Tool

Unit Title: Teaching the UDHR through The Crucible

Unit Introduction: This curriculum unit provides a human rights lens through which to study the issues of Arthur Miller's play *The Crucible* (1995), which is a commonly taught work of American literature in public high schools across the United States. The unit incorporates the UDHR and

Table 9.1 Unit Block Plan

Week One	Personal Context of Human Rights. Human Rights "Show and Tell."	Historical Context of Human Rights. Introduction to the UDHR and its history	Understanding the UDHR. Group work analysis of the UDHR. Human Rights Research Project explained. Letter of Intent assigned.
Week Two	Mob Mentality and Human Rights. Analysis and discussion of the McMartin Preschool Trials.	Introduction to the Salem Witch Trials. Explore the chronology of the witch trials, connecting them to human rights.	Introduction to *The Crucible*. Anticipation Guide and biographical information on Miller. Start reading and discussing Act One. Assign Dialectical Journals.
Week Three	Act One Analysis. Concept focus on character motivations jigsaw	Research Topics given out. Work on research in computer lab; assign note cards for research.	Human Rights focus. The rights of children. Start reading and discussing Act Two.
Week Four	Act Two Analysis. Concept focus: Religious allusions, religious inclusion	Human Right focus: Religious Tolerance. Read news article on France's *burqa* ban.	Quiz on Acts One and Two
Week Five	Act Three Analysis. Concept focus: Equity in the justice system	Historical Fiction Assignment. Read samples and discuss	Human Rights focus: Juvenile Justice and the Death Penalty. Read closing arguments for Lee Malvo trial.
Week Six	Act Four Analysis. Concept focus: Activism and human rights.	"Reimaging *The Crucible*" Assigned	Work on research paper in computer lab
Week Seven	Student performances for "Reimaging *The Crucible*"	Review for the test. Notes and team Jeopardy!	Test on *The Crucible*

includes lesson plans that encourage looking at "American" history through the eyes of the oppressed, particularly women and religious and/or ethnic minorities.

The pedagogical approach used in this unit is rooted in the principles of HRE—education about human rights, through human rights, and for human rights. It is based on an education model that connects academic knowledge to students' prior experiences. The goal is to use *The Crucible* as a conduit through which to both educate and empower young people about their own human rights.

This unit is intended to last about seven weeks of class. The two major aspects of the unit, *The Crucible* and human rights, are taught together (Table 9.1). For instance, while the students read Act One of the play for homework, the class develops its understanding of human rights and connects the themes of the play to their personal lives. The unit was designed for a class that takes place on a block schedule three times a week, on Monday and Thursday for two hours, and on Wednesday for 55 minutes. The block lessons, however, are easily converted into two-hour-long lessons for teachers who see their students every day.

Summary of Major Activities in the Unit

Human Rights "Show and Tell." Before starting with the history of human rights, this activity connects the essence of human rights to students' own lives, for it connects human rights with their personal experiences and helps to create a positive and respectful classroom community in which students may share their ideas and experiences freely. Students are asked to bring in anything that represents what they associate with human rights, such as a visual, a poem or excerpt of a story, personal object, song, etc. If possible, post the offerings on the wall for the rest of the unit. With student consent, I also incorporate their objects and stories into the lessons throughout the unit. For instance, a Jewish student brought in her family's immigration papers from when they were fleeing the Holocaust during World War II. When we read a news article later that month about the Holocaust, I incorporated the papers into the class discussion and lesson.

Human Rights Research Paper. The Human Rights Research Paper is a comprehensive study of a specific violation of each student's choosing. Every student must research a different topic; no overlaps are allowed. To pick topics, the students write "Letters of Intent" which are a way for them to practice persuasive writing with a tangible goal. If more than one student chooses the same topic, the topic is awarded to the student with the most persuasive letter. While setting up the students in competition to one another may seem to be divisive, the students are also encouraged to give follow-up preferences. When it is truly difficult to choose among students, topics can often be broken up so that two students can work on different aspects of the same issue. For instance, Gay Rights in the United States tends to be a popular topic. This, however, can be broken up into the right to marriage, the right to safety, freedom from torture, etc.

Historical Fiction Assignment. This is the creative writing aspect of the research project. The Historical Fiction Assignment requires the students to write a narrative from the perspective of someone who has suffered from the human rights violation they are researching. The goal of this activity is for students to practice narrative writing, including imagery, persuasive writing techniques, and awareness of audience. Many students choose to write imagined letters or diary entries from the viewpoint of people suffering from human rights violations.

Presentation of Human Rights Research. Students share their research in presentations that must incorporate visuals, information, the arts, and a call to action. This encourages students to utilize ethos, pathos, and logos, and also to express themselves on violations that they are passionate about. I have seen students play songs on guitar, sing, read original poetry, make movies, and so on. Students are welcome to read their Historical Fiction assignment to the class as part of their presentation. With 30 students, the presentations generally take about a week of class.

"The Crucible" Dialectical Journals. This is an ongoing homework assignment throughout the unit. To work on their writing and analysis as well as to engage personally with the text, students write Dialectical Journals for the play. The students choose lines from the play to respond to and write both an analysis of their selection as well as a reflection on how the text relates to their personal experience. The goal of this activity is for students to develop their own meaning from and relationship with the literature.

Reimaging "The Crucible." In groups, students rewrite a section of the play from the perspective of one of the disempowered characters. They may use lines from the play as written, but also are encouraged to alter dialogue in order to convey the new perspective to the audience. Possible character choices include Tituba, Elizabeth, Abigail, or any of the other girls. The brief section is then performed in front of the class. After each performance, students explain their rationale for their revision.

Lesson One: Personal Context of Human Rights

Essential Question: How are human rights applicable to students' personal experiences?

Objectives: Students will explain the significance of their personal items that relate to human rights and listen to others ideas, responding as appropriate.

Standards: Common Core English Language Arts (ELA) Grades 11–12: Speaking and Listening 1.

Time: Two hours.

Materials Needed: Students and teacher should bring in personal objects that relate to human rights. Personal objects can be a picture, poem, story, song, or item. Some students may want to talk about an experience or idea that relates to human rights.

Introductory Activity: Start class by playing a song related to human rights violation. I chose to play a song on the guitar that I wrote about a human rights issue that is personal to me—violence against women. I find that being vulnerable with my students and sharing my interests and talents with them allow them to feel more free themselves to participate.

Steps: Ask students to share their personal objects and talk about them. Provide positive encouragement and hang up items on the board as is possible. Allow students time to ask questions and talk about their ideas. Be sure to monitor discussion for emotional sensitivity. Each student will have a few minutes to share. Debrief with students; ask them what they learned about each other in general. I usually end the class with an acknowledgment of everyone's contribution to make sure that the classroom feels like an emotionally safe place for all students.

Assessment: Students will demonstrate their understanding and connection to human rights in their verbal presentations. Other students are encouraged to ask questions and respond appropriately.

Lesson Two: Historical Context of Human Rights

Essential Questions: What is the history of human rights? What is the UDHR? How can the UDHR apply to students' lives?

Standards: Common Core ELA Grades 11–12: Reading Informational Texts 2, 3, 8

Objectives: Given the history of the UDHR, students will analyze the reasons for the UDHR and write/discuss ways in which they can work for human rights in their daily lives

Time: One hour.

Materials Needed: Access to a short video called "The History of Human Rights" from the website www.youthforhumanrights.com. History of the UDHR from "The World As It Could Be" program, available at www.theworldasitcouldbe.org

Introductory Activity: Students will watch a short clip called "The History of Human Rights." After watching the clip, lead a brief discussion on this clip. Ask students what rights related to the personal objects brought in for the previous class.

Steps: Students will receive a handout edited from "The World As It Could Be" program about the history of the UDHR. Read aloud and discuss as reading. Ask students to write their thoughts on why World War II inspired international human rights discourse. Students will also write a response to the Eleanor quote given in the reading.

> Where, after all, do universal rights begin? In small places, close to home… Such are the places where every man, woman, and child seek equal justice, equal opportunity, equal dignity without discrimination. Unless these rights have meaning there, they have little meaning anywhere. (Roosevelt, as cited in *The World As It Could Be*, 2014, p. 4)

They will write and discuss how they can work for human rights in their everyday life. For homework, ask students to talk to someone not in the class about human rights.

Assessment: Students will demonstrate their understanding through discussion and through their written responses.

Lesson Three: Understanding the UDHR

Essential Questions: What specific rights are protected by the UDHR, and how are those rights violated and/or upheld in today's world?

Objectives: Given the UDHR, students will be able to analyze and interpret specific articles and how they relate to today's world

Standards: Common Core ELA Grades 11–12: Reading Informational Texts 4, 7, 8

Time: Two hours.

Materials Needed: Butcher paper and markers. The full text of the UDHR, available at: http://www.un.org/en/documents/udhr/. Handouts from the Human Rights Research Paper and the Letter of Intent are included at the end of the unit.

Introductory Activity: Have students respond to the following question: What are ten rights you think all people should have? Students may work on this with a partner. Then they will share their ideas with me. This assignment is good for "cold calling"—to call on students without them raising their hands – because they will all have something to say.

Steps: Students will receive the UDHR. Place students in groups of three or four. Assign each group three to four different articles of the UDHR.

On a piece of butcher paper, students should write the articles in their own words, provide examples of when the rights are upheld or broken, and illustrate their examples. Go around the room and hear the interpretations from each group. Provide examples from current events as well, to supplement student examples. This is a good way to introduce possible topics for the research papers. Post student work around the classroom. After this activity, give out the assignment sheet for the Human Rights Research Paper and Letter of Intent and answer questions.

Assessment: Students will verbally explain their specific article to the class. They will also write down each other's plain language version on their own handout as is necessary.

Lesson Four: Mob Mentality and Human Rights

Essential Questions: How do current events relate to human rights? How does mob mentality threaten human rights?

Objectives: Given new articles on the McMartin Trial, students will analyze the roots and dangers of hearsay and mob mentality both in society and in the justice system.

Standards: Common Core ELA Grades 11–12: Reading Informational Texts 2, 3, 7, 6

Time: Two hours.

Materials Needed: Articles and information on the McMartin Preschool Trial, available at http://law2.umkc.edu/faculty/projects/ftrials/mcmartin/mcmartin.html.

Introductory Activity: Ask students to write about the following question: What is something you would NEVER want to be accused of, even if you were ultimately found innocent? Why? Students will write individually, then discuss in pairs, and then we will have a class discussion.

Steps: After the introductory activity, introduce students to the facts about the McMartin Preschool Trial. Have students read the letter sent to parents by the police. Ask students to discuss how their parents would react if they received such a letter, or how they would feel if they received such a letter. Students will then read and annotate a commentary on the trials, available at http://law2.umkc.edu/faculty/projects/ftrials/mcmartin/mcmartin account.html. In small groups, have students list and explain problematic aspects of the trials, and discuss whom they viewed as the greatest victims in the McMartin Preschool Trials. In the closing discussion, identify how the rights violated in the trials connect to human rights. Ask students to identify specific articles of the UDHR that were violated during this event.

Assessment: Students will turn in their writing. Student participation will be assessed by their writing, annotation, group work, and class discussion.

Lesson Five: Introduction to the Salem Witch Trials

Essential Questions: What were the Salem Witch Trials? How do the Salem Witch Trials relate to human rights?

Objectives: Given historical background on the Salem Witch Trials, students will connect this historical event with the McMartin Preschool Trials and analyze the human rights violations that took place during this time.

Standards: Common Core ELA Grades 11–12: Reading Informational Texts 1, 3, 7, 8

Time: One hour.

Materials Needed: Primary sources and other documents related to the history of the Salem Witch Trials are available at: http://law2.umkc.edu/faculty/projects/ftrials/salem/SALEM.HTM.

Introductory Activity: Ask students to respond to the following questions: Are children trustworthy? If a child accused an adult of doing something bad, would you believe him or her? Why or why not?

Steps: After discussing the introductory question, have students read "Chronology of Events Related to the Salem Witch Trials" aloud, popcorn style. This is available at: http://law2.umkc.edu/faculty/projects/ftrials/salem/ASAL_CH.HTM. Throughout the reading, discuss the hypocrisy and underlying motives in the people's behavior. Other appropriate topics include the injustices in the legal system, such as the assumption of guilt rather than innocence, use of spectral evidence as proof, slavery, and the lack of proper defense and appeals for suspected witches. After reading this, ask students whether such a trial could happen again. Have students write their answers, pair share, and then discuss with class. Then show students the parallels between the McMartin Trial and the Salem Trials, available at: http://law2.umkc.edu/faculty/projects/ftrials/mcmartin/salemparallels.htm. This is not in References section. To close, ask students: What human rights violations took place during the Salem Witch Trials? Write student ideas on the board as they speak.

Assessment: Collect student writing. Student participation will be assessed through their writing, pair sharing, and speaking to the class as a whole.

Lesson Six: Introduction to The Crucible

Essential Questions: What are the main themes explored in Arthur Miller's play *The Crucible*? How do these themes relate to human rights?

Objectives: Given *The Crucible* Peer Interview Worksheet, students will analyze and discuss the major themes of *The Crucible*. Students will also begin reading and discussing Act One of the play in class.

Standards: Common Core ELA Grades 11–12: Reading 1, 2, 3, 5, 9
Time: Two hours.
Materials Needed: There are many different versions of "*The Crucible* Anticipation Guide" available online. I use one that allows students to write responses to various statements that address the themes in the play. Biographical information about Arthur Miller is available online through many different sources. I found the following website to be useful: http://www.pbs.org/wnet/americanmasters/episodes/arthur-miller/none-without-sin/56/. Students will also need the text of the play, which should be provided by the school. A PDF of the full text of the play is also available at: http://asbamericanlit.edublogs.org/files/2011/10/21078735-The-Crucible-Arthur-Miller-2hmdzot.pdf.

Introductory Activity: Have students write a response to the following quote from John F. Kennedy: "The rights of every man are diminished when the rights of one man are threatened." Good questions to discuss: When are the rights of man "diminished"? How does diminishing one person's right affect other people's rights?

Steps: After discussing the Kennedy quote, students will be given a copy of "The Crucible Anticipation Guide." Working alone or with a partner, students will consider and respond to the major themes of the play and discuss them with each other. After they write (which usually takes about 10–15 minutes), facilitate a class discussion on the questions. The questions are open-ended and often provide a lot of discussion. This is a day when every single person can participate verbally in class. After discussion of the themes, students will read about and discuss Arthur Miller's life and how he connected the Salem Witch Trials to the Red Scare of the 1950s. Through discussion, also connect this to the McMartin Trials. After providing this context, begin reading the play aloud with class. Allow students to volunteer for parts.

Assessment: All students will participate verbally. Journals and student interviews may also be collected. Assign Dialectical Journals for homework.

Letter of Intent

Write me a letter of at least one paragraph in which you state what human rights violation you will focus on. This should tell what human right is being broken as well as where it is being broken. You will briefly explain why you chose to research this issue, and why *you* should be the one to research this topic. If more than one student wants the same topic, the topic will be awarded to student who writes the most effective letter. Effective letters are thoughtful, persuasive, and well written. In case you don't get your first choice topic, give at least two others you would be interested in researching.

Possible Topic Ideas: The following is a list of possible topics, but you are more than welcome to choose something not on this list.

Rwandan Genocide	Widow's Rights—India
Genocide in Darfur	Rape—United States
Kurdish Genocide	Torture—GITMO
Discrimination against Roma (gypsies)	Terrorism—IRA
Discrimination against Muslim people	Terrorism—Islamic Fundamentalists
Gay Rights—United States	Torture—Abu Ghraib
Death Penalty	Child Soldiers
North Korea – Freedom of Speech	Immigrant Rights
China – Freedom of Speech	Homeless Rights
Persecution of Tibetan people	Rape (country/region—not United States)
Sex Trafficking	Child Abuse (country/region)
Gay Rights (country/region)	Corporal Punishment in US schools
Child Abuse in the United States	Police Brutality—United States
Women's Rights—Middle East	Police Brutality (country/region)
Women's Rights—Africa	Right to Health Care/Medicine

Human Rights Project

This is your major paper for the quarter. Choose a specific human rights violation to research. You can choose a domestic or foreign violation; the key is that it should be something that you are concerned with. While the type of violation is a broad topic, you will focus on one specific incident. Topics may not be older than 1980.

There are two aspects of this research project. You will:

1. Give a *presentation* of your violation
   —visuals (power point or poster)
   —between five and six minutes
2. Write a *research paper*: the details of this human rights violation
   —see back for specific instructions and details
3. Write a work of *historical fiction* from the viewpoint of the victim(s)
   —creative writing piece with realistic details

Human Rights Project: Research Paper

Your research paper will most likely be six-to-eight pages long. The first half of the paper is a synthesis of the factual information that you discovered during your research. It is *essential* that you cite your sources—if you don't cite your sources, your paper will be considered plagiarized.

How to Structure Your Research and Your Essay

Introduction (One to Three Paragraphs)

Use an interesting story or fact that you learned during research, something that will grab the reader's attention. Summarize the information *in your own words*. (Cite your sources.)

Research Topic (One to Two Paragraphs)

Explain the topic of your research paper. State why this topic is important, which articles of the UDHR are in violation, and what you think should be done about it.

Background Information (Three to Five Paragraphs)

Give an overview of your topic, including the roots of the issue. (Cite your sources.)

Violations of the UDHR (Three to Five Paragraphs)

What human rights have been violated? How were they violated? Use the articles of the UDHR to frame this section. Choose two to four articles from the UDHR, and write a paragraph (or two) about each one. Include specific information from your research to explain how these articles were violated. (Cite your sources.)

What Is Being Done about This Violation? (Three to Five Paragraphs)

Who is working to stop it (government groups, militia groups, political groups, human rights organizations, nonprofit organizations)? What are they doing? Is it working? Why or why not? (Cite your sources.)

Proposed Solution (One to Three Paragraphs)

What do you think should be done? Why?

Why I Chose This Topic (One to Two Paragraphs)

Explain here why you chose this human rights violation.

Your Personal Experiences with this Issue (One to Three Paragraphs)

Even if you haven't ever experienced this violation yourself, you can share your feelings about the fact that this right is being violated in others.

Reflection/Summing Up (One to Three Paragraphs)

What did you learn from this project? Restate your thesis. Restate the main facts of this violation, and close with a final call to action, urging your audience to do something to help.

Helpful Websites for the Unit

The following list consists both of materials used in the unit and of websites that provide supplemental resources to teaching through an HRE lens. As for connecting the human rights issues to today's world, I suggest that teachers find current news articles that are relevant to students' lives.

Linder, D. (2003). *McMartin preschool abuse trials of 1987 to 1990*. Retrieved May 25, 2014, from http://law2.umkc.edu/faculty/projects/ftrials/mcmartin/mcmartin.html.

Linder, D. (2009, September). *The Salem witchcraft trials of 1692*. Retrieved May 25, 2014, from http://law2.umkc.edu/faculty/projects/ftrials/salem/SALEM.HTM.

Miller, A. (1952). *The crucible*. Retrieved May 25, 2014, from http://asbamericanlit.edublogs.org/files/2011/10/21078735-The-Crucible-Arthur-Miller-2hmdzot.pdf.

PBS American Masters. (2006, August 23). *Arthur Miller—None without sin*. Retrieved May 25, 2014, from http://www.pbs.org/wnet/americanmasters/episodes/arthur-miller/none-without-sin/56/.

United for Human Rights. (n.d.). *Youth for human rights*. Retrieved May 25, 2014, from http://www.youthforhumanrights.org/.

United Nations. (1948, December 10). *The Universal Declaration of Human Rights*. Retrieved May 25, 2014, from http://www.un.org/en/documents/udhr/.

United Nations. (2011). *United Nations Declaration on Human Rights Education and Training*. Retrieved from http://www.hre2020.org/UN-Declaration-on-Human-Rights-Education-and-Training.

United Nations. (n.d.). *United Nations cyberschoolbus*. Retrieved May 25, 2014, from http://www.un.org/cyberschoolbus/ I don't find this in the text.

The World As It Could Be. (2014). *The world as it could be: Human rights education program*. Retrieved May 25, 2014, from http://www.theworldasitcouldbe.org/.

References

Christie, A. (2011). *Murder on the Orient Express: A Hercule Poirot mystery*. New York: Harper Collins.

Curren, R. (2009). Education as a social right in a diverse society. *Journal of Philosophy of Education* 43(1): 45–56.

Darby, D. and Levy, R. E. (2011). Slaying the inequality villain in school finance: Is the right to education the silver bullet? *Kansas Journal of Law and Public Policy* 20(3): 351–387.

Miller, A. (1995). *The crucible*, 20th edn. New York: The Penguin Book.

National Governors Association Center for Best Practices, Council of Chief State School Officers. (2010). *Common Core State Standards Initiative* | Home. Retrieved from http://www.corestandards.org/.

Print, M., Ugarte, C., Naval, C., and Mihr, A. (2008). Moral and human rights education: The contribution of the United Nations. *Journal of Moral Education* 37(1): 115–132.

Reyes, X. E. (2010). Educational equity and access and universal human rights: Effects on teacher education in the U.S. *International Online Journal of Educational Sciences*, 2(1): 1–21.

Spero, A. M. (2012). Human rights education and the performing arts. *Peace Review* 24(1): 28–35.

United Nations. (1948, December 10). The Universal Declaration of Human Rights. *Welcome to the United Nations: It's Your World*. Retrieved from http://www.un.org/en/documents/udhr/index.shtml.

United Nations. (1989). *Convention on the Rights of the Child*. Retrieved from http://www.ohchr.org/en/professionalinterest/pages/crc.aspx.

United Nations. (1996). *Human rights questions: Human rights questions including alternative approaches for improving the effective enjoyment of human rights and fundamental freedoms* (A/51/506). Retrieved from http://www.un.org/documents/ga/docs/51/plenary/a51-506.htm.

United Nations. (2011). *United Nations Declaration on Human Rights Education and Training*. Retrieved from http://www.hre2020.org/UN-Declaration-on-Human-Rights-Education-and-Training.

United Nations Decade for Human Rights Education. (1995–2004). (n.d.). *OHCHR Homepage*. Retrieved from http://www2.ohchr.org/english/issues/education/training/decade.htm.

CHAPTER 10

Reframing a Community College Social Problems Course through a Human Rights Perspective

Lindsay Padilla

As a sociology professor in northern California, I have become truly appreciative of the wide array of opportunities and rewarding experiences that the community college system can offer its student population. In one century (Cohen and Brawer, 2008), these institutions have opened significant doors of opportunities to a wide swath of people, particularly those who have been socially and economically marginalized. At its very core, the community college provides higher education to those who would otherwise not receive it (Boggs, 2010; Prentice, 2007). The open admissions process powerfully "subvert[s] the assumption of college for the select few" (Boggs, 2010, p. 4). By their very nature, community colleges espouse the human rights ideal that education is a right, not a privilege (Herideen, 1998, p. xiii). They are the only "distinctly American form of higher education... [with] an explicit and implicit commitment to accessibility, community development and social justice" (p. xv).

Serving nearly half of all United States undergraduate students (about 10.5 million people), two-year community colleges have appropriately been called "the people's college" (O'Banion and Gillet-Karam, 1996) and "democracy's college" (Boggs, 2010). Historically, community colleges have enrolled roughly half of all undergraduate students of color (American Association Of Community College (AACC), 2013; Snyder and Dillow, 2011) and

45 percent of the nation's first-time freshman (AACC, 2013). As such, the US community college system serves a distinctly nontraditional population. Underrepresented or "nontraditional" students in higher education constitute the more vulnerable groups in larger society. The common definition of nontraditional includes "adults beyond traditional school-age (beyond the early twenties), ethnic minorities, women with dependent children, underprepared students, and other groups who have historically been underrepresented in higher education" (Kim, 2002, p. 85).

My own community college classroom reflects these realities. Many of my students are first-generation college students, parents, reentry, and undocumented. With the most to gain from human rights recognition, these populations are more equipped to claim their rights if they know why they are excluded. The purpose of this chapter is to situate community colleges as the ideal institution to integrate introductory concepts of human rights into course syllabi and into the teaching practice of its professors as well as to articulate the valuable connection between human rights education (HRE) and service learning. I describe my rationale for teaching human rights, share student responses, and discuss the impact on my teaching, my students, and our local community.

The Universal Declaration of Human Rights

The clearest definition of human rights is the rights one has for being human; or as Brunsma (2010) beautifully states, "Because one is a member of the human family, because one is a member of this planet, because of one's humanity, because one *is,* so they have rights *as humans*" (p. 14). The term "human right" is applicable to all individuals, regardless of their complex identities and encompasses civil and political rights and economic, social, and cultural rights. The Universal Declaration of Human Rights (UDHR) outlines the 30 articles required for the recognition of our full, and shared, humanity. All these rights are equally important and interconnected. The UDHR offers a glimpse of shared global norms and values that can be utilized in educating community college populations, or in the words of the UDHR, "a common standard and achievement for all peoples and all nations" (United Nations, 1948).

However, access to or knowledge about these rights is not widespread. A 1997 study by Human Rights USA showed that 93 percent of people in the United States had never heard of the UDHR (Flowers, 2003). The survey results showed that while they had opinions about human rights issues, only 8 percent of adults and 4 percent of youth had any notion of the UDHR. When informed of its existence, they overwhelmingly supported it and wanted more information (Flowers, 2003). Since my students most likely will start my course not having heard of the UDHR, I asked the question: What would knowledge and application of these rights mean for my students?

Upon presenting the UDHR to the General Assembly of the United Nations in 1948, Eleanor Roosevelt declared: "It is not a treaty; It is not and does not purport to be a statement of law or of legal obligation. It is a Declaration of basic principles of human rights and freedoms" (Roosevelt, 1948). Unlike the legally binding treaties that followed, the UDHR was intended as a document embodying aspirational principles. This fact provides all the more reason to introduce human rights, through education, as a tool for democratic participation, a peak into a future not yet realized, rather than a set of rules.

In my experience, framing a course from a human rights perspective and supporting it with the UDHR helped my students see the multiple connections between social justice, education, and the world in which they live. Understanding the central tenets of human rights and the UDHR provides the context for my pedagogical tool: a syllabus for the social problems course. I chose to include the syllabus here because it demonstrates the framing of the course and the power of service learning as an assessment tool. The organization of this chapter is as follows: the first section sets the stage for my choice of pedagogical tool by discussing why HRE belongs at the community college; the next section discusses the power of service learning as an assessment tool; and the final section contains my reflections.

HRE in My Community College Course

As a way to pursue human rights in our community, our nation, and the world, HRE provides the vehicle for us to know our rights and create an inclusive campus culture. As defined by Amnesty International (n.d.), HRE is

> a deliberate, participatory practice aimed at empowering individuals, groups and communities through fostering knowledge, skills and attitudes consistent with internationally recognized human rights principles...Its goal is to build a culture of respect for and action in the defense and promotion of human rights for all. (http://www.amnesty.org/en/human-rights-education)

There are many definitions of HRE, but this one clearly articulates my pedagogy and worldview. HRE is necessarily collaborative and action oriented. It embodies Paulo Freire's (1970, 2000) educational philosophy, which argues that a typical classroom environment does not allow teachers or students to be human, denying students the ability to critically reflect on the world in which they live and detaching the school environment from their everyday lives. According to Freire (2000), education is a form of intervention in the world: "If we have any serious regard for what it means to be human, the teaching of contents cannot be separated from the moral formation of the learners. To educate is essentially to form" (p. 39). Freire's philosophy of education is a guiding pedagogy and ethical judgment for the implementation of HRE in my community college course. His understanding of a transformative education exemplifies human dignity.

Ironically, the community college system, which claims to embody the ideals of democracy, does not provide its students with the analytical tools to contemplate social order and see the "discrepancy between [these] ideals and reality" (Zinn, 2005, p. 69). If democracy and social justice represent the means to achieve universal values and human dignity as embodied by the UDHR, an important place to inculcate this viewpoint is in the community college system. The focus on community college is important for HRE because the students who attend these institutions are likely to have human rights violated and would benefit from a holistic, action-oriented pedagogy. This unique learning environment and acceptance policy rightfully positions community colleges to take a leadership role in human rights curriculum.

HRE holds the instructor accountable for perpetuating the democratic ideals of the community college mission. I work at a crucial site for social change, and my vocation contains tools for change. Shor (1999) describes the importance of teaching: "no learning process is value-free, no curriculum avoids ideology and power relations. To teach is to encourage human beings to develop in one direction or another" (p. 22). From this perspective, I believe the student, the discipline, and our community should remain at the center of inquiry. The intention behind each assignment and activity for my social problems course keeps this point in focus. I asked myself: What do I want my students to become in four months time? How will this reflect the human rights community I envision?

The purpose of the incorporation of HRE into schools, then, is to prepare students to participate in society *and* to develop fully as individuals. The application of HRE in schools purports to:

(a) Integrate the teaching of human rights standards, values, and action skills into the curriculum;
(b) Promote knowledge of and respect for the rights contained in the UDHR, create awareness of human rights violations, and provide tools for action to end violations; and

(c) Teach the values of human dignity, tolerance, multiculturalism and nonviolence, and the skills of critical analysis and civic participation. (Belisle and Sullivan, 2007, p. 3)

In order to apply HRE to my social problems course, I began by incorporating the UDHR. I combed through my course outline and the content to be covered in the semester. Next, I corresponded each topic with related articles in the UDHR and added International Treaties and Conventions, for example: Convention on the Elimination of All Forms of Discrimination Against Women (CEDAW) and Convention on the Rights of the Child (CRC). To make the connection clearer, I also designed a graphic organizer as a reference for my students. (Refer to the syllabus at the end of this chapter for more details.)

Once the semester outline was done, I grappled with how to accomplish (b) and (c) of Belisle and Sullivan's (2007) description of HRE. I wanted my students to have a learning experience that helped them relate emotionally and intellectually to course material, connect their personal biographies and narratives to world events, and "transform their own lives so they are consistent with human rights norms and values" (Tibbitts, 2008, p. 3). This is where the course activities, assignments, and assessments brought HRE to life, prompting the questions: What violations will we look at? What actions will we take?

I knew that the UDHR would be the instrument connecting students' lives with others. However, according to Blau (n.d), it is more than just a tool to apply; it is also a tool to create a culture of respect:

> Human rights are grounded in respect for the rights and dignity of others. For this reason human rights are not simply legal instruments, but also everyday practices, rooted in community culture and in rhythms of everyday life. They are collective like democracy is— the more people participate the better the outcome for everyone and encompass the rights of distant others. (http://www.humanrightscities. org/human_rights/index.html)

The UDHR may connect students to their realities, but as the professor, I have to offer space to analyze these realities. As a result, I had to reconsider the structure of my class. Students needed the opportunity to explore and debate the ethical concerns that inevitably arise around human rights violations. Henry's (2006) classroom experience and research supports my decision, as she explains how "human rights norms and standards can provide clarification and analysis for often emotionally driven issues" (p. 108). HRE helps students develop moral agency, but they need to develop it on their own. Henry argues that if a teacher honors the students' agency embedded in human rights, then college students are able to see human rights as "liberating, not as a set of rules" (p. 111). The design of the course allows students to choose what social problem to study, has them connect the UDHR to their issue, and provides space for an action around that issue. The UDHR becomes a tool rather than a set of rules.

Teaching students to see and learn about the value-laden nature of human rights issues trains them to be critical thinkers and encourages them to *act* on their choices, fulfilling a desired outcome of HRE. In the following student reflection, the UDHR provides a blueprint for social change to this learner:

> This class has helped me to understand that if I am to be effective in the fight for human rights, I must: first, recognize the rights that are being violated; second, recognize my own privileges and power of influence given to me because of my social location in society; third, use my position to evoke positive change in society—change geared toward expanding and broadening the reach of human rights. (Student reflection assignment, 2012)

Not only is the UDHR a standard to be applied to the lives of my students and their communities, but also it serves as a motivating force that connects citizens across the globe:

> The framework of the UDHR has inspired me to pursue studies in social justice and social movements. The principles of the UDHR have reinvigorated my desire to engage the public in new and exciting ways. I am now more confident that my activism will be supported, and perhaps even endorsed, by a global community of consciously aware, caring human beings. (Student reflection assignment, 2012)

My students' reflections highlight the value of incorporating human rights into the community college classroom. Throughout the semester, I guided my students through the process of connecting what they are reading to what they have experienced in their lives and at their service-learning sites. These connections are vital in developing empathy for others and realizing our shared humanity. I encouraged action and reflection throughout the semester, which are both important components of social change. In the following section, I suggest how service learning and reflections are important components for realizing the promise of HRE at the community college level.

HRE and Service Learning

Service learning is a methodology wherein participants learn about community issues and academic content through active participation in service and reflection (Belisle and Sullivan, 2007). Belisle and Sullivan (2007) find that service learning can provide:

> experiences that are eye-opening, challenging and satisfying. It allows [students] to see the influence and impact that each individual can have on their community, and ultimately, it empowers them to use that influence toward the creation of a better, more humane world for all. (p. 1)

By combining HRE education and service learning in my classroom, students engaged in action-oriented service projects that teach about current issues, promote human rights values, and provide essential life skills. Working in the classroom and "in the field," a crucial link is established between the content of a discipline and the various realities that exist in the world. Service learning became a vehicle for students to transcend the classroom walls and focus on *doing* human rights, thereby providing hands-on experiences that students can apply in their lives and careers. One student reflected on this notion:

> My service learning experience and our [school-wide human rights] awareness campaign have helped me become aware of human rights, which has encouraged me to become a human rights advocate. I now know how human rights are violated and how I can be a change that hopefully could improve things for future generations... Spreading change and speaking truth is a revolutionary act and something everyone should learn. (Student reflection assignment, 2012)

Service learning also assists students in seeing human rights in the context of personal responsibility and realizing that individuals—past and present—make a difference:

> I am most joyous for giving my services and in return, I have been encouraged, emboldened to work at my activism. Specifically, this summer I will start an awareness blog as a small way of igniting cultural value changes. (Student reflection assignment, 2012)

I was concerned about perpetuating inequalities through service work. The work of Herzberg (1994) argues that for service learning to enhance academic outcomes, critical analysis of the issue regarding service is necessary; otherwise it is simply charity. Barber (1998) expands on the concern:

> Serving others is not just a form of do-goodism or feel-goodism, it is a road to social responsibility and citizenship. When linked closely to classroom learning...it is an ideal setting for bridging the gap between the classroom and the street, between the theory of democracy and its much more obstreperous practice...Service is an instrument of civic pedagogy...In serving the community, the young forge commonality; in acknowledging difference, they bridge division; and in assuming individual responsibility, they nurture social citizenship. (p. 232)

Therefore, assessment design is paramount to alleviating concerns around charity. Reflection, through journal writing, in-class discussions, class presentations, and papers, is crucially important to positive, academic outcomes (Gwin and Mabry, 1998). Eyler and Giles (1999) have called reflection "the hyphen in service-learning: it is the link that ties the student experience in the community to academic learning" (p. 171).

I required reflection and analysis throughout my course. In particular, I had students write on a class blog. This allowed them to read what others were experiencing and to engage in conversations, both in and out of class, about their service sites, activities, and the content of the course. I also required a final written reflection that had them review all their entries, discuss their strongest entry and most difficult entry, as well as reflect on what they learned and how they changed. The final reflections brought out insights that the students only discovered because they were looking at their work over the entire semester.

Eyler and Giles (1999) found service learning had a positive impact on students' motivation, a deepened understanding of the subject matter and social complexity, an increased awareness of community needs. This experience fostered a feeling of connection to the surrounding community, and I found similar results. Combining sociological inquiry with service learning enabled my students to move beyond the individualistic explanations of social phenomena and to courageously raise awareness and inquiry about structure, ideology, and social justice. The HRE curriculum provided the structure for their analysis. Two students' reflections exemplify this point:

> Now that I have a better understanding of my community, I feel like human rights awareness can inspire a community to come together, bound by common beliefs in equality, justice, and human compassion.

> Human rights have a way of inspiring the good in people, and that is the very substance that turns a group of neighbors into a working community. (Student blog post, 2012)
>
> This class has encouraged me to be a better human altogether. Having compassion for everyone: every race, ethnicity, and background. I've kind of always been that way, but this class has showed me how to bring what I have to the table and help in any way that I can. (Student blog post, 2012)

Studying human rights through a sociological lens offers the framework for critical analysis and inquiry. Students leave my class with the ability to understand the content of my discipline, analyze how their individual service connects with social structure and the potential for social change, and apply this perspective in order to become active community members.

Final Reflections

> Our human condition is one of essential unfinishedness...we are incomplete in our being and in our knowing...we are 'programmed' to learn, destined by our very incompleteness to seek completeness, to have a 'tomorrow' that adds to our 'today'. (Freire, 2000, p. 79)

This chapter outlined the necessity for including HRE at the community college level and using service learning to achieve course goals. As a way to pursue human rights in our community, our nation, and the world, education allows us to know our human rights. Unlike normative education, which primarily views students as lucrative investments, I argue that HRE and service learning can facilitate student empowerment by nurturing the development of students and offering the opportunity for praxis. By emphasizing critical thinking, authentic dialogue, and creativity, HRE and service learning provide a worldview of emancipation necessary for restoring our humanness and assisting students in becoming agents of change.

The foundations of HRE stress the importance of theoretical knowledge and its relevance to local situations, connection between theory and practice, and belief in democratic, anti-racist ideas. Helping our students discover that "because one is a member of the human family, because one is a member of this planet, because of one's humanity, because one *is*, so they have rights *as humans*" (Brunsma, 2010, p. 14). Teachers may hesitate to incorporate HRE because human rights are often seen as unrealistic, idealistic, and remote, outside of the mainstream of events, something that happens in a distant land, or as a luxury for the fortunate. This is where service learning, with the proper pedagogical implementation, provides a remedy for this concern. HRE and service learning offer the framework to facilitate students' understanding of the commonalities between the local and the global; furthermore, this curriculum educates the students to live and work in a pluralistic society. A human rights perspective emphasizes critical thinking and demands the instituting of respect in the classroom and across campus.

Fundamental changes, not just a class by class or a student code of conduct implementation, must be made in order to foster a human rights culture on our campuses. To study human rights through one or two *required* classes or the celebration of a thematic month further reifies and objectifies the notion of culture and universal rights, possibly perpetuating "otherness." We need a curriculum that not only discusses human rights, but also works on making human dignity a world reality. This curriculum aims to do just that: it begins to connect students' knowledge acquisition to their respective communities and to humanity. The service-learning project (SLP) stresses the importance of theoretical knowledge and its relevance to local situations, connects theory and practice, and encourages democratic, anti-oppressive mindsets.

I am a sociologist, and thankfully the American Sociological Association (ASA) is supportive of my endeavor to include human rights into my teaching. On August 17, 2005, the ASA released a statement in defense of scholarly work and freedom of thought as it relates to human rights. On August 12, 2009, the ASA affirmed and expanded on the original statement to include a more comprehensive discussion of human rights, recognizing that "human rights and the violation of human rights are embedded in societies and communities which are fundamental subjects of sociological study" (American Sociological Association, 2009, para 1). This pronouncement confirms my belief in the power of HRE, particularly when united with service learning, in declaring that the ASA strives to "serve the public good, including the advancement of human rights and freedoms" (para 4). My discipline also affirms that social change can occur in the classroom as we empower students by helping them reach their intellectual potential.

Through HRE, community college students can find a way to make their rights a reality and reduce the atrocities to which we bear witness. Educators are implicated in this process too. We must provide an education that enlightens and liberates. In teaching and in education at large, "our shared humanity is more apt to flourish" (Brunsma and Overvelt, 2007, p. 71). Once students and educators have the ability to translate private feelings into public issues, social change is possible (Mills, 1959). Teachers who recognize the empowering possibilities of HRE must continue to liberate and heal within the walls of their classrooms and work on branching into the community, because, in affirming human rights, the possibility for social change can be realized.

Pedagogical Tool: Course Syllabus

SOC 2: Introduction to Social Problems Course Description

This course presents a sociological framework for understanding and engaging major social problems in the United States and around the world. Through a human rights perspective, we will explore the issues of human rights and examine social problems as they relate to the violation of rights. Working in the classroom and within our community, we will investigate a variety of areas where social problems occur (the economy, education, work, the environment, etc.) and look at how these problems evolve and change. All students will participate in a service learning project (SLP) that offers the opportunity not only to analyze social problems "in the field," but also to participate in efforts to address social problems themselves. Another component of this process will include educating others about human rights. While SLPs may not present complete "solutions" to social problems, this course equips students with the sociological theories and concepts to understand and evaluate problems, as well as the ways in which people struggle to change them.

Student Learning Outcomes

- Examine different social problems from a variety of sociological perspectives, including a human rights framework
- Understand basic sociological concepts and how to apply them to analyzing social problems
- Investigate the interactions between structural inequality and human agency
- Examine, analyze, and address social problems in surrounding communities by applying the UDHR
- Enter, participate in, and exit a community with respect and integrity
- Demonstrate reciprocity and responsiveness in service work with surrounding communities
- Develop critical thinking and writing skills that combine the analytical tool of a sociological imagination with civic engagement.

Text Requirements

Textbook: Dolgon, C. and Baker, C. (2010). *Social Problems: A Service Learning Approach*, 1st edn. Sage Publishing.

Course Requirements

Participation 10%: Since the class relies on discussion as well as small group in-class exercises as important pedagogical tools, attendance is essential. Studies show that those students, who regularly attend classes and are active participants, do better than those whose attendance is irregular and do not participate. Your classmates depend on your participation. This class requires *respectful interaction* of students who, by the nature of their own lived experiences, will have differing viewpoints on how we know what we know. It is crucial that each student participate through sharing personal experiences, observations, or by actively listening.

Weblog 20%: An ongoing requirement of this class is a demonstration of knowledge gained combined with your service experience. Students will a keep an online blog of your experiences where you respond to questions or problems presented to you in class. The blogging will be graded on quality and not quantity.

Photo "Essay" 10%: A 20-page photo essay (can be turned into a photo book) reflecting the state of your chosen UDHR article in your neighborhood. The components of this "essay" include: a dedication, an overview of the article, a statement, and analysis of the problem in your neighborhood, a short biography, and a reflection piece.

Leading Class Discussion 10%: Once during the semester you will lead a discussion of one or more readings assigned for the week. This discussion should include a creative, interactive, and engaging response to the reading(s) and two discussion questions for the class to consider.

Service Learning Project (SLP) 30%: Over the course of the semester you will have the opportunity to learn about the diversity and needs of our community, first hand. You will engage in a SLP, whereby you actively apply the knowledge you have gained in the classroom by providing your time and services to address real community needs. This class will work with several community organizations to actively address social issues in our community. The requirements for this project are: (1) 20 hours of service over the semester, (2) creating a learning opportunity for the population you are working with about human rights, (3) service learning and Human Rights Research Paper, and (4) presentation during the last week of classes (Table 10.1).

Table 10.1 Course Schedule

Lecture Topic	Required Reading	Assignment Due
Introductions	Syllabus	
Service Learning (SL)	Chapter 1 *Sociological Imagination* Sign up for Discussion Leading	**SL Application & Best Practices** Set up Weblog
Human Rights	*UDHR*	Weblog 1
SL Organizations	*The Vanity of Volunteer ism* Guest Speakers: Community Partners	Weblog 2 Comment
The Whole Wide World Around: Globalization and its Discontents	Chapter 10 *What should a billionaire give and what should you?* *The New Politics of Consumption*	**Choose Service Site** Weblog 3 Comment
Who Has, Who Doesn't? Poverty, Inequality, and Homelessness	Chapter 2 *Covenant on Economic, Social & Cultural Rights;* *Covenant on Political & Civic Rights* **UDHR: Article 25**, Film: End of Poverty	**Schedule Interviews** **SL Plan & Agreement** Weblog 4 Comment
On the Job—Work, Workers, and Changing Nature of Labor	Chapter 3 **UDHR: Articles 13,14, 23–24** Film: Fight in the Fields	Weblog 5 Comment
Finding Ourselves—Race, Gender, Sexuality, Multiculturalism and Identity	Chapter 2 *Convention on Genocide* **UDHR: Article 1–3** Case Study: Rwanda Film: Shake Hands with the Devil	Weblog 6 Comment
Continue: Race, Gender, Sexuality, Multiculturalism, and Identity	Chapter 4 **UDHR: Article 1–3** Film: Shake Hands with the Devil	Weblog 7 Comment

continued

Table 10.1 Continued

Lecture Topic	Required Reading	Assignment Due
Continue: Race, Gender, Sexuality, Multiculturalism, and Identity	Chapter 4 *Covenant of the Elimination of All forms of Discrimination Against Women* **UDHR: Article 1–3** Guest Speaker from Marriage Equality	**Research Proposal**
Be it Ever So Humble—Changing Families in a Changing World	Chapter 5 *Covenant on the Rights of the Child* **UDHR: Article 4,16**	Weblog 8 Comment
Who Breathes Easy? Protecting and Designing our Environments	Chapter 6 **UDHR: Article 25**	Weblog 9 Comment
Why Can't Johnny Read? Education in Crisis	Chapter 7 **UDHR: Articles 26–27** Speaker from Public Library	**Time Log (you) & Performance Evaluation** (agency)
What Price is Justice? Deviance, Crime, and Building Community	Chapter 8 *The New Jim Crow* **UDHR: Articles 5–12; 21,** Ella Baker Center	Weblog 11 Comment
An Apple a Day? Health and Health Care for All	Chapter 9 **UDHR: Article 25**	**Photo Essay**
A World that is Truly Human	Course Wrap Up! Presentations	Weblog 12 Comment

Weblog Assignment

Our "Social Problems and Human Rights Blog" is a way for you to keep an informal online journal recording your thoughts and reflections on the readings. Using the Blogger platform, you will document your insights, thoughts, opinions, and questions regarding course readings and experiences. You can explain what you find the most important, significant, or troubling; make connections to your particular community, social or cultural group, your nation, or the global community; explore how alternative ways of approaching these issues, questions, problems, or solutions may be obtained; or identify other material which helps further explain, interpret, or solve the particular set of readings. These blogs foster critical thinking, understanding context, and engaging other learners.

Community Service Learning Project

Final Research Paper (100 points)

You will write a 5-7-page paper integrating library research on a social problem, how it relates to human rights and the articles in the UDHR, ICESPR, and ICCPR that address your problem, and your personal experience addressing the social problems and needs of your community. This paper should also address some of the main themes and issues discussed in the readings, lectures, and films this semester.

For this research paper you want to pick ONE social problem that your agency addresses and do some investigative research on that social problem. For example, if you are working with *Si Se Puede* you might want to do research on racial/ethnic educational inequality. You will combine your library research of this problem and your own personal experiences working in your community organization to answer the following questions in your paper:

1. What social problems does your agency address?
2. Why did you pick this specific social problem?
3. How does your agency specifically address the social problem you researched?
4. How is your work in the agency part of the strategy to address this problem?
5. Why does this social problem exist in our nation and our communities?
6. How does your social problem relate to human rights and the articles in the UDHR, ICESPR, and ICCPR that address your problem?
7. Is the social problem you researched related to some of the social problems we examined over the semester? How and why?
8. Based on your service work experience, how can individuals create social change and address social problems in their community?

Service Learning Presentation (50 points)

You will make a short (5–10-minute) presentation to the class on the following:

1. Relating your service work to the themes/issues/articles/international documents discussed in class and your research of a social problem
2. Providing an overview of your work this semester
3. Presenting your vision for social change – what we need to do!

References

Alexander, M. (March 9, 2010). The new Jim Crow. *HuffPost: The blog.* Retrieved from http://www.econ.brown.edu/fac/glenn_Loury/louryhomepage/teaching/Ec%20137/The%20New%20Jim%20Crow-from%20The%20Nation.pdf.

American Association of Community Colleges. (2013). *American Association of Community Colleges: 2013 Fact Sheet.* Washington, DC: American Association of Community Colleges.

American Sociological Association. (2009). *Statements by ASA Council.* Retrieved from http://www.asanet.org/about/Council_Statements.cfm (June 05, 2014).

Amnesty International (n.d.). Human rights education. [Web page]. Retrieved from http://www.amnesty.org/en/human-rights-education.

Barber, B. R. (1998). The apprenticeship of liberty: Schools for democracy. *The School Administrator.* Retrieved from http://aasa.org/SchoolAdministratorArticle.aspx?id=15264.

Belisle, K. and Sullivan, E. (2007). *Service learning lesson plans and projects.* New York: Amnesty International and Human Rights Education Associates.

Blau, J. (n.d.). *Human rights week.* [Web page]. Retrieved from http://www.humanrightscities.org/human_rights/index.html.

Boggs, G. R. (2010). Democracy's colleges: The evolution of the community college in America. *Prepared for the White House Summit on Community Colleges, Washington, DC: American Association of Community Colleges.* Retrieved from Google Scholar.

Brunsma, D. L. (2010). We are the ones we've been waiting for: Human rights and us/U.S. *Societies Without Borders* 5(1): 1–20.

Brunsma, D. and Overfelt, D. (2007). Sociology as documenting dystopia: Imagining a sociology without borders—A critical dialogue. *Societies Without Borders* 2(1): 63–74.

Cohen, A. M. and Brawer, F. B. (2008). *The American community college.* San Francisco, CA: Jossey-Bass.

Dolgon, C. and Baker, C. (2010). *Social problems: A service learning approach.* New York: Sage.

Eyler, J., and Giles. D. (1999). *Where's the learning in service-learning?* San Francisco, CA: Jossey-Bass.

Flowers, N. (2003). What is human rights education? *A survey of human rights education,* pp. 107–118. Gütersloh, DE: Bertelsmann Verlag.

Freire, P. (1970). *Pedagogy of the oppressed.* New York: Herder and Herder.

Freire, P. (2000). *Pedagogy of freedom,* 2nd edn. Lanham, MD: Rowman and Littlefield.

Henry, M. (2006). Human rights in the college classroom: Critical thinking about their complex roots. *Peace and Change* 31(1): 102–116.

Herideen, P. E. (1998). *Policy, pedagogy, and social inequality: Community college student realities in post-industrial America. Critical studies in education and culture series.* Westport, CT: Greenwood Publishing Group.

Herzberg, B. (1994). Community service and critical teaching. *College Composition and Communication* 5: 307–319.

Kim, K. A. (2002). ERIC review: Exploring the meaning of "nontraditional" at the community college. *Community College Review* 30(1): 74–89.

Mills, C. W. (1959). *The sociological imagination*. New York: Oxford Press.

O'Banion, T., and Gillet-Karam, F. (1996). The people's college and the street people: Community colleges and community development. *The Community College Journal* 67(2): 33–37.

Prentice, M. (2007). Social justice through service learning: Community colleges as ground zero. *Equity and Excellence in Education* 40(3): 266–273.

Roosevelt, E. (1948). *Statement to the United Nations' General Assembly on the Universal Declaration of Human Rights*. Retrieved from http://www.gwu.edu/~erpapers/documents/displaydoc.cfm?_t=speeches&_docid=spc057137.

Shor, I. (1999). What is critical literacy? In I. Shor and C. Pari (eds.) *Critical literacy in action: Writing words, changing worlds*, p. 22. Portsmouth, NH: Boynton/Cook Publishers.

Singer, P. (2006). What should a billionaire give-and what should you? *New York Times*. Retrieved from http://www.nytimes.com/2006/12/17/magazine/17charity.t.html?pagewanted=all&_r=0.

Snyder, T. and Dillow, S. (2011). *Digest of Education Statistics: 2010 (NCES 2011–015)*. Washington, DC: US Department of Education, Institute of Education Sciences, National Center for Education Statistics.

Student Reflection Assignment. (December, 2012).

Tibbitts, F. (2008). Human rights education. *Encyclopedia of peace education*. Teachers College: Columbia University. Retrieved from http://www.tc.edu/centers/epe/entries.htm.

United Nations. (1948). *Universal Declaration of Human Rights*. UN General Assembly Resolution 217A. Retrieved from: http://www.refworld.org/docid/3ae6b3712c.html.

United Nations. (1979). *The Convention on the Elimination of All Forms of Discrimination Against Women*. UN General Assembly. Retrieved from http://www.un.org/womenwatch/daw/cedaw/text/econvention.htm.

United Nations. (1989). *The Convention on the Rights of the Child*. UN General Assembly. Retrieved from http://www.ohchr.org/en/professionalinterest/pages/crc.aspx.

Zinn, H. (2005) *On democratic education*. Boulder, CO: Paradigm Publishers.

CHAPTER 11

Teaching and Learning Asian American Leadership: A Human Rights Framework

Melissa Ann Canlas

In class, we were taught that leadership is everything we can practice in our daily life, but it is really hard to do so. As an Asian woman, *I am so used to being invisible*... Yet, I believe that as long as I am willing to practice more, I will internalize exercising leadership for the benefit of my communities. (City College of San Francisco—CCSF student)

[Asian Americans] always found ways to fight back. Even if it's a little thing like if it was changing jobs or something big like going into the court system to fight back. You find out about all these leaders or past leaders in the community who found all of these ways to fight back. And I think it kinda does empower us to fight back. To find ways to help out our community since there are so many problems right now. (CCSF student)

These quotations from students in my Asian American leadership course at City College of San Francisco (CCSF) reflect challenges, lessons learned, and possibilities imagined from a curriculum that honors the histories and leadership of Asian Americans. Asian American students rarely see themselves represented in their schools' curriculum; and examples of Asian American leadership, past and present, are rarely a part of students' educational experiences. This chapter examines the right to education for Asian American students and asserts that critical leadership development is a necessary component of a comprehensive human rights education.

All students have the right to an education that is "directed to the full development of the human personality and the sense of its dignity"—an education that "strengthen[s] the respect for human rights and fundamental freedoms" (Article 26, The Universal Declaration of Human Rights, 1948). I argue that Asian American students deserve to be taught histories that center their communities' experiences and realities, and that highlight the leadership of Asian Americans, past and present. In this chapter, I explore the design of a critical leadership development curriculum that is grounded specifically in the histories and communities of Asian American students and their on-going struggles for social justice and human rights. I focus on the case study of the International Hotel (I-Hotel) in San Francisco: a multi-racial, multi-issue, intergenerational struggle led by Asian Americans in San Francisco, beginning in the 1960s. Teaching and learning about the I-Hotel offers multiple ways for all students – not only Asian Americans – to explore critical leadership, Asian American history, community organizing, and human rights issues. Throughout the chapter, I share reflections from my students and my own thoughts as a critical educator of Asian American studies. As my students' quotations suggest, teaching and learning the histories of Asian American leadership can inspire and encourage students to act as leaders themselves for social change and in pursuit of human rights for all.

Critical Leadership Development and Right to Education

> Unless Asian-Americans are provided a comprehensive education, they do not have access to equal education (Ms. Phan, high school teacher, as cited in Pang, 2006, p. 68)

How is critical leadership development a human rights issue? Leadership development is an often overlooked component of education and educational equity (Omatsu, 2006; Pang, 2006). Pang (2006) argues that a comprehensive education for Asian American students must include a curriculum that highlights strong Asian American leadership models so that students can see themselves as "empowered beings rather than passive ones" (p. 68).

Only by more fully educating about Asian Americans and critical leadership can we fully realize the right to education as defined in Article 26 of the Universal Declaration of Human Rights (UDHR):

> Education shall be directed to the full development of the human personality and to the strengthening of respect for human rights and

fundamental freedoms. It shall promote understanding, tolerance and friendship among all nations, racial or religious groups, and shall further the activities of the United Nations for the maintenance of peace.

Critical leadership development works to realize these rights, by developing students' understanding of themselves as leaders and as agents for change.

Asian American critical leadership development also addresses Article 1 of the International Covenant on Economic, Social and Cultural Rights (1966): "All people have the right to self determination. By virtue of that right, they freely determine their political status and freely pursue their economic, social, and cultural development." The fields of Asian American Studies and Ethnic Studies were founded in the 1960s on the central tenet of "self determination," by students and allies who demanded that educational curriculum should include the histories and contributions of people of color, so that all students could fully participate in the decisions that inform and shape their lives (Wei, 1993). In other words, in order to achieve self determination and the "full development of the human personality," Asian Americans and all students deserve to be educated about their stories in a way that portrays them as fully realized human beings—not as stereotypes, not absent from history, and not only as victims of oppression and discrimination, but as leaders with both the capacity and responsibility to act in the service of human rights.

Critical Leadership Development: Counter-Narratives of Asian American Leadership

Well, for me, learning about the history of Asian Americans in the U.S, I kinda feel bad sometimes because they were put down a lot and they were discriminated against. But then later on you learn about how much they fought... And it makes you feel proud that you were part of this, you know, Asian heritage... And it's kinda like if they can survive it in the past, then why can't I? It makes you feel more empowered. (CCSF student)

Asian Americans as a whole are largely underrepresented and marginalized in official leadership positions, despite high levels of educational achievement (Jung and Yammarino, 2001). Asian Americans comprise approximately 5.6 percent of the US population (17.2 million) yet make up only 0.3 percent of corporate officers, less than 1 percent of corporate board members, and about 2 percent of college presidents (Sy et al., 2010). These statistics encourage the question: Why are there so few Asian American leaders?

Many believe that Asian Americans fail to hold leadership positions because there exists a shortage or deficiency of Asian American leaders. This belief is often paired with an assumption that Asian cultures lack leadership skills. Research suggests that Asian Americans are perceived to be both hardworking and high achieving, but also too passive, too inwardly focused, and lacking the assertiveness and authority to be effective leaders (Jung and Yammarino, 2001; Kwon, 2010; Liu, 2009; Pang, 2006). These perceptions fit a familiar narrative that suggests that Asian cultures are inherently deficient and that Asian Americans should address these cultural deficiencies in order to gain access to White, Western, male leadership culture.

Through critical leadership theory, this chapter asserts a counter-narrative of Asian American leadership: Asian American leaders have always existed, and Asian Americans continue to be leaders in their communities. In fact, Asian Americans, like all groups who experience oppression, possess a wealth of leadership, strength, resistance, resilience, and power (Solorzano and Yosso, 2002; Yosso, 2005). These leaders are numerous and have faced historical and systemic barriers in obtaining formal positions of power; but these leaders continue to assert their power nonetheless, especially in fighting back against discrimination and inequalities. Articulating and teaching counter-narratives of Asian American leadership allows Asian Americans to be more fully humanized and respected in classrooms and curriculums. These counter-narratives move beyond simplistic stereotypes of Asian Americans, allowing students to recognize and acknowledge the leadership that exists within their own families and communities. These counter-narratives offer students a framework within which they can understand their own power and capacity as leaders as well.

Critical Leadership Theory in the Classroom

Critical leadership theory offers a lens to reshape and dismantle the essentialized definitions of what it means to be both Asian American and a leader. In utilizing the term "critical" leadership, I refer to Leonardo's (2009) definition of a critical education as one that engages students in the process of debate and critique and that "encourages students to become aware of, if not actively work against, social injustice" (p. 18). I define the term "Critical Leadership" broadly, drawing upon the theories of Shared Leadership (Omatsu, 2006), Transformative Leadership (Shields, 2010), and Critical Leadership Praxis (CLP) (Daus-Magbual, 2011; Tintiangco-Cubales, 2012). Each of these models of leadership seeks equity and justice as its goal. As Shields (2010) writes of Transformative Leadership, such leadership "begins with questions of justice and democracy; it critiques inequitable practices" (p. 559). Similarly,

Tintiangco-Cubales (2012) articulates CLP as a pedagogical process that "focuses on practicing leadership *skills* that directly engages a *purpose* that is rooted in equity and social justice" (p. 7).

Rather than assuming that Asian cultures and communities lack strong leaders, critical leadership development poses the following questions: What roles do race and racism play in the underrepresentation of Asian Americans in leadership? Are there historical and institutional barriers that have limited access to power and leadership for Asian Americans? What roles do stereotypes play in the perception that Asian Americans do not make good leaders? In teaching and learning about Asian American critical leadership, these questions form an engaging starting place for students to begin to critique structures of race, racism, power, and inequality.

In my classes, investigating stereotypes of Asian Americans has proven to be an accessible introduction to critical leadership development. Most students are easily able to articulate stereotypes of Asian Americans. Identifying stereotypes allows for the opportunity to examine these stereotypes through a critical lens. Although Asian Americans are an immeasurably complex and diverse population—in language, ethnicity, immigration status and histories, and socioeconomic class—popular stereotypes and representations often essentialize Asian Americans into a singular culture or people. For Asian Americans, these stereotypes most often fall into two major categories: the "forever foreigner" and the "model minority." The forever foreigner stereotype suggests that Asian Americans, regardless of their citizenship and immigration histories, are consistently viewed as foreigners and considered less than fully American (Gee, 2004; Lee, S. J., 2005; Takaki, 1998). The model minority stereotype defines Asian Americans as passive, hardworking achievers who have strong family values, and great respect for authority (Lee, S. J., 2005; Lee, S. S., 2006). These stereotypes are also gendered. Asian American women are often portrayed as a "Lotus Blossom": passive and self-sacrificing, and/or as a "Dragon Lady": hyper-sexual and alluring, but threatening (Ono and Pham, 2009). Stereotypes of Asian American men often characterize them as emasculated geeks, less powerful and attractive than their White (or Latino or African American) counterparts (Ono and Pham, 2009).

Once these stereotypes are identified, they can be problematized and critically analyzed in a classroom. Are these stereotypes true? Do these stereotypes play a role in how we perceive (or do not perceive) Asian Americans as leaders? Do these stereotypes suggest that Asian Americans are culturally unsuited for leadership? In fact, a study of racial perceptions of Asian Americans in leadership (Sy et al., 2010) suggests that a "subtle and complex stereotyping process" may limit leadership opportunities and create barriers for Asian Americans (p. 917). The model minority stereotype defines Asian Americans as successful achievers who have great respect for authority, but who are unsuited to be authority figures themselves (Lee, S. J., 2005; Lee, S. S., 2006; Wei, 1993). These stereotypes also serve to justify an "official neglect of programs and services for Asian American students" that obscures the myriad educational and economic needs of Asian Americans (National Commission on Asian American and Pacific Islander Research in Education, 2008, p. 3).

These stereotypes assume that there exists a static, passive, monolithic Asian American culture, one that is unsuited for leadership. Discussing the connections between stereotypes and essentialism can assist students in identifying these narratives of cultural deficiency. As Gorski (2013) writes:

> The practice of essentialism attributes stereotypical characteristics to large swaths of people based solely on a single identity dimension such as race, gender, or class…essentialism leads to deficit thinking because it encourages us to look for the source of the problems…in stereotyped understandings of the 'cultures' of those students rather than in the educational and social systems that repress them. (p. 86)

By engaging in this kind of critique, critical leadership development allows students to move from an assumption of cultural deficiency to a broader, critical examination of the inequitable power structures and institutions that continue to marginalize Asian Americans and others.

When students understand that cultural narratives and structures of power are created, they can also understand that these cultural narratives can be rewritten, and power structures can be changed. Cultures are, in fact, not simplistic and static, but immeasurably complex and fluid. And while culture can be used as a form of domination (Rosaldo, 1989; Williams, 1977), culture and social narratives can also be rewritten in ways that empower Asian Americans and others. Similarly, definitions of leadership can be rewritten and rearticulated, as well as directed toward the purpose of human rights and social change.

Students can be encouraged to critique notions of leadership that define a leader as an individual who holds a position of influence, authority, and power over others (Omatsu, 2006). A leader, by this definition, is a rare and exceptional individual, and one who is most often White, Western, wealthy, and male. In contrast, critical leadership defines leadership as a collaborative, ongoing practice of caring, commitment, and community action directed toward social equity. Critical leadership also draws upon other models of leadership and community research that emphasize the importance of connectedness and giving (Silver, 2011), caring, empathy, and shared responsibility (Pang, 2006) within communities. Unlike traditional leadership models where a leader is defined as a rare and uniquely gifted individual, critical leadership acknowledges that anyone who shares and practices these values can be a leader.

Teaching these counter-narratives and broadening definitions of leadership to include and acknowledge the leadership of Asian Americans can have a profound impact on students. Critical leadership theory respects the multiple cultures of Asian Americans as a source of strength, rather than a deficiency to be overcome. The histories and communities of Asian Americans are filled with examples of courageous women and men, youth and elders, who resisted oppression, challenged discriminatory laws, organized labor unions, built families and communities, innovated technologies, and asserted their rights to be treated equally as Americans (Takaki, 1998; Zia, 2001).

Learning these histories and redefining leadership is often both challenging and inspiring to many students. As one student stated:

> I thought leadership was like being alone at the top and you control the people downwards. But then as like what I've learned [in class], leadership is about helping each other and bringing everyone up. It's not just about one person, it's about everyone. (CCSF student)

Students often report that learning alternative models of leadership leads to a sense of empowerment and encouragement to act against injustice. One student wrote:

> Before that I think leadership is not my thing, I just think it's about the principal or chairman about some unions. Most of us just follow what they say or something like that. [But] now I think we can stand up, speak out, and fight for our rights. (CCSF student)

Perhaps one of the most personally rewarding aspects of teaching critical leadership development is hearing students say that our classes have taught them to be more engaged with and respectful of their own families and communities. One student stated, "I guess it just really opened my eyes on a lot of the problems that we usually just overlook in the community." Another reported:

> I'm really interested in helping immigrants that can't speak English really. At home I'm used to helping my parents and grandparents fill out forms

and read their mail because they can't speak English. When I was little I used to think that it was a really big burden... [but now] I want to help them. (CCSF student)

The practicing of applying leadership skills to one's own family and communities speaks to the core of universal human rights. In her 1958 speech to the United Nations, Eleanor Roosevelt famously stated that human rights begin "in small places, close to home" (United Nations, n.d., para 3). Teaching and learning Asian American leadership has the potential for each of us to practice these skills and to take action in the places closest to our homes and hearts.

Legacies of Leadership

Many times, people will choose to be in silence about the unfairness and violation toward them, because they are afraid of standing out or being targeted. However, if we never speak out and let people hear our voice, then no one could help us and the justice would never come. Seeing and understanding the students, tenants [of the I-Hotel] and workers bravely striving for their rights, I am empowered to stand up for what is right. (CCSF student)

The following lesson plan is a three-part unit designed to introduce students to the decades-long struggle for the International Hotel (I-Hotel)—a community struggle in San Francisco that directly addressed issues of race, class, immigration, affordable housing, and human rights. The disciplined, nonviolent, strategic, and committed leadership of the I-Hotel tenants and their allies provides powerful examples of Asian American critical leadership. Youth and college students played a significant role in the I-Hotel struggle, and the unit challenges students to ask themselves about their own commitments to human rights in their communities. A brief background to the I-Hotel struggle is included in the lesson plan.

The campaign to prevent the eviction of Asian American elders from the I-Hotel was often framed as a struggle for housing as a human right. Article 25 (1) of the UDHR states,

Everyone has the right to a standard of living adequate for the health and well-being of himself and of his family, including food, clothing, housing and medical care and necessary social services, and the right to security in the event of unemployment, sickness, disability, widowhood, old age or other lack of livelihood in circumstances beyond his control.

The tenants of the I-Hotel were primarily elder Filipino and Chinese immigrant men whose rights to housing and security were threatened by the proposed eviction and demolition of the I-Hotel—a place that had been home and community to these elders for many decades. The slogan "Housing is a human right" appeared in many of the posters, speeches, and protests of I-Hotel tenants and allies during the nine years of protest to save the I-Hotel tenants from eviction.

The following lesson plans were designed to examine concepts of critical leadership development through defining key terminology (racism, oppression, power, and leadership) and through the case study of Asian American leadership in the I-Hotel struggle. The unit also contains an experiential learning component created for students to investigate human rights issues in their communities directly by speaking with community leaders and advocates.

These lesson plans were developed specifically for Asian American Studies classes at CCSF and could also be adapted for high school students and other undergraduate classes. The majority of the students in the Asian American studies courses at CCSF identify as Asian or Asian American; these include American born students, immigrants, international students, and English Language Learners. However, the material is applicable and important for students of all racial or ethnic backgrounds, especially because the I-Hotel struggle involved a broad coalition of diverse groups, and serves as an excellent example of interracial and intergenerational alliance building.

Student reflections and dialogue are a key component of the unit, and the struggle of the I-Hotel often has a dramatic and emotional impact on students. Viewing Curtis Choy's film "The Fall of the I-Hotel" (2005) never fails to elicit strong emotions from students. During discussion and reflections about the film, students often express a range of responses and emotions—from empathy, sadness, and anger to pride and inspiration. Below are excerpts from different students' responses to the unit.

> The lengths the *manongs* (elders) and community were willing to go in order to save the I-Hotel was just phenomenal to watch. The sense of community and unity is just overwhelming. It's astounding. And it amazes me how disciplined the people were (and are, even today with present protests) when being faced with physical abuse.
>
> I felt sympathetic to the older tenants in I-Hotel. I also feel great when I see other people helping the tenants to protect I-Hotel, regardless [of whether or not] they were tenants, [of different] races, and ethnicity.

The film and discussions also bring up challenging feelings of anger and even despair. The violent eviction of the I-Hotel tenants in 1977 is chronicled in the film, and many students remark on their disgust, anger, and discouragement at the mistreatment of the elder I-Hotel tenants. As one student responded, "If a group of organized citizens couldn't prevent the eviction...then what is the point?" Although the I-Hotel was eventually rebuilt in 2005, the tragedy of the eviction and the losses to the tenants and their allies was undeniable.

However, although many students are rightfully angered by the injustice of the eviction, many students are also able to make connections between the I-Hotel struggle, human rights, and the need for systemic change, both past and present. Perhaps just as importantly, students often feel encouraged and empowered to act. Below is a sampling of responses from different students on viewing the film and reflecting on the I-Hotel:

> Overall, this film made me more sad than angry. What greater injustice is it than for a person to be kicked out from a place he considered home for more than half his life? A place he believed that he would live in until his death? And yet, the owner of the building and the city were within their legal rights to evict the tenants of the I-Hotel. Does that make it fair or right in any way? No. Certainly not. It just shows that something needs to change in the legal system. An eviction as sudden as the one forced on the I-Hotel tenants should not have been allowed. Watching the struggle and the eventual loss was just upsetting.
>
> Affordable housing in San Francisco is still a relevant issue today. I also learned that addressing income inequality is an essential step in providing affordable housing to low-income San Francisco residents. Like myself, I couldn't afford to rent a room for myself and my mother, so I have to live and share a two bedroom apartments with eight other relatives in my first year of arrival in the U.S.
>
> I believe housing is and should continue to be a human right. At the current day, we have the power to house everyone in the United States and even feed them. It is my belief that if we have the power to do something good, it should be our duty to pursue that act.
>
> It teaches me fighting for what I believe in is important. We should cling together in times of trouble. We should stand out, speak out and control our own life...Even the hotel was destroyed, their struggles were not to be in vain, and there is a rebuilt I-Hotel. Although not all result is what we want, we have to struggle. Only we struggle, we have the chance to get what we want.

In teaching this, and other human rights or social justice lesson plans, dialogue and reflection are crucial. It is important to emphasize to students that the work for human rights is a long and ongoing *process*, one that includes struggles, defeats, and also victories. The work for human rights also requires empathy, alliances, community, self-care, compassion, and fortitude. Examples like the I-Hotel struggle offer students an opportunity to examine both the complex successes and challenges of community leaders, *and also* the continual work that still needs to be accomplished. The eviction of the I-Hotel tenants was nothing short of heartbreaking; the struggle trained and galvanized a generation of allies, many of whom were instrumental in teaching future generations and assisting in the rebuilding of the I-Hotel in 2005. Struggles for affordable housing and an epidemic of homelessness and income inequality persist, as numerous community organizations and advocates work tirelessly to address these issues every day. Our communities experience loss and heartbreak; and we also have reserves of courage, strength, and leadership to rebuild. Examining these complexities, including students' complicated responses and emotions, provides a dialogue necessary for practicing and sustaining human rights and critical leadership.

As an Asian American woman and a human rights and social justice educator, I am continually challenged to recommit to my own work; and I am nurtured and sustained by the work and example of my students. In my classroom, I have seen the ways in which critical leadership development has been transformative for my students and my own communities. Perhaps for me, the greatest lesson of the I-Hotel, and ultimately of human rights, is that of critical hope (Duncan-Andrade, 2009)—a hope rooted in the knowledge that there are always courageous leaders working toward justice, even in the presence of discrimination, loss, and inequality. This hope is, as Leonardo (2009) writes, perhaps the "ultimate act of defiance" within oppressive systems (p. 31). This is a hope firmly grounded in the histories of the Asian American critical leaders who came before us and in the power and examples of Asian American leaders who surround us in our communities. This critical hope can sustain our work as critical leaders to transform unjust systems to be the service of human rights for all.

Pedagogical Tool

Unit Title: Legacies of Asian American Leadership: The Fall and Rise of the I-Hotel

Unit Introduction: The following is a three-part unit designed for high school or undergraduate college students to examine critical leadership through the case study of the I-Hotel. The units are designed to be taught sequentially,

but Lesson One and Lesson Two may also be taught as standalone units. Lesson Three may also be useful as an introduction to an extended research project for students to investigate other examples of community issues and human rights leadership.
Essential Questions:

1. How do we define the following concepts: power, oppression, racism, resistance, leadership? How can understanding these terms assist in the process of working toward human rights?
2. How do these definitions relate to the experiences of Asian American communities? How can redefining these terms help us to understand critical Asian American leadership?
3. Explore the following questions about the I-Hotel, San Francisco:
   - What can the I-Hotel teach us about leadership, Asian Americans, human rights, and resistance?
   - In what ways are the struggles represented by the I-Hotel still present?
   - How can we exercise leadership in our own communities in present day?

Background Information: *The Fall and Rise of the I-Hotel*: The I-Hotel was a residential hotel built in the early 1900s on Kearny Street, in San Francisco, in a neighborhood that was once Manilatown. The I-Hotel primarily housed low-income, immigrant men, mostly Filipino and Chinese laborers. The struggle of the original I-Hotel, from 1968 to 1977, focused on the elderly tenants resisting eviction from the I-Hotel in a neighborhood that was quickly gentrifying. The demographics of the hotel in the 1960s tell a remarkable story about the immigration laws and structural barriers that faced the tenants throughout their lives in America. Curtis Choy's film, "The Fall of the I-Hotel" (2005), chronicles the stories of these *manongs* (respectful term for Filipino elders), their immigration to the United States during the 1930s and 1940s, and their experiences with economic exploitation, fierce nativism, and anti-Filipino violence. Many of these elders had been relegated to work low-wage jobs in service industries and as migrant farm workers. When many of these *manongs* immigrated to the United States, laws existed to deny Asian immigrants the right to own land, or to earn naturalized citizenship. Additionally, Filipina women were largely discouraged to immigrate; and due to anti-miscegenation laws, many Filipino men were unable to start families in the United States. For these men, the I-Hotel, and the surrounding businesses of Manilatown, provided not only low-income housing, but also home and community.

By the late 1960s, each of the small businesses of Manilatown was slowly sold as the neighborhood was gentrified to make way for the emerging financial district. In 1968, the now-elder tenants received an eviction notice so that the building could be torn down to build a parking garage. The tenants organized themselves with a broad range of community allies, including college students and community advocates for numerous issues: low-income housing, elder rights, labor unions, ethnic studies, and immigration. This sustained struggle was often framed as a human rights issue, with advocates insisting that housing is a human right. Despite the efforts of this coalition, at 3 am on August 4, 1977, San Francisco police, armed in riot gear, carried out the eviction, violently pushing past a human barricade of 5000 nonviolent protestors to evict the tenants. The City of San Francisco spent over $250,000 in overtime pay for the 300 police officers and sheriff's deputies for the eviction, but made no effort to relocate or provide services for the tenants (Sorro and Habal, n.d.). The eviction was devastating for the tenants and their allies, and many of the tenants were forced to relocate out of San Francisco.

However, the I-Hotel story continued, and the parking lot was never built because of continuous community pressure. After many more decades of community struggle, many of the original I-Hotel allies, along with a new generation of community advocates, were able to rebuild the I-Hotel in the same location where the original building stood. The new I-Hotel, reopened in 2005, respectfully honors the legacy of the original tenants, the larger community of allies, and continues the spirit of struggle and resistance for Asian Americans and their communities.

Lesson One: Asian American Critical Leadership and Human Rights: Defining Key Terminology

Essential Questions: How do definitions of power, oppression, resistance, and leadership help us to understand the experiences of Asian American communities and human rights? How can redefining these terms help us to understand critical Asian American leadership?

Objectives: Critically define the following concepts: power, oppression, racism, resistance, leadership, and human rights.

Time: 1.5 hours or more.

Materials Needed: Easel paper, tape, markers.

Steps:

1. Provide students easel paper and markers, and organize the students into small groups. Assign each group one of the following terms: Leadership, power, equality, oppression, racism, and justice. Ask

students to illustrate what they think this term means, in images, symbols, or text.
2. When complete, post these items around the room and do a "gallery walk" for students to look at each other's work. Hang a blank easel paper next to each drawing, so that students in all groups can add their contributions and illustrations to each term.
3. Allow each group also to share and describe the terms that they illustrated.
4. Discuss the posters and definitions, and then contextualize these terms within Asian American communities and experiences. Questions for discussion may include:

How does racism "work"?

- What are some of the dimensions of racism? Is racism only individual action? Is racism (and other forms of discrimination) also embedded in our institutions (schools, governments, laws, law enforcement)?

How do we define power?

- Is power defined only in terms of money, wealth, authority, and status?
- Can our communities be powerful even if they are not wealthy?
- Is power a positive and/or negative thing? Are our communities powerful? How?

How do we define resistance?

- What are we resisting against? Do we participate in resistance in our daily lives?
- Consider the following definition of transformational resistance:
  ○ Transformational resistance is "political, collective, conscious, and motivated by a sense that individual and social change is possible [and]...based on an awareness and critique of social oppression and motivated by an interest in social justice" (Solorzano and Delgado Bernal, 2001, p. 320).

How do we define leadership?

- Critically analyze the definition of leadership: By these definitions, who can be considered a leader? Are women included in this definition? Youth? People of color? Elders?
  ○ Are leaders only those who are elected to formal leadership positions?

- Do we see examples of leadership in our communities? What other qualities of leadership should be included in this definition (e.g., collaboration, empathy, self-reflection, and community)?
- Are Asian Americans often considered leaders? Do you consider yourself a leader? Why/not?

Note: This part of the unit could be extended over several class sessions, if desired (i.e., defining power or leadership could easily take an entire class session) or revisited throughout the course of a semester.

Assessment: Conclude by discussing, "What does leadership for social justice and human rights look like? Can we participate in working for justice? How?" Ask students to write a reflection journal about the discussion and/or any of the questions posed during the activity.

To prepare students for Lesson Two of the unit, you may choose to assign the article "No Evictions, We Won't Move!" (Solomon, 2003) as a homework assignment for students, before viewing the film "The Fall of the I-Hotel" (Choy, 2005).

You may also choose to have students view the website for the I-Hotel, and photographs of the original tenants:

- http://manilatown-heritage-foundation.org/.
- http://www.manilatown.org/ihlifehome.htm(contains photographs of the original tenants).

Lesson Two: Asian American Leadership in Action: "The Fall of the I-Hotel"

Essential Questions: Explore the following questions about the I-Hotel: What does the I-Hotel story have to teach us about leadership, human rights, and resistance? In what ways are the struggles represented by the I-Hotel still present? How can we exercise leadership in our own communities in present day?

Objectives: Analyze the case study of the I-Hotel, San Francisco, as a site of multiethnic, multigenerational resistance and human rights organizing, led by and for Asian Americans. Apply the critical definitions from Lesson One to the examples given from the I-Hotel film.

Time: Viewing "The Fall of the I-Hotel": Two hours minimum, includes 58-minute film and one-hour discussion.

Introductory Activity: Begin with a discussion about the question, "Is housing a human right? Why or why not?" If you have assigned homework in preparation for the film, you may ask students to share their impressions of the readings.

Steps:

1. View the film "The Fall of the I-Hotel," directed by Curtis Choy, 2005, 58 minutes.
2. Distribute the attached viewing guide to "The Fall of the I-Hotel" and ask students to consider the following questions as they watch the film.
3. After the film, facilitate a discussion on the film and the students' responses. This dialogue might best be done in two distinct discussions. The film elicits strong emotions, and it may be necessary to allow students to process their emotional reactions before attempting a critical analysis of the film. During the critical discussion, refer to the terminology defined during Lesson One of this unit.
4. After the film, you may choose to show additional media clips that discuss the rise of the new I-Hotel (opened in 2005).
   a. The following YouTube clips are from a six-part series created by students at San Francisco State University, documenting both the fall and the rise of the I-Hotel. These brief clips work well to supplement the film.
      i. Part 1: http://www.youtube.com/watch?v=WfY9deqRQ3Y&list=PLD0B0CBFD82D9F6A3.
      ii. Part 2: https://www.youtube.com/watch?v=fD9Jwpdb9IU&list=PLD0B0CBFD82D9F6A3&index=2.
      iii. Part 3: https://www.youtube.com/watch?v=pxWSkq7m8pI&index=3&list=PLD0B0CBFD82D9F6A3.
      iv. Part 4: https://www.youtube.com/watch?v=lTryMwpNbo0&list=PLD0B0CBFD82D9F6A3&index=4.
      v. Part 5: https://www.youtube.com/watch?v=ckdgi0xuUQA&index=5&list=PLD0B0CBFD82D9F6A3.
      vi. Part 6: https://www.youtube.com/watch?v=tBoCeq7MT5k&list=PLD0B0CBFD82D9F6A3&index=6.

Assessment: Assign students to write a response to the film and discussion and/or selected questions from the viewing handout.

Lesson Three: Legacies of Asian American Leadership: A Visit to the I-Hotel. Experiential Learning Component

Essential Questions: In what ways have communities learned from the lessons of the I-Hotel? How do communities continue to respond to issues such as affordable housing and/or other human rights issues? In what ways can we exercise our own leadership and participate in this work?

Objectives: Conduct experiential research by visiting and touring the I-Hotel and interviewing members of the Manilatown Heritage Foundation about the continuing legacies of the I-Hotel. If students are unable to visit the I-Hotel, an alternate field trip or experience could be arranged. For example, students could identify a housing rights organization and arrange a visit to the organization to interview someone from the organization. Faculty could also arrange for guest speakers who deal with housing rights to speak to the class.

Time: Varies. If planning a visit to the I-Hotel, allocate approximately three hours for the tour, plus travel time.

Introductory Activity: To prepare students for this activity, have students share their written responses from Lesson Two, and brainstorm questions to ask about the current I-Hotel and the work of the Manilatown Heritage Foundation.

Steps:

1. Arrange a visit and tour to the I-Hotel to speak with the members of the Manilatown Heritage Foundation. Alternatively, students could attend and/or volunteer for one of the cultural events sponsored at the I-Hotel.
2. Prepare questions to ask the hosts about the I-Hotel. Some questions may include:
    - How does the new I-Hotel honor the history of these *manongs* and *manangs*?
    - What leadership does the I-Hotel and the Manilatown Heritage Foundation take in responding to current issues in our communities?
3. After the experience, discuss with students: What are some of the lessons to be learned from the I-Hotel? What does the I-Hotel, past and present, teach us about the leadership of Asian American communities? To assess the unit as a whole, ask students to write a reflection based on some of the following questions. See reflection worksheet below.

Handout: Viewing Questions: The Fall of the I-Hotel

1. How did you feel watching the film? What people, moments, or images stood out to you most from the film?
2. The I-Hotel struggle could have simply been the story of victimized individuals evicted from a building when the building was sold. But Choy and the I-Hotel tenants and allies tell a much deeper story. How does Choy's film frame the story of the I-Hotel and its tenants? Why are the histories of the *manongs* important to understanding the I-Hotel struggle?

3. How are Asian Americans portrayed in the film? How is this similar to or different from the ways that Asian Americans are portrayed in mainstream media, past and present? How are these representations similar to or different from what you experience in your families and communities?
4. Asian Americans are often stereotyped as the "model minority"—economically successful, high achieving, passive, and immune from racism or discrimination. How does the struggle for the I-Hotel challenge this stereotype?
5. The struggle for the I-Hotel was sustained over decades. In addition to the protests, what other kinds of leadership and tasks were necessary to sustain this struggle? In what ways did the *manongs* and their allies exercise leadership through this long struggle?
6. Who were some of the I-Hotel allies? Do we still see Asian Americans building interracial, intergenerational alliances today?
7. The *manongs* and their allies assert, "Housing is a human right." Human rights are rights given to every person, regardless of their race, class, gender, citizenship, ability, etc. Do you believe housing is (or should be) a human right? Why/why not?
8. Is affordable housing in San Francisco still a relevant issue today? Do we hear or know about communities fighting for the right to affordable housing today? What can we do to contribute to changing these issues in present day?
9. Consider the definitions of power, oppression, resistance, and leadership. Does learning about the I-Hotel struggle expand, confirm, or challenge your definitions of leadership? What kind of leadership do you notice exercised today by members of your community? (Students? Immigrants? Women? Elders?)
10. What are the lessons that we should learn and teach about the I-Hotel struggle?

Reflection Worksheet

Reflection questions adapted from "The three levels of reflection on community service learning worksheet" (Cooper, 2006).

Write a 2–3-page reflection based on what you learned and experienced during this unit. In your reflection address some of the questions below:

Internal and interpersonal reflections: What have I learned about myself through this unit? How has learning this information impacted my understanding or empathy toward others? How have class discussions and activities impacted my understanding of "community" and my willingness to serve to others? Have my own stereotypes or prejudices been challenged? Have I allowed myself to be challenged? What have been my "take-aways" from this learning process? How have these experiences informed the way I understand human rights? How have these experiences influenced the way that I understand myself and my own power and potential as a leader? Will I be able to translate these experiences into how I think, feel, and act, both toward myself and toward others? How?

Institutional reflections: From this unit, are you able to identify any underlying or overarching issues that define Asian Americans, immigrants, elders, working-class communities, and others? What could be done to change these situations? What actions are already being taken? How might these understandings alter your future commitments and actions?

References

Cooper, M. (2006). Reflection: Getting learning out of serving. *The Volunteer Action Centre at Florida International University.* Retrieved from http://sites.stfx.ca/service_learning/sites/sites.stfx.ca.service_learning/files/Reflection_%20Getting%20Learning%20Out%20of%20Serving.pdf.

Choy, C. (Producer) and Choy, C. (Director). (2005). *The fall of the I-Hotel* [DVD]. USA: Third World Newsreel. (Original work published 1983. Revised 2005).

Daus-Magbual, A. S. (2011). *Courageous hope: Critical leadership praxis of Pin@y Educational Partnerships.* San Francisco, CA: San Francisco State University. Unpublished dissertation.

Duncan-Andrade, J. (2009). Note to educators: Hope required when growing roses in concrete. *Harvard Educational Review* 79(2): 181–194. Retrieved from http://mcli.maricopa.edu/files/success/2011/Keynote%20Presentation%20Duncan%20Andrade.pdf.

Gee, H. (2004). From Bakke to Grutter and beyond: Asian Americans and diversity in America. *Texas Journal on Civil Liberties and Civil Rights* 9(2): 129–158.

Gorski, P. C. (2013). Teaching against essentialism and the "culture of poverty." In P. C. Gorski, K. Zenkov, N. Osei-Kofi, and J. Sapp (eds.) *Cultivating social justice teachers,* pp. 84–107. Sterling, VA: Stylus Publishing.

International Covenant on Economic, Social and Cultural Rights. (1966). Retrieved March 22, 2011, from http://www.ohchr.org/EN/ProfessionalInterest/Pages/CESCR.aspx.

Jung, D. I. and Yammarino, F. J. (2001). Perceptions of transformational leadership among Asian Americans and Caucasian Americans: A level of analysis perspective. *Journal of Leadership Studies* 8(1): 3–21.

Kwon, M. L. (2010). The impact of the model minority stereotype on Asian American college student leadership involvement. *Dissertation Abstracts International Section A: Humanities and Social Sciences* 70(9-A): 33–69.

Lee, S. J. (2005). *Up against whiteness: Race, school, and immigrant youth.* New York: Teachers College Press.

Lee, S. S. (2006). Over-represented and de-minoritized: The racialization of Asian Americans in higher education. *InterActions: UCLA Journal of Education and Information Studies* 2(2): 1–16. Retrieved from http://escholarship.org/uc/item/4r7161b2.

Leonardo, Z. (2009). *Race, whiteness, and education.* New York: Routledge.

Liu, A. (2009). Critical race theory, Asian Americans, and higher education: A review of research. *InterActions: UCLA Journal of Education and Information Studies* 5(2): 1–12. Retrieved from http://escholarship.org/uc/item/98h4n45j.

National Commission on Asian American and Pacific Islander Research in Education. (2008). *Asian Americans and Pacific Islanders: Facts not fiction: Setting the record straight.* New York, NY: New York University.

Omatsu, G. (2006). Making student leadership development an integral part of our classrooms. In E. W.-C. Chen and G. Omatsu (eds.) *Teaching about Asian Pacific Americans: Effective activities, strategies, and assignments for classrooms and communities*, pp. 183–194. Lanham, MD: Rowman and Littlefield Publishers.

Ono, K. A. and Pham, V. N. (2009). *Asian Americans and the media.* Cambridge, MA: Polity Press.

Pang, V. O. (2006). Fighting the marginalization of Asian American students with caring schools: Focusing on curricular change. *Race, Ethnicity & Education* 9(1): 67–83. Retrieved from http://0-search.ebscohost.com.ignacio.usfca.edu/login.aspx?direct=true&db=aph&AN=19606838&site=eds-live&scope=site.

Rosaldo, R. (1989). *Culture and truth: The remaking of social analysis.* Boston, MA: Beacon Press.

Shields, C. M. (2010). Transformative leadership: Working for equity in diverse contexts. *Educational Administration Quarterly* 46(4): 558–589.

Silver, N. L. (2011). *Telling the whole story: Voices of ethnic volunteers in America.* Berkeley, CA: Community Initiatives.

Solomon, L. R. (2003). *Roots of justice: Stories of organizing in communities of color.* San Francisco, CA: John Wiley.

Solorzano, D. G. and Delgado Bernal, D. (2001). Examining transformational resistance through a critical race and LatCrit theory framework: Chicana and Chicano students in an urban context. *Urban Education* 36(3): 308–342.

Solorzano, D. G. and Yosso, T. J. (2002). Critical race methodology: Counter-storytelling as an analytical framework for educational research. *Qualitative Inquiry* 8(23): 23–44.

Sorro, B. and Habal, E. (n.d.). Family of tenants: life in the I-Hotel. Retrieved October 17, 2013, from http://www.manilatown.org/images/panel10a.jpg.

Sy, T., Shore, L. M., Strauss, J., Shore, T. H., Tram, S., Whitely, P., and Ikeda-Muromachi, K. (2010). Leadership perceptions as a function of race-occupation fit: The case of Asian Americans. *Journal of Applied Psychology* 95(5): 902–919.

Takaki, R. (1998). *Strangers from a different shore: A history of Asian Americans.* New York, NY: Little, Brown, and Company.

Tintiangco-Cubales, A. (2012). *Kilusan 4 kids: Critical language for elementary school students*, vol. 1. Santa Clara, CA: Phoenix Publishing House International.

United Nations. (1948) *The Universal Declaration of Human Rights*. Retrieved May 4, 2012, from http://www.un.org/en/documents/udhr/.

United Nations. (n.d.). Retrieved from http://www.un.org/en/globalissues/briefing papers/humanrights/quotes.shtml.

Wei, W. (1993). *The Asian American movement*. Philadelphia, PA: Temple University Press.

Williams, R. (1977). *Marxism and literature*. Oxford, England: Oxford University Press.

Yosso, T. J. (2005). Whose culture has capital? A critical race theory discussion of community cultural wealth. *Race, Ethnicity and Education* 8(1): 69–91.

Zia, H. (2001). *Asian American dreams: The emergence of an American people*. New York: Farrar, Straus and Giroux.

CHAPTER 12

Female Genital Mutilation: A Pedagogical Tool to Explore Global Violence against Women

Onllwyn Cavan Dixon

Why design a pedagogical tool focused on female genital mutilation (FGM)? The answer is quite simply, "Why not?" The seeds for this pedagogical tool were planted in 2007 while I was a doctoral student at the University of San Francisco. At the time, I had been left emotionally shattered after reading the 2011 book *Desert Flower: The Extraordinary Journey of a Desert Nomad* by author and activist Waris Dirie. I couldn't stop thinking about Dirie's story and all of the millions of unknown girls and women who had been subjected to FGM by the people who were supposed to love and protect them. I was especially moved by the following words:

> I feel that God made my body perfect the way I was born. Then man robbed me, took away my power, and left me a cripple. My womanhood was stolen. If God had wanted those body parts missing, why did he create them? I just pray that one day no woman will have to experience this pain. It will become a thing of the past. People will say 'Did you hear, female genital mutilation has been outlawed in Somalia?' Then the next country, and the next, and so on, until the world is safe for all women. What a happy day that will be, and that's what I'm working toward. In'shallah, if God is willing, it will happen. (Dirie, 2011, p. 240)

For the first time, as a committed children and women's rights advocate, I was left completely unsure of how I could do *anything* about such a complex and far reaching issue. When I was required to design a human rights focused pedagogical tool for the human rights education (HRE) course I was enrolled in at USF, I poured all of my passion, uncertainty, outrage, revulsion, and hope into learning as much about FGM as possible. I quickly realized, "To live is to choose. But to choose well, you must know who you are and what you stand for, where you want to go and why you want to get there" (Annan, 1997). I present this tool to educators wanting to engage their students in a broader discussion about FGM as well as the universality of gender oppression of women around world. I wholeheartedly believe it is possible through awareness, dialogue, and reflection, for men and women, to make it possible for girls and women to thrive.

The following tool was designed for instructors or student affairs professionals who focus on gender, sexuality, culture, or international studies in a two- or four-year college setting and are interested in implementing HRE into their instruction. The intended audience is English-speaking college students. In addition, the tool may be used with older audiences; however, it is not recommended for groups younger than 16 years old. Due to the sensitive nature of the material, the facilitator should allow for enough time to debrief with the group following each session. It is recommended authorization be obtained prior to presenting or using this pedagogical tool. In addition, as often as possible, the teacher should present background information, instructions, and activities in a way that is mindful of the various ways students learn and process new knowledge. It may be beneficial to look at various learning style models about how to approach teaching in a manner that addresses multiple student modalities. In addition, it could be helpful to peruse the work of critical pedagogues for ideas for integrating critical praxis.

Introduction

In an interview appearing in *Warrior Marks: Female Genital Mutilation and the Sexual Blinding of Women*, Senegalese activist Awa Thiam states, "When you cut off a woman's genitals, when you sew them together, when you open them to have sexual relations, when you sew them up again when the husband is absent...there's no need for explanation—everything is clear. You control the woman..." (as cited in Walker and Parmar, 1996, p. 288). Sharing her deeply personal insights about FGM, Dayla, a university student in Iraqi Kurdistan, reveals, "'I remember that there was a lot of blood and a large fear. This has consequences now during my period. I have emotional and physical pain and fear from the time when I saw the blood. I don't even go to school when I have my periods because there's too much pain'" (Khalife, 2012, p. 239). Like foot binding in China and breast ironing in Cameroon, the practice of FGM is ultimately about the oppression of girls and women.

According to hooks (1990) and Mohanty (2003), sexism and misogyny undergird and fuel the values of many of the world's social and political institutions. As a result, "millions of women and girls begin life hampered by personal status laws that claim to protect women but in fact restrict their choices in life, including whom they marry and divorce, decisions that affect health for a lifetime, and their family and society" (Worden, 2012, p. 5). At its core, the sexual mutilation of women is an attempt to control women's sexuality, their very bodies. FGM and other practices of violence against women, including rape, domestic battery, and sexual assault, are not only issues of women's rights but also of human rights (Bunch, 2012).

FGM is a violation of the human rights of women and girls as recognized in numerous international and regional human rights instruments. Early human rights instruments do not specifically refer to FGM, but they provide a foundation for the right of women to be free from various forms of violence. For example, Article 1 of the Convention on the Elimination of All Forms of Discrimination against Women (CEDAW) (1979) defines discrimination against women as:

> any distinction, exclusion or restriction made on the basis of sex which has the effect or purpose of impairing or nullifying the recognition, enjoyment or exercise by women, irrespective of their marital status, on a basis of equality of men and women, of human rights and fundamental freedoms in the political, economic, social, cultural, civil or any other field.

FGM fits this broad definition of discrimination against women as set forth in CEDAW because it interferes with their attainment of fundamental human rights. Moreover, FGM results in short- and long-term physical and mental harm to its victims and perpetuates subordination of women and girls. Further support for the principle that FGM is a form of gender discrimination, as outlined in CEDAW, can be found in the General Recommendation Nos. 14, 19, and 24 from the Committee on the Elimination of Discrimination against Women. These recommendations emphasize the severe health and other consequences for women and girls subjected to FGM, identify FGM as a form of violence against women, and recommend state parties implement stringent measures to eliminate the practice. Because the practice of FGM is predominantly carried out on girls under the age of 18, the issue is fundamentally one of protection of children's rights. As such, the Convention on the Rights of the Child (CRC) (1990) acknowledges the role of parents and family in making decisions for children. However, it places the ultimate responsibility for insuring the rights of a child in the hands of governments. The CRC also establishes the "best interests of the child" standard in addressing the rights of children. FGM is recognized as a violation of that best interest standard and a violation of children's rights. The CRC mandates governments to abolish traditional practices that impact the health of children.

Furthermore, in December 2012, the UN General Assembly unanimously passed a resolution banning FGM. One hundred and ninety-four UN Member States urged countries to condemn the practice and to take necessary measures, including awareness raising, allocating sufficient resources to protect women and girls from this form of violence, and enforcing legislation. They also called for paying special attention to the protection and support of women and girls who have been subjected to FGM and those at risk, including refugee women and women migrants. Nevertheless, examining FGM is not a justification for some groups to condemn others for culturally specific forms of violence against women. A continuum of violence against women exists in all countries of the world, and it manifests itself in specific and often complex ways (Kristoff and WuDunn, 2009; Worden, 2012).

The World Health Organization (WHO) defines FGM as all procedures involving partial or total removal of the external female genitalia or other injury to the female genital organs whether for cultural, religious, or other non-medical reasons. There are different types of FGM known to be practiced today. FGM has been practiced for thousands of years in countries throughout Africa and the Middle East, and to a lesser extent in Asia. It is not known when or where the tradition of FGM originated but several differing theories have been proposed. Some believe the practice began in ancient Egypt. Others believe it started with the arrival of Islam or developed independently in sub-Saharan Africa prior to the arrival of Islam as a part of puberty rites. While FGM is illegal in most Western and African nations, many of the laws are not enforced due to cultural norms or religious decree.

FGM is a topic that touches on many sensitive issues and should be approached with care and intention. Therefore, the facilitator should carefully consider the makeup of their class (such as age, gender, group dynamics, and prior knowledge) and tailor the sessions accordingly. The sessions are not meant to be an exhaustive list of possible activities, but rather they are a suggested framework for introducing students to the key concepts for understanding the global nature of violence against women and how they may individually and collectively address the underlying issues.

Final Thoughts

In the summer of 2009, I was fortunate to pilot this tool while working with a group of 20 first year college students who were participants in a two-week transition program for incoming first-generation students. The students were ethnically diverse, approximately half male and female, most identified as heterosexual, and they came from a variety of geographic locations. In addition, the students had decided upon a range of majors from business to performing arts. The mission of the program was to provide academic and social preparation for the rigors of the first year of college.

I taught a course focused on contemporary issues and chose to emphasize FGM. For many of the students, it was their first exposure to FGM or HRE for that matter. To be honest, it was initially extremely frustrating to prevent students from remaining perpetually revolted, framing much of what we discussed from a largely Western point of view. I could see the judgment written all over their faces! I could only imagine what they were thinking as I introduced the topics we would cover over five sessions.

Nevertheless, I persevered because I believed I could provide the students with a transformative learning experience, one that could motivate them to find their own ways to become human rights defenders. I am happy to say I was right. At the conclusion of the class, many of the students expressed their gratitude for my willingness to take them on a journey that was often uncomfortable. Specifically, one student, the daughter of an Iranian father and French American mother, approached me on the last day of class and boldly stated, "I am a human rights defender! I'm going to be as courageous as Waris Dirie."

Three years later, I happened to run into this same student on campus. She proudly announced she was preparing to graduate with her bachelor's degree in international studies. The student also thanked me for providing an opportunity for her to begin to learn about human rights issues. It was this very experience that was the impetus for her to decide to join the Peace Corps after graduation. It was one of my proudest moments as an educator. I offer you this resource in the hopes that it will inspire you to tackle the difficult topic with your students, joining the global community of people who advocate for human rights.

Introducing the Tool

Begin by playing the song "Bravebird" by Amel Larrieux for the class (https://www.youtube.com/watch?v=qwnuYU_FsWk) and have them discuss the lyrics of the song. The song is also available from several online sellers. Discussion questions can include:

- What images do the lyrics evoke?
- How do the lyrics make the listener feel?
- What emotions do you think the songwriter/narrator is attempting to convey?

Session One Objectives

By the end of the session students should be able to:

1. Understand the broad meaning of "tradition";
2. Identify gender based traditions which are prevalent in their communities; and
3. Generate constructive ideas of how to change harmful traditional practices.

Defining tradition:

- Ask students: How do they define tradition?
- Let students discuss the question in small groups and have a scribe take notes on the discussion to share with the class.
- Have the class agree on a definition.

Examining of cultural values and traditions in small groups: Divide students into small groups and ask them to:

- Identify practices or traditions they are aware of and decide whether they are beneficial, harmful, or neutral (neither beneficial nor harmful) to women. If the list does not include them suggest terms like: plastic surgery, dieting, using cosmetic products, etc.

Session Two Objectives

By the end of the session the students should be able to:

1. Describe the structure and functions of female external genitalia;
2. Define FGM; and
3. Describe types of FGM.

Diagram exercise:

- Have enough large posters with an unlabeled diagram of the female external genitalia for each small group.
- Give the students labels the names of the different structures and their functions written on them with some type of adhesive on the back.
- Ask the students to paste the labels on the appropriate structures on the diagram.

Use a diagram similar to the following (Figure 12.1):

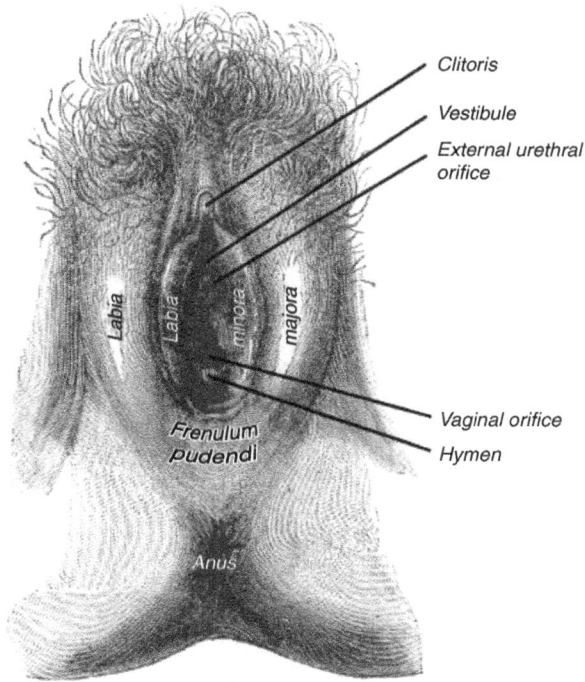

Figure 12.1 Diagram: Female External Genitalia.

Note: This faithful reproduction of a lithograph plate from *Gray's Anatomy*, a two-dimensional work of art, is not copyrightable in the United States as per Bridgeman Art Library v. Corel Corp.; the same is also true in many other countries, including Germany. Unless stated otherwise, it is from the *20th U.S. edition of Gray's Anatomy of the Human Body*, originally published in 1918 and therefore lapsed into the public domain. http://en.wikipedia.org/wiki/File:Gray1229.png.

216 • Onllwyn Cavan Dixon

Defining FGM: Ask students if they know what FGM is.
Share the following definition with the class:
FGM is the partial or complete removal of the external female genitalia or other injury to female genital organs for non-medical purposes. It is usually performed on girls between four and twelve. In some cases, FGM is performed on infants or women before their marriage.

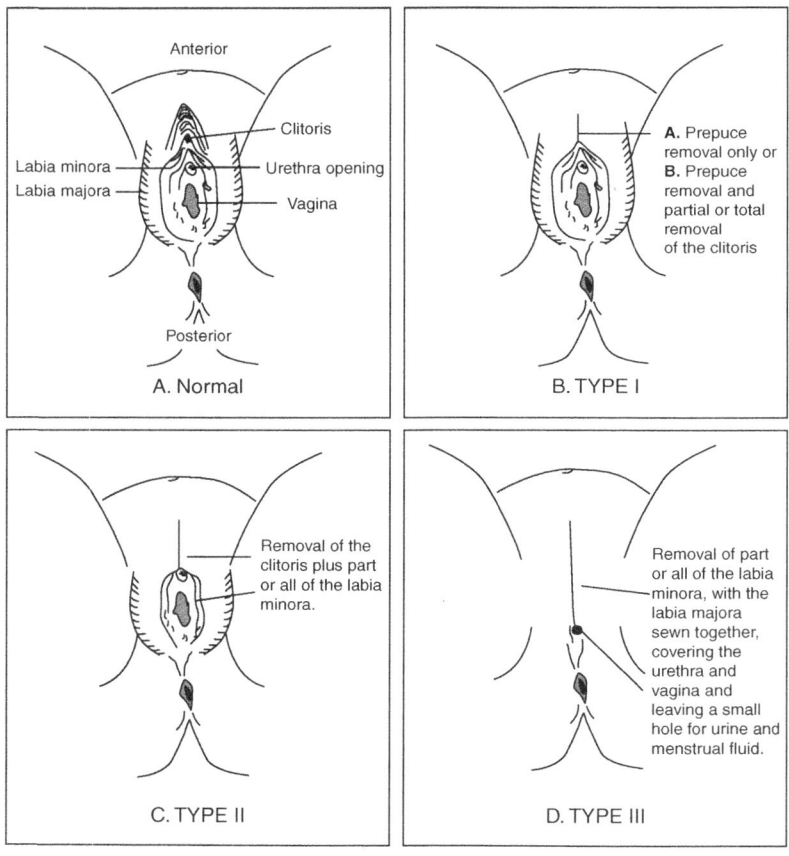

Figure 12.2 Diagram: FGM. This work has been released into the public domain by its author, Kaylima at the Wikipedia project. This applies worldwide. Kaylima grants anyone the right to use this work for any purpose, without any conditions, unless such conditions are required by law http://commons.wikimedia.org/wiki/File:FGC_Types.jpg.

Types of FGM include:

- *Type I* – excision of the prepuce (the fold of skin around the clitoris) with or without excision of part or all of the clitoris (clitorectomy);
- *Type II* – excision of the clitoris with partial or total excision of the labia minora (excision);
- *Type III* – excision of part or all of the external genitalia and stitching/narrowing of the vaginal opening (infibulation); and
- *Type IV* – There are a range of procedures including: pricking, piercing or incising of the clitoris and/or labia; stretching of the clitoris and/or labia; cauterization by burning of the clitoris and surrounding tissue; scraping of tissue surrounding the vaginal orifice (*angurya* cuts) or cutting of the vagina or inserting herbs into the vagina to cause bleeding or for the purpose of tightening or narrowing (*gishiri* cuts); introduction of corrosive substance.

It is suggested a diagram similar to Figure 12.2 be used to illustrate the types of FGM:

The most common type of FGM is excision of the clitoris and the labia minora, accounting for up to 80 percent of all cases; the most extreme form is infibulation, which constitutes about 15 percent of all procedures.

Material for sessions one and two extracted and adapted from *Female Genital Mutilation: Teacher's Guide by the World Health Organization* found at http://www.who.int/gender/other_health/en/teachersguide.pdf.

Session Three (Part I) Objectives

By the end of the session the students should be able to:

1. Identify the reasons given by communities for performing FGM; and
2. Give estimates of the prevalence of FGM in the countries where it is practiced.

Why FGM Is Practiced?

FGM is perpetuated for a number of sociocultural and religious reasons. FGM is traditionally practiced as a ritual signifying the acceptance of a woman into society and establishing her eligibility for marriage. It is often believed to inspire submissiveness in young women. Some reasons given for FGM range from beliefs that touching the clitoris will kill a baby during childbirth, altering female genitalia promotes better hygiene, fertility is enhanced, and chastity is ensured. In many communities, the main reason given for FGM is the belief that it reduces women's sexual desire, reducing the likelihood of sex outside marriage.

In communities where FGM is practiced, it is extremely difficult, if not impossible, for women to marry if they have not undergone mutilation. Marriage is often the only role available for women in FGM practicing communities because they receive little education and are discouraged from pursuing a profession. In the case of infibulation, a woman is "sewn up" and "opened" only for her husband. Family honor is seen as dependent upon controlling a woman's sexuality. Therefore, restricting women's sexuality is believed to be vital. Other justifications include the belief that FGM enhances fertility and promotes survival of children. FGM is practiced among some adherents of Islam, Christianity, and Judaism. FGM is also practiced among some animists. It has been erroneously linked to religion but predates Christianity and Islam. However, some practitioners of these religions believe the practice is obligatory for followers of the religion.

Because of this faulty link to various religions, especially Islam, religious leaders have an important role to play in distancing FGM from religion. For example, while FGM is practiced in Egypt, which is predominantly Muslim, it is not practiced in many other countries with predominantly Muslim populations like Saudi Arabia and Pakistan. Many Muslim scholars and theologians have refuted the association of FGM with Islam, saying that FGM is not prescribed in the Quran and is indeed contradictory to the teachings of Islam.

Note: To illustrate this point show a clip of a debate between Malika Zarrar, lecturer on Islamic religious law, and Muhammad Wahdan, Al Azhar University lecturer, (https://www.youtube.com/watch?v=rUvrHsPaTSo). Have students identify the main points of the two arguments and discuss them.

Prevalence of FGM

FGM is sometimes performed by doctors, but the majority of the time it is performed by women who are not medically trained. Instruments such as pieces of broken glass, scalpels, and tin cans are often used. Most of the girls and women who have undergone genital mutilation live in countries in southern Asia, the Middle East, and Africa. However, the practice has been increasingly found in immigrant communities in Australia, Europe, and North America. Share the following statistics with students perhaps in a PowerPoint or Prezi:

- FGM is increasing rather than decreasing as countries become more modernized
- Type I and Type II are the most common FGM procedures, accounting for more than 85 percent of all procedures
- The number of girls and women who have been subjected to FGM is estimated at between 100 and 140 million
- An estimated 6,000 girls and women experience FGM every day
- More than 3 million girls on the African continent alone are at risk of undergoing this practice every year
- 10 countries with highest percentage of FGM performed: Somalia (98 percent), Guinea (96 percent), Djibouti (93 percent), Egypt (91 percent), Eritrea (89 percent), Mali (89 percent), Sierra Leone and Sudan (88 percent), Gambia and Burkina Faso (76 percent)
- Egypt has the largest number of women who have undergone FGM (27.2 million)

Data extracted from *Female Genital Mutilation/Cutting: A Statistical Overview and Exploration of the Dynamics of Change* found at http://www.unicef.org/media/files/FGCM_Lo_res.pdf.

Session Three (Part II) Objectives

By the end of the session the students should be able to:

1. Describe the immediate and the long-term physical complications of FGM;
2. Understand some of the psychosocial and sexual complications of FGM; and
3. Have a general idea of international conventions and resolutions against FGM.

Health Consequences of FGM

- Immediate complications include: severe pain, shock, hemorrhage, urine retention, ulceration of the genital region, and injury to surrounding tissue. Severe hemorrhaging and infection can lead to death.
- Long-term consequences include: cysts and abscesses, keloid scar formation, damage to the urethra resulting in urinary incontinence,

recurrent urinary tract and pelvic infections, dyspareunia (painful sexual intercourse), increased risk of fistulas, sexual dysfunction, and difficulties with childbirth.
- Psychosexual and psychological health: Genital mutilation may leave a lasting mark on the lives and minds of the girls and women who have undergone FGM. In the long-term, girls and women may suffer feelings of incompleteness, anxiety, low self-esteem, post-traumatic stress disorder (PTSD), depression, and other mental health problems.

Information extracted from http://www.hrw.org/news/2010/06/10/qa-female-genital-mutilation.

International Human Rights Laws Addressing FGM

The Universal Declaration of Human Rights (1948) became the foundation for two multilateral covenants, the International Covenant on Economic, Social and Cultural Rights (1966) and the International Covenant on Civil and Political Rights (1966). These covenants form the foundation for international human rights laws. In addition there are several conventions that protect girls' and women's rights, including Convention on the Elimination of All Forms of Discrimination Against Women (1979), Convention against Torture, and other Cruel, Inhuman or Degrading Treatment or Punishment (1984), and Convention on the Rights of the Child (1990).

These Covenants and Conventions form the basis for many of the laws that have been enacted to protect girls and women from the practice of FGM. There has been a shift away from thinking about FGM as primarily a health issue and towards considering it an issue of both women's health and human rights. The *2005 Female Genital Mutilation/Cutting: A Statistical Exploration*, published by United Nations International Children's Emergency Fund, states,

> At the international level, the human rights implications of FGM/C have been broadly recognized over time. In Vienna in 1993, the UN World Conference on Human Rights called for the elimination of all forms of violence against women to be seen as a human rights obligation. In particular, the World Conference stresses the importance of working towards the elimination of violence against women in public and private life ... and the eradication of any conflicts which may arise between the rights of women and the harmful effects of certain traditional or customary practices. (p. 2) (http://www.unicef.org/publications/files/FGM-C_final_10_October.pdf)

According to WHO, the key rights that should be protected are:

- The right to health;
- The right to be free of cruel and degrading practices;
- The right to sexual and corporal integrity; and
- The right to reproduce.

The following link to *Female Genital Mutilation: The Prevention and the Management of the Health Complications: Policy Guidelines for Nurses and Midwives* (2001) provides more in depth information on FGM and human rights violations (pp. 7–10). (http://whqlibdoc.who.int/hq/2001/WHO_FCH_GWH_01.5.pdf)

- The facilitator should trace the timeline of development of key human rights documents and how they address FGM.
- As a follow-up activity, have students journal about whether a difference exists between women's rights and human rights. Is FGM a human rights violation? If so, what international laws does it violate? Should FGM be considered torture? (Responses can be discussed as a larger group.)
- In addition, students can research laws in the US and abroad that address FGM. The Female Genital Cutting and Education Network website provides an overview of such laws at http://www.fgmnetwork.org/legisl/index.php.

Session Four Objectives

By the end of the session the students should be able to:

1. Humanize the practice of FGM; and
2. Connect FGM to the larger issue of violence and oppression of women in their local communities.

Possible Activities

- Reading of interview with Fauziya Kassindja (Togo and United States), conducted by Kerry Kennedy Cuomo at (http://www.pbs.org/speaktruthtopower/fauziya.html) or reading and discussion of excerpts from *Do They Hear You When You Cry* by Fauziya Kassindja and Layli Miller Bashir (1999)
- Reading and discussion of testimony by Waris Dirie at http://www.fgmnetwork.org/articles/testimonies.php

- View BBC Two special panel on FGM https://www.youtube.com/watch?v=2OXoV7FPX8Y&list=PLaras6O4sh0ewTaCxzQxCahof2pvIa8fT and https://www.youtube.com/watch?v=30RGrOkEVcM&list=PLaras6O4sh0ewTaCxzQxCahof2pvIa8fT
- Reading and discussion of excerpts from *Possessing the Secret of Joy* by Alice Walker (1992)
- Viewing and discussion of 2009 documentary *The Cut: A Documentary* http://www.thecutdocumentary.org/
- Viewing and discussion of the 1993 documentary *Warrior Marks* directed by Pratibha Parmar. Information is available at http://www.wmm.com/filmcatalog/pages/c49.shtml

Session Five (Part I) Objectives

By the end of the session the students should be able to:

Better understand how the U.S. culture perpetuates violence against women, in particular how this is reflected in gender representations in advertising.

Activity

- View and discuss the 2000 documentary *Killing Us Softly 3* by Jean Kilbourne, Ed.D. Information about the film including a study guide is available at http://www.mediaed.org/videos/MediaGenderAndDiversity/KillingUsSoftly.

Session Five (Part II) Objectives

By the end of the session the students should be able to:

Understand the relationship between pop-cultural imagery and the social construction of masculine identities.

Activity

- View and discuss the 1999 documentary *Tough Guise Violence, Media & the Crisis in Masculinity* featuring Jackson Katz, Ed. M. and directed by Sut Jhally. Information about the film and a print-ready study guide is available at http://www.mediaed.org/videos/MediaGenderAndDiversity/ToughGuise

Community Reflection

After all the sessions have been completed, it is imperative that the group be able to answer what, when, where, by whom, and why questions. Ultimately, the group should discuss how what they have learned has contributed to a deeper understanding of global violence against women. The following provides a useful model for engaging in community reflection:

Phase I (The problem)

- Name the problem
- Put the problem in context (history, origin, and causes)
- Identify elements of the problem
- Identify consequences of the problem

Phase II (The personal)

- How does what you have learned contradict, expand, differ, or support your personal experiences?
- What feelings and emotions were brought up by this topic?

Phase III (Creative/Transformative)

- What action can I/we take based on our reflections?

References

Annan, K. A. (1997). *Commencement address: Massachusetts Institute of Technology.* Retrieved from http://newsoffice.mit.edu/1997/annansp.

Bunch, C. (2012). How women's rights became recognized as human rights. In M. Worden (ed.) *The unfinished revolution: Voices from the global fight for women's rights*, pp. 29–39. New York: Seven Stories Press.

Dirie, W. (2011). *Desert flower: The extraordinary journey of a desert nomad.* New York: William Morrow Paperbacks.

hooks, b. (1990). *Yearning: Race, gender, and cultural politics.* Boston, MA: South End Press.

Khalife, N. (2012). Lasting wounds: Female genital mutilation. In M. Worden (ed.) *The unfinished revolution: Voices from the global fight for women's rights*, pp. 239–248. New York: Seven Stories Press.

Kristof, N. D. and WuDunn, S. (2009). *Half the sky: Turning oppression into opportunity for women worldwide.* New York: Alfred A. Knopf.

Mohanty, C. T. (2003). *Feminism without borders: Decolonizing theory, practicing solidarity.* Durham, NC: Duke University Press.

Office of the High Commissioner for Human Rights. (2014). *Convention on the Rights of the Child.* Retrieved from http://www.ohchr.org/en/professionalinterest/pages/crc.aspx

United Nations. (2009). *Convention on the Elimination of All Forms of Discrimination against Women.* Retrieved from http://www.un.org/womenwatch/daw/cedaw/text/econvention.htm.

United Nations. (2009). *General recommendations made by the Committee on the Elimination of Discrimination against Women.* Retrieved from http://www.un.org/womenwatch/daw/cedaw/recommendations/recomm.htm.

Walker, A. and Parmar, P. (1996). *Warrior marks: Female genital mutilation and the sexual blinding of women.* San Diego, CA: Harcourt Brace and Company.

Worden, M. (2012). Revolutions and rights. In M. Worden (ed.) *The unfinished revolution: Voices from the global fight for women's right*s, pp. 1–13. New York: Seven Stories Press.

Afterword: Will Human Rights Education Be Decolonizing?

K. Wayne Yang

This book leads us to this question, to this edge, about what human rights education (HRE) will do in a world of empire. The voices in this book whispered, and sometimes shouted, descriptions of human rights beyond the current legal definitions of human rights. They described the intimate, personal, and profound rights to a heartbeat, to a self-determined future, to a sexuality, a culture, a language, and an intact being—"the basic right to be who you are" in Olga Talamante's words (Foreword, this book). These diminutive yet profound human rights are real and real important. Human Rights are related yet not the same: they are a legal promise that one day all people will have the entitlements that only the privileged enjoy. While reading this book, the edge between human and the Human kept appearing for me at the borders between the personal and powerful nation-state formations like the United States and the United Nations. Talamante's organizing for the tortured and disappeared in Argentina, and Durán's discussion of the UN human rights mission in Haiti (chapter 7, this book), teaches us that sometimes the promise-makers must be kept at arms reach. Too often, if not always, the very powers that enforce Human Rights are the human rights violators, as felt so keenly by the Black Panther Party SF8 (Blundell, chapter 3, this book). The violators can be invisible, hidden behind structures of violation. Sometimes we may gain some human entitlements by gaining access to structures that violate, "humiliate and mutilate" someone else elsewhere, to draw on the words of Malcolm X (1964b, p. 75).

This book illuminates human rights contradictions. How is it that everyone is supposed to have them, yet the reality is that most people do not? How is that the United Nations guarantees them, but the United Nations violates them? These contradictions must be confounding for students. For me, the roots of these contradictions lie in the modern condition, which is a colonial condition.

Decolonizing education stems from traditions of interrogating one's colonial condition as a local problem and a world problem at once. Ruth Wilson Gilmore (2014) says it is the Black Radical Tradition, drawing on the words of Cedric Robinson and on the life of Harriet Tubman. For Gilmore, this tradition "has accumulated since the first instant that chattel slavery came into being" (p. 232). Not just limited to people of African descent, the Black Radical Tradition is shorthand for freedom fighting and freedom dreaming that is lifetimes long, for which "the survival of the collective is the purpose of life…our lives should unroll as a narrative of freedom" (p. 232).

Decolonizing education also stems from Indigenous survivance—life narratives of vitality and active presence beyond naked survival (Vizenor, 1999). Linda Tuhiwai Smith (1999) states that for now, the decolonizing imperatives before Indigenous communities are clear: "the survival of peoples, cultures, languages; the struggle to become self-determining, the need to take back control of our destinies" (p. 142). Because colonialism is vested in the settlement of Indigenous lands, and the enslavement of Indigenous people-turned-property, then to decolonize is to unsettle Indigenous lands and to abolish slavery, that is, to abolish the carving of land/people into pieces of property (Spillers, 1987; Tuck and Yang, 2012).

So on the surface, decolonizing and HRE may seem perfectly compatible. However, the legal concept of "Human" has continued to mean a settler and a property owner whose "Rights" to land, life, and liberty are actually entitlements enforced by settler nation-states. For people of color in the United States, achieving human status has historically meant to masquerade as propertied settlers. Consider the US Supreme Court civil rights cases of Takao Ozawa (1922) and Bhagat Singh Thind (1923). Each appealed for rights by actually suing for status as a white propertied man. Human status might provide a pathway toward human rights. But achieving it may require you to act like "the man": anti-black, anti-Indigenous, pro-empire, and pro-settler. In this way, settler nations offer a seductive way for you or I to solve an individual problem of nonhuman status: become a settler. But this won't solve the collective problem of colonialism.

For HRE to be decolonizing depends on our willingness to denaturalize the category of Human, to practice red pedagogy (Grande, 2004) as an alternative to critical pedagogy (Freire, 2000). Whereas critical pedagogy highlights the human as the unit of liberation, a red pedagogy already understands how the human cannot be exceptionalized from land, water, and from "nature." A red pedagogy interrogates human rights vis-a-vis Indigenous land rights. We might start by contrasting the Universal Declaration of Human Rights (UDHR) with the United Nations Declaration on the Rights of Indigenous Peoples (UNDRIP). We might proceed by following the ghost of Malcolm X.

Malcolm X Said Human Rights Are a Strategy for Decolonization

As a young teacher in the 1990s, I viewed HRE with suspicion. I associated it with a liberal look toward the international by Americans looking for sites to stake their activist identities. Turning international sometimes meant turning a blind eye toward your present place and moment. For me, that present place was Oakland, and other North American cities like it: cities built and building upon histories of settlement/displacement, gentrification/ghetto-ization; cities hatch-marked by the sharp contradictions between urban realities and urbane privileges. I was particularly discouraged when the Amnesty International student club at Oakland High, where I was teaching at the time, decided that US political prisoner, Mumia Abu-Jamal, had indeed murdered Philadelphia police officer Daniel Faulkner, and thus deserved a state-administered death sentence. The students came to these conclusions themselves, after reviewing all available evidence under the guidance of a progressive teacher. If HRE was about evaluating who does and doesn't deserve state violence, then I wanted nothing to do with it.

Admittedly, I was pretty darn ignorant of the scope of human rights activism. Plus, my feel for political change was fairly parochial. I needed this book. I needed to see the strategic value of human rights in anti-colonial movements, the synergy between transnational and local human rights activism, and the ways queer people, people of color, and stateless people instrumentalize while transgressing the limits of the UDHR. One such person was El-Hajj Malik El-Shabazz, commonly known as Malcolm X.

> America is a colonial power...depriving us of first-class citizenship, actually by depriving us of human rights. She has not only deprived us of the right to be a citizen, she has deprived us of the right to be human beings, the right to be recognized and respected as and men and women. (Malcolm X, 1964a, pp. 50–51)

Human rights for Malcolm X was a political strategy that went beyond the US nation-state, and thus beyond the ways in which civil rights legislation had limited Black dreams for freedom into a promise of someday equality with whites, or more precisely limited Black dreams into the fantasy of a someday white status.

> [W]e are the victims of America's colonialism or American imperialism... [O]ur problem is not an American problem; it's a human problem. It's not a Negro problem; it's a problem of humanity. Not just in this life but in our past life. It's not a problem of civil rights but a problem of human rights. (Malcolm X, 1964c, para. 1)

Malcolm X said our present local struggle was transnationally and transhistorically significant – not just this life but in our past life. Furthermore, colonialism/empire is the transnational and transhistorical problem that connects the Black struggle in America to struggles in other places and other times. For me, Malcolm X provided a shared vocabulary for these struggles: human rights, colonialism, empire.

We Need a yPAR Project on Human Rights Violations

It was a decade later, in 2007, that I first engaged in HRE—alongside educators Jeff Duncan-Andrade and David Philoxene, who organized their Senior Advanced Placement English curriculum around the UDHR. In a yearlong, youth Participatory Action Research project (yPAR), students researched how different nation-states met or failed to meet the standards laid out by the 30 articles in the UDHR. Each research group designed a comparative study between human rights in an Oakland community context and a community in another part of the world. However, what I wish to highlight here is not the curriculum, but the ghetto context. We had all just survived firsthand experience of human rights violation, in the form of a state-administered school execution.

East Oakland Community High School (EOC) was a public, noncharter school created by the youth, their families, and educators in 2004. Our mission was education for self-determination and social justice. The school was inspired by and named after the Oakland Community School, the original Black Panther Party school that was open from 1971 to 1982 (Huggins and LeBlanc-Ernest, 2009). Before the first class could graduate, our school was shut down by the State of California in the summer of 2007. At the time, Oakland Unified School District had a single overseer with absolute power—the "State Administrator"—who very much served as a colonial governor over the public school system.

Following the death of EOC, David Philoxene negotiated asylum in the United Neighborhood Improvement Association (UNIA), a descendent of Marcus Garvey's organization. UNIA granted use of a large Victorian house in West Oakland (Paperson, 2010) to our small group of educational refugees. We were about one-quarter of the original founding class, and one-twelfth the total EOC student body. This was the context: colonial government, educational refugees, asylum for a lucky few within an old Pan-Africanist headquarters.

In the ghetto context, the rights to work, leisure, adequate living conditions, and to education (UDHR Articles 22, 23, 24, 25, and 26 respectively) were not unmet rights but rights actively destroyed by the state. In other words, the problem wasn't just state failures to meet human rights standards, but indeed state interventions against the self-determined efforts of our community to provide them for ourselves. Ghettos, and similar places of manufactured crises, must be understood as sites of active human rights violations.

The scope and degree of these violations, like so many other contexts of state crimes against humanity, are difficult to document—as the state does not measure them. I think of how "statistics" comes from the German *statistik*, meaning "the science of state data." I think how the East German State (GDR) stopped recording suicides in 1977, and how suicides were the basis for Emile Durkheim's (1897) sociology of the urban condition. Similarly, the State Administration stopped recording any data about our youth after killing EOC; all along we were a population to be eliminated, whose destinies were of no account. Around this country, statistiks are used to close schools and yet statistiks never measure the effects of school closure. By closing EOC, the state also stopped gang unity summits, barred advocates within housing and youth authority, expunged all Advanced Placement coursework from student transcripts, and dried up real scholarships and work opportunities. I will not name nor count for you the youth murdered, incarcerated, and jobless as a direct result of school closure; our community knows their names. My point is, the official record does not.

We need a yPAR project on human rights violations. Perhaps it could be an online resource where yPAR groups could document and share the violations in their communities. The statistik of high stakes accountability—No Child Left Behind, Race to the Top, or whatever its current catchphrase may become—is a state science of educational terror. Even equity-minded educators are seduced by these yardsticks of deficiency and their promises of someday sameness. We need a counter-statistik to stop "seeing like the state," to borrow a phrase from James Scott (1998), and to see the state for the violations it commits. HRE can help us look beyond the horizon of the white test score—that is, the impossibility of equal test-scores with whites—and toward standards of human dignity actually worth fighting for.

The Rights of Indigenous Peoples Are Not Just Human Rights

Malcolm X understood that Black people lie outside of, or more precisely, underneath the nation-state. In the months between 1964 and his assassination in 1965, he adopted human rights as a strategy to go above US sovereignty. He appealed directly to the Organization of African Unity to bring the case against the United States of human rights violations to the United Nations on behalf of African Americans.

> Our freedom struggle for human dignity is no longer confined to the domestic jurisdiction of the United States government. (Malcolm X, 1964b, p. 76)

Again, context matters. This was the era of colonial independence, with 34 newly independent African nations by 1964 when Malcolm X attended the second meeting of the Organization of African Unity in Cairo, and nearly 20 more to be born. Former colonies literally doubled the UN General Assembly in the decade of the 1960s, tipping the scales toward a Third World majority. The United Nations itself was just a teenager, and still figuring out its own power and ideological leanings. In this anti-colonial international atmosphere, Malcolm X felt that the UDHR could be an instrument to internationalize the Black anti-colonial struggle.

Malcolm X had not known about the burgeoning movement by American Indians toward a revitalized sovereignty. These events would take the international media stage just a few years within his death: the Occupation of Alcatraz by the United Indians of All Tribes in 1968, and the rise of the American Indian Movement in 1969. However, he understood that self-determination requires mutual recognition among sovereign entities. Rather than "trying to prove [Black people] are Americans," he noted, "We are fighting for recognition as human beings" (1964a, pp. 51–52). Malcolm X worked for mutual recognition between African nations and Africans in America in 1963. In 2014, wouldn't he be working toward mutual recognition between Black people and Indigenous nations?

Today's context is dramatically different. The United States frequently co-opts the language of "human rights" as an excuse for military invasions and economic warfare. Postcolonial nation-states have not lived up to our revolutionary expectations. However, struggles for human rights have also created unexpected political possibilities. One significant outcome has been the UNDRIP, passed by the UN General Assembly in 2007.

I think any Human Rights curriculum ought to compare these two documents—the UDHR as spearheaded by Eleanor Roosevelt in the context of post-WWII UN, and the UNDRIP as collectively argued, devised, and deliberated by hundreds of distinct Indigenous peoples for the new millennium. There are some important similarities, like how the United States, Canada, Australia all initially refused to sign. There are some even more important differences. Unlike the UDHR, which locates Human Rights within the realm of nation-states, the UNDRIP treats States as useful but not supreme units of government. States can always be refused by Indigenous peoples. It asserts Indigenous peoples' right to self-determination (Article 3), autonomy and self-government (Article 4), which includes "distinct political, legal, economic, social and cultural institutions, while retaining their right to participate fully, if they so choose, in the political, economic, social and cultural life of the State" (Article 5).

Most importantly, UNDRIP asserts the land rights of Indigenous people. This part is the most interesting and difficult for settlers whose "human rights" to housing and resources and national belonging depend on the occupation of Indigenous lands. Articles 8, 10, 25 to 30, and 32 state that Indigenous peoples cannot be dispossessed of lands, and further, stolen lands must be restored or adequately redressed. "Indigenous peoples have the right to the lands, territories and resources which they have traditionally owned, occupied or otherwise used or acquired" (Article 26). Settlers' rights to own land stem from a philosophy of property, enforced by the state. Indigenous relations to land are inherent, and more profound than the claims of states or settlements, and even social justice or human rights claims.

Calling Out an Empire

As I write, the US military is gearing up airstrikes against the Islamic State of Iraq and al-Sham (ISIL) in the name of human rights. The human rights "abuse-excuse" is insidious because it exploits real human rights crises to justify invasion and its accompanying horrors; and in the case of Iraq, to re-narrate the horrific US war machine as an antidote to the atrocities committed by ISIL. However, scratch the surface of the official narrative, and anyone can uncover how past and *current* US policy foment the very conditions for revolutionary and reactionary violence. If we look at Iraq before and after the 2003 US-induced "regime change," we see massive dislocations of people, more than 130,000 civilian deaths from the invasion, the destruction of a nearly free universal hospital system, the establishment of one of the most corrupt governments in the world, and the rise in firepower and fundamentalist fear in deciding the fate of the peoples within its borders.

US airstrikes will not deliver human rights. Only self-determination for local Sunni living in ISIL territory can do that. In this regard, President Obama's analysis is correct: the only real solution involves empowering the local Sunni people who were shut out of the US- sponsored Iraqi state after fighting on behalf of US empire during the first invasion. No one believes they will fight for the United States again, nor for the Iraqi state against ISIL. That fight does not lead to self-determination, nor to human rights. Yet the United States is hardly ever loudly called out as the human rights violator. Instead, it is the United States who claims to be an empire of human rights.

Another example, and there are many, of human rights in service of empire was the 2012 "Stop Kony" campaign, which enjoyed widespread American populist support for seeking out and arresting/assassinating Joseph Kony, a militia cult leader formerly operating in Uganda indicted of war crimes and crimes against humanity. The *2012 Kony* feature film sported a poster of a Republican elephant and Democrat donkey intimately joined in peace, with the slogan "One thing we can all agree on": get Kony. Stop Kony sports a self-congratulatory imperialist logic where Americans can "unite" under the "common cause" of eradicating an Orientalized enemy other, the "savage Black African warlord." Such logic squashes any kind of meaningful dissent to US militarism and disciplines the everyday American to become pro-Empire while feeling like a human rights activist. Out goes an abuser; in comes an empire.

In contrast to imperial interventions, Olga Talamante's organizing as mentioned earlier, in many ways, called out US empire, quite literally out of Argentina. Similarly, in the 2014 #BringBackOurGirls campaign for the return of over 200 schoolgirls abducted in Chibok, Nigeria, activists have called out US military intervention which will assuredly not bring back the girls alive. Jumoke Balogun (2014) writes to American hashtag activists:

> Consequently, your calls for the United States to get involved in this crisis undermines the democratic process in Nigeria and co-opts the growing movement against the inept and kleptocratic Jonathan administration. It was Nigerians who took their good for nothing President to task and challenged him to address the plight of the missing girls. It is in their hands to seek justice for these girls and to ensure that the Nigerian

government is held accountable. Your emphasis on U.S. action does more harm to the people you are supposedly trying to help and it only expands and sustains U.S. military might....

Don't join the American government and military in co-opting this movement started and sustained by Nigerians (para 12–13).

Balogun (2014) offers an alternative to American human rights imperialism: support the self-determined efforts of Nigerians to fight child-abduction, child-soldiering, and state corruption as well as Western militarism. "If you must do something, learn more about the amazing activists and journalists like ['Gbenga Sesan, Chioma Agwuegbo, and Oby Ezekwesili,] just to name a few, who have risked arrests and their lives as they challenge the Nigerian government to do better for its people within the democratic process" (para 13). In addition to learning, Americans can and should support self-empowered activists materially, by directly funding them. One avenue for this is Global Fund for Women (2014), a grantmaking foundation that operates from "a rights based approach, rather than a development led approach" (pt. 2). Such an approach literally invests in and mobilizes resources into the hands of women's organizations and movements. It puts faith not in Western powers, but in transformative shifts in power, so that women on the ground can realize their own rights and create lasting solutions to the world's problems.

Such efforts teach us how to call *out*, not call *in*, empire. They also describe profound human rights rooted in the sovereignty of the person, not supremacist sovereignty. The difference is easy to test, supremacist sovereignty calls to "save the children." Sovereignty of the person calls for self-determination.

In the spirit of Detroit Red, Malcolm Little's *nom-de-guerre* before Malcolm X, before El-Hajj Malik El-Shabazz, I wish to conclude that empire must too be called out of America's ghettos. As I write, the bankrupt City of Detroit has shut off the water on 100,000 of its residents as a punishment for delinquent payments. The master plan for Detroit will be achieved when Detroit is done auctioning off its real estate, and urban farms are bulldozed, people displaced, land resold for speculative profits. These are human rights violations. They are part and parcel to settler colonialism. State and vigilante violence in this urban "frontier" reverberates as a transhistorical, translocal problem: bullets fly in Ferguson while I write in 2014, and in Sanford in 2012, Oakland in 2009, New Orleans in 2005, Los Angeles in 1992, Detroit in 1967, and Watts in 1965, and the list goes on...Natalia Anciso (2014), whose artwork graces the cover of this book, traces State and vigilante violence in the urban frontier to that in *la frontera*, specifically in the Texas borderlands against Mexican and Indigenous peoples then and now. Yet, grassroots groups like Detroit Summer also continue the work of self-determination; an example is the creation of urban farms toward local economies and food security. Their theory of change is the same one that the late poet, teacher, warrior June Jordan (1978) presented at the United Nations for the women of South Africa: *we are the ones we have been waiting for*. A decolonizing HRE can attend to Malcolm's insights: Ghetto colonialism is an internal manifestation of empire and of American settler colonialism; human rights are not achievable in a colonial setting; human rights are achieved through self-determination.

References

Anciso, N. (2014). Selected works. *Natalia Anciso: Oakland-based artist of the Texas borderlands*. Retrieved from http://www.nataliaanciso.com/#!selectedworks/ckiy.

Balogun, J. (2014). Dear Americans, your hashtags won't #BringBackOurGirls: You might actually be making things worse. *The World Post*. Retrieved from http://www.huffingtonpost.com/jumoke-balogun/hashtags-wont-bring backourgirls_b_5292312.html.

Durkheim, E. (1897/1966). *Suicide, a study in sociology*. New York: Free Press.

Freire, P. (2000). *Pedagogy of the oppressed*. New York: Continuum.

Gilmore, R. W. (2014). Afterword. In E. Tuck and K. W. Yang (eds.) *Youth resistance research and theories of change*, pp. 230–233. New York: Routledge.

Global Fund for Women. (2014). *How we grant*. Retrieved from http://www.global fundforwomen.org/what-we-do/how-we-grant.

Grande, S. (2004). *Red pedagogy: Native American social and political thought*. Lanham, MD: Rowman and Littlefield Publishers.

Huggins, E. and LeBlanc-Ernest, A. D. (2009). Revolutionary women, revolutionary education: The Black Panther Party's Oakland Community School. In D. F. Gore, J. Theoharis, and K. Woodard (eds.) *Want to start a revolution?: Radical women in the Black freedom struggle*, pp. 161–184. New York: New York University Press.

Jordan, J. (1978). *Poem for South African women*. Retrieved from http://www.june jordan.net/poem-for-south-african-women.html.

Malcolm X. (1964a/1990). The Black revolution. In G. Breitman (ed.) *Malcolm X speaks: Selected speeches and statements*, pp. 45–57. New York: Grove Weidenfeld.

Malcolm X. (1964b/1990). An appeal to African heads of state. In G. Breitman (ed.) *Malcolm X speaks: Selected speeches and statements*, pp.72–85. New York: Grove Weidenfeld.

Malcolm X. (1964c). Malcolm X: A problem of human rights. Interview transcript. Retrieved from http://www.civilrightsdefence.org.nz/tuhoe/.

Paperson, L. (2010). The postcolonial ghetto: Seeing her shape and his hand. *Berkeley Review of Education* 1(1): 5–34.

Scott, J. C. (1998). *Seeing like a state: How certain schemes to improve the human condition have failed.* New Haven, CT: Yale University Press.

Smith, L. T. (1999). *Decolonizing methodologies: Research and indigenous peoples.* London: Zed Books.

Spillers, H. J. (1987). Mama's baby, Papa's maybe: An American grammar book. *Diacritics: a Review of Contemporary Criticism* 17(2): 65–81.

Tuck, E. and Yang, K. W. (2012). Decolonization is not a metaphor. *Decolonization: Indigeneity, Education and Society* 1(1): 1–40Bottom of Form.

Vizenor, G. R. (1999). *Manifest manners: Narratives of postindian survivance.* Lincoln, NE: University of Nebraska Press.

Contributors

Annie S. Adamian is a public school teacher, currently in her 13th year of teaching science at Bidwell Junior High School in Chico, California. She is a doctoral candidate in International and Multicultural Education with a concentration in Human Rights Education at the University of San Francisco.

Barbara J. Arduini taught high school English in California for over seven years, and is now in Plovdiv, Bulgaria, on a Fulbright English Teaching Assistantship. She earned an MFA in Creative Nonfiction from St. Mary's College of California, and is currently working on her MA in International and Multicultural Education with a concentration in Human Rights Education at the University of San Francisco.

Jessie Blundell is a literacy specialist at Dr. Charles Drew Elementary School in the Bayview/Hunters Point neighborhood in San Francisco, California. She is also a doctoral candidate in International and Multicultural Education with a concentration in Human Rights Education at the University of San Francisco.

Erin Brennan has been an elementary educator for eight years. She has an MA degree in International and Multicultural Education with concentration in Human Rights Education from the University of San Francisco. She currently is teaching at an international school while living in Puebla, Mexico.

Melissa Ann Canlas has been working in education in San Francisco for over 15 years. Melissa currently teaches in the Asian American Studies and Women's Studies departments at City College of San Francisco (CCSF). She is also the Project Director of APALU: Asian Pacific American Leaders United, a critical leadership development program at CCSF funded by an Asian American Pacific Islander Serving Institutions grant from the US Department of Education. Melissa's research interests include critical pedagogy, critical leadership theory, oral history, gender studies, and youth development. She is currently a doctoral student in International and Multicultural Education with a concentration on Human Rights Education at the University of San Francisco.

Puja Kumar Clifford is an English teacher at San Francisco International High School, where she collaborates with Jacqueline Fix to create curriculum for English language learners. Puja earned her MA and teaching credentials from Stanford University's Teacher Education Program in 2010. She is currently on a one-year leave of absence, living and working at an outdoor school in New Zealand.

Kelly Delaney has taught seventh and eighth graders English, World History, and AVID at a public middle school in Northern California. She is also a teacher educator at Notre Dame de Namur University in Belmont, California, teaching classes with an emphasis on human rights, social justice, and equity in education. She is currently working on collecting narratives of Palestinian people living in exile and under occupation for her doctoral dissertation in International and Multicultural Education with a concentration in Human Rights Education at the University of San Francisco.

Onllwyn Cavan Dixon is an adjunct faculty member in the Department of International and Multicultural Education at the University of San Francisco, where he received his Ed.D. His passions include critical pedagogy and human rights education, youth advocacy, decolonizing methodologies, social constructions of race, class, and gender, and nonprofit program management and evaluation.

Victoria Isabel Durán was born and raised in San José, California. Victoria established a foundation for community activism and commitment to education from her public school experience. She is a doctoral candidate in International and Multicultural Education with a concentration in Human Rights Education at the University of San Francisco. She is a passionate and creative social studies teacher at Calero High School in San José, California. Victoria enjoys exercising her creativity, listening to music, and immersing herself in travels to experience new cultures and adventures.

Jacqueline Fix is the instructional coach at San Francisco International High School and was the founding English teacher when the school opened in 2009. She earned an MA from the University of San Francisco in International and Multicultural Education with a concentration in Human Rights Education.

Susan Roberta Katz is Professor and Chair of International and Multicultural Education at the University of San Francisco, where she co-founded the concentration in Human Rights Education in 2008. In 2014, she was awarded the Sarlo Prize that recognizes teaching which exemplifies the mission of the university. A former San Francisco middle school teacher, she received her MA and PhD in Education in Language and Literacy at the UC Berkeley Graduate School of Education. She has received Fulbright research and teaching fellowships in both Hungary and Ecuador. Her scholarly work has been published in such journals as *Teachers College Record*, *Urban Education*, and *Intercultural Education*.

Lindsay Padilla is a full-time professor of sociology at Solano Community College in Fairfield, California. She was a 2011–2012 Stanford Human Rights Education Initiative (SHREI) fellow, which encouraged collaboration with other human rights educators across the community college system in California. Lindsay received her BA and MA from San Diego State University. She received her EdD in International and Multicultural Education with a concentration in Human Rights Education at the University of San Francisco.

Andrea McEvoy Spero serves as the Director of Education at The Martin Luther King, Jr. Research and Education Institute at Stanford University and an adjunct professor at the University of San Francisco. As the first University of San Francisco doctoral graduate with a concentration in Human Rights Education, her research focused on the use of performing arts to teach human rights in an urban high school setting. Before attending the University of San Francisco, Andrea taught high school social studies in Los Angeles and the Bay Area.

Olga Talamante is currently the executive director of the Chicana/Latina Foundation, a nonprofit organization that promotes the professional and leadership development of Latinas. Olga migrated from Mexico in the early 1960s to Gilroy, California, where she and her family worked in the farm fields. As a youth, she was increasingly active in the farm workers and Chicano student movements. During the mid-1970s, she became well known for her experience as a political prisoner in Argentina. As a result of a successful grassroots campaign, she was released after spending 16 months in an Argentine prison. Upon her return to the United States in 1976, she remained active in the Chicano, Latin American solidarity, LGBT, and progressive political movements. To this day, Olga is widely respected for her community activism and leadership, as evidenced in numerous awards, including the "Women Making History Award" from the San Francisco Commission on the Status of Women.

Felisa Tibbitts is the founder and senior advisor of Human Rights Education Associates, which she directed from 1999 to 2011. She has taught courses in numerous institutions, including the Harvard Graduate School of Education, Teachers College at Columbia University, the UN University for Peace, and the University of San Francisco. Cofounder of the US Human Rights Educators Network, Felisa is actively promoting human rights education in US schools. Over the past 25 years, she has worked with numerous government and international agencies all over the world in developing curriculum and policies that support the integration of human rights into teaching and training.

K. Wayne Yang is Associate Professor in Ethnic Studies at the University of California, San Diego. In 2004, he cofounded the Avenues Project, a youth development nonprofit organization, as well as East Oakland Community High School, which were inspired by the Survival Programs of the Black Panther Party. Currently, he is collaborating with Roses in Concrete to create a K-12 school center in Oakland. His research interests include: ghetto colonialism, decolonization, popular culture, and social movements.

Index

9/11, Islamophobia and, 89
10 Tactics for Turning Information into Action, 123

Academic Conversations (Zwiers and Crawford), 40
activism, for adequate standard of living, 62–3
Ada, Alma Flor, 23
Adamian, Annie S., 7
adequate standard of living, 47–64.
 See also Universal Declaration of Human Rights (UDHR), Article 25 of
 activism and, 62–3
 children's experiences and, 54–5
 creating change for, 51–2
 group project for, 58–60
 pedagogical tools for, 55–63
 team building project for, 60–2
 and wants *versus* needs, 56–7
 women's rights and, 51
Advancement Via Individual Determination (AVID), 87–8, 96
advertising. *See also* media
 children as targets of, 95
African Americans, human rights for, 35–7
Agwuegbo, Chioma, 233
Aladdin, 88, 101
 as embodiment of Islamophobia, 91–3

American Indian Movement, 230
American Sociological Association, human rights and, 178
Amnesty International, 12
 HRE defined by, 171
 Our World, Our Rights of, 53
Anciso, Natalia, 233–4
Arabs
 negative stereotypes of, 88
 racial profiling of, 92
Aristide, Jean-Bertrand, 108, 111, 113
Aristide Foundation, 112
Asian immigrants, and denial of citizenship, 198
Asian American leadership, 187–207.
 See also International Hotel (I-Hotel)
 counternarratives of, 189–90
 and critical leadership theory, 190–4
 "Fall of the I-Hotel" and, 195–6, 198, 201–2
 leadership legacies and, 194–7
 pedagogical tool for, 197–205
 reflection worksheet and, 204–5
 statistics on, 189
 and student visits to I-Hotel, 202–4
Asian Americans, stereotypes of, 191–2

Bajaj, Monisha, 25
Balogun, Jumoke, 232–3
Bashir, Layli Miller, 221
basic social conditions, defined, 50

Bell, Herman, 36
bias. *See also* stereotypes
  awareness of, 10
bilingual instruction, Proposition 227 and, 70
bin Laden, Osama, 89
bioethics
  dignity and, 76–8
  responsibilities and practices of, 67
Bitter Cane, 121
Black Panther Party, 4, 225
  Civil Rights Movement and, 37
  FBI and, 33
  history and context of, 32–7
  history and legacy of, 31–46
  New Orleans police and, 36
  pedagogical tool, 38–45
  teaching legacy of, 40–5
  Ten Point Program of, 33
  use of symbols and, 42
Black Panther Party school, 228–9
Black Power Movement, and refashioning of collective memory, 34–5
Black Radical Tradition, 226
Boal, A., 34
Boggs, Grace Lee, 18
Bowman, John, 36
"Bravebird," 213–14
Brennan, Erin, 8
Bridgefort, Ronald Stanley, Jr., 36
Bridges, Ruby, 37
BringBackOurGirls campaign, 232–3
Brown, Richard, Black Panther unit and, 31, 33, 36, 37, 40, 41, 44–5
Brown v Board of Education, 37
Building a Strategy for HRE in U.S. Schools, 13

California Proposition 187, 70
California Proposition 227, 70
Campaign to Free the SF8, 31–2, 225
Carter, Jimmy, 20
case study approach, 24
  in science classroom, 67–70

cell model project, in science classroom, 75–6, 80–1, 81t
charity, *versus* service learning, 176
children. *See also* Convention on the Rights of the Child (CRC)
  HRE and, 53–4
Children's Services Council, 52
Choy, Curtis, 195, 198, 202
Christensen, Linda, 39
Civil Rights Era, 4, 11
  collective memory and, 34–5
  one-dimensional approach to, 37
Clements, Charlie, 25
coalitions, Black Panther unit and, 42–3
COINTELPRO, Black Panthers and, 33
collective memory, refashioning of, 34–5
collective rights, 4
  versus individual rights, 152
  UDHR and, 171–2
Columbia University, Peace and Human Rights Education at, 25
Committee for the Defense of Human Rights, 36
Committee on the Elimination of Discrimination against Women (CEDAW), 211–12
Common Dreams, 122
community colleges, human rights ideals and, 169–70
compassion, human rights violations and, 10
conscientization, Freire's concept of, 89
Convention against Torture and Other Cruel, Inhuman or Degrading Treatment or Punishment, 4, 220
Convention on the Elimination of All Forms of Discrimination against Women (CEDAW)
  Article 1 of, 211
  social problems course and, 173
  US failure to sign, 19
Convention on the Rights of the Child (CRC), 4, 8, 10, 220
  FGM and, 212

food security and, 49
Haiti and, 112
Islamophobia as violation of, 92–3
social problems course and, 173
US and, 19, 152
Convention Relating to the Status of Refugees, 10
Cool Drink of Water, A (Kerley), 62
Cornell notes, 96, 97
critical leadership theory, 190–4
  key terminology in, 199–201
  versus traditional leadership models, 192–3
critical media analysis, in Islamophobia unit, 98
critical pedagogy, 23
Crucible Anticipation Guide, The, 163
Crucible unit, 149–67
  dialectical journals and, 158
  and historical context of human rights, 159–60
  historical fiction and, 158
  human rights project in, 164–6
  human rights research and, 157–8
  human rights "Show and Tell" activity and, 157
  letter of intent in, 163–4
  major activities for, 157–8
  McMartin Preschool Trial and, 161–3
  mob mentality and, 161
  pedagogical tool for, 155–66
  and personal context of human rights, 158–9
  reimaging activity, 158
  Salem Witch Trials and, 162
  themes of play in, 162–3
  UDHR and, 160–1
  UDHR violations and, 165
  unit block plan for, 156t, 157
  websites for, 166
cultural narratives, rewriting, 192
cultural norms, gender and, 152, 214
Cuomo, Kerry Kennedy, 221

Darfur genocide, 24
Declaration on Human Rights Education and Training, 18
decolonization
  HRE and, 225–35
  human rights as strategy for, 227–8
  yPAR project and, 228–30
Department of Homeland Security, and reshaping of Civil Rights Era, 34–5
Detroit, human rights violations in, 233
Dirie, Waris, 209, 213, 221
Do They Hear You When You Cry, 221
Doctors without Borders, in Haiti, 111
dropout rates, increased, 150
Duncan-Andrade, Jeff, 228
Durán, Victoria, 225
Durkheim, Emile, 229

economic rights. *See also* International Covenant of Economic, Social & Cultural Rights (ICESC)
  US and, 19
education. *See also* human rights education (HRE)
  decolonizing, 225–36
  Freire's philosophy of, 171–2
  human rights and, 57–8
  market-driven approach to, 20–1
  right to, 5–6 (*see also* Universal Declaration of Human Rights (UDHR), Article 26 of)
elementary classrooms. *See also* adequate standard of living; Black Panther Party
  HRE in, 53–4
empire, human rights in service of, 231–4
empowerment
  as HRE goal, 21–2
  through social problems course, 178
English Language Learners (ELLs)
  curriculum for, 130
  Know Your Rights unit and, 132–44
equality, *versus* equity, 74–5
Erdelatz, Ed, 36

essentialism, 90
  stereotypes and, 192
ethics, human rights education and, 151–3
exceptionalism, US, 18–20
Extraordinary Journey of a Desert Nomad, The (Dirie), 209
Ezekwesili, Oby, 233

"Fall of the I-Hotel, The," 195–6, 198, 201–2. *See also* Asian American leadership
  viewing questions for, 203–4
Farewell to Manzanar, A, 140–1
  understanding UDHR and, 131–2
Faulkner, Daniel, 227
Federal Bureau of Investigation, Black Panthers and, 33
Female Genital Cutting and Education Network website, 221
female genital mutilation (FGM), 209–24
  health consequences of, 219–20
  international human rights law and, 220–1
  pedagogical tool for, 213–23
  prevalence of, 218–19
  religious/sociocultural rationales for, 217–18
  types of, 212, 216f, 217
  UN conventions pertaining to, 220
  UN resolution banning, 212
  WHO and, 212
Female Genital Mutilation: The Prevention and the Management of the Health Complications; Policy Guidelines for Nurses and Midwives, 221
food banks, role of, 52
food security
  Convention on the Rights of the Child and, 49
  defined, 49
  versus nutrition security, 50
Frayer-style Vocabulary activity, 136, 145f

Free the SF8 campaign, 35–7
Freire, Paulo, 6, 23, 34, 89, 171–2
Fuentes, Emma, 25
funding, school, communities of color and, 70

gender
  cultural norms and, 214
  social construction of, 68
gender roles, oppressive, 152
genetically modified organisms (GMOs), 67
genetics research, handout for, 84t
genitalia, female, 214–16, 215f, 216f. *See also* female genital mutilation (FGM)
genocide, Darfur, 24
gentrification, housing rights and, 198
Gillian-Smiley, Anita, 16
Gilmore, Ruth Wilson, 226
Global Human Rights Education listserv, 12
government, role of, 9
gradual release approach, 39–40
graduate studies at USF, 22–3, 25
Grant, Oscar, 15
grassroots organizations, HRE and, 6
Gregorc Activity, 74–5
group work, in science classroom, 74–5

Haiti
  colonization of, 109–10, 116
  Doctors without Borders in, 111
  history of resistance in, 115
  human rights in (*see* human rights in Haiti)
  infrastructure in, 119
  literacy rate in, 109
  photos of, 123f–6f
  post-earthquake conditions in, 108
  worker wages in, 110
"Haiti: After the Quake," 118–19
Haiti Grassroots Watch, 110
Haiti Justice Alliance, 109
Hamer Academy, 15–18

Harvey Milk Civil Rights Academy
  Black Panther pedagogical tool and, 38–45
  classroom context of, 38–9
health, poverty and, 50–1
health care, International Covenant on Economic, Social and Cultural Rights and, 50
Herz, Ansel, 111
high school classrooms, HRE in. See *Crucible* unit; human rights in Haiti; *Know Your Rights: Understanding the Universal Declaration of Human Rights (UDHR)*
hooks, bell, 89
housing, as human right, 194, 201. *See also* Universal Declaration of Human Rights (UDHR), Article 25
human, legal concept of, 226
human rights
  contradictions of, 226
  culture of, 9
  leadership development and, 188
  needs and, 135
  personal context of, 158–9
  in service of imperialism, 231–4
  student definitions of, 135–6
  student knowledge of, 76
  transnational-local synergy of, 227
  types of, 7–8
  value-laden nature of, 174
  versus women's rights, 221
human rights education (HRE)
  as alternative pedagogical approach, 153–4
  Amnesty International definition of, 171
  building movement for (*see also* human rights education movement)
  challenges and triumphs of teaching, 15–28
  challenges to, 18–22
  core competencies in, 10–11
  critical need for, 15–18
  decolonization and, 225–35
  as effective educational model, 153–4
  as ethical educational model, 151–3
  goals of, 172–3
  graduate studies in, 22–3
  history of, 3–5
  implementing, 154–5
  informal education and, 6
  key features of, 7–9
  legal dimension of, 7–8
  narrow approach to, 11–12
  need for, 151–5
  normative content of, 8
  objectives of, 22
  outcomes of, 5
  pedagogies of, 8–9
  preventive intent of, 7
  right to, 5–6
  service learning and, 175–7
  UN definition of, 5
Human Rights Education Associates, 12
human rights education movement
  international, origins of, 3
  in US, 3–14, 11–13
human rights educators, identifying as, 21–2
human rights in Haiti, 107–27, 225
  action project and, 122–3
  Constitution and, 111–12
  earthquake impacts and, 109–11
  education and, 113, 121–2
  future of, 114
  gallery walk and, 119–20
  gallery walk photos and, 123f–6f
  resistance songs and, 120–1
  restavèks and, 121–2
  slavery legacy and, 112
  survivor mixer and, 118–19
  UDHR and, 108–9, 115–16
human rights law, FGM and, 220

human rights standards.
  See also specific covenants and treaties
  evolution of, 3–5
  international, 7
  resistance to, 4
Human Rights USA, 12, 170
human rights violations
  East Oakland and, 15–18
  ethical concerns and, 173–4
  in US cities, 233–4
  yPAR project on, 228–30
Hunger Games, The (Collins), 150
Hurricane Katrina, 24
Hutton, Bobby, 33

immigrants
  Asian, and denial of citizenship, 198
  undocumented, Proposition 187 and, 70
Immortal Life of Henrietta Lacks, The (Skloot), 77
imperialism, human rights in service of, 231–4
Indigenous peoples
  rights of, 230–1
  survivance of, 226
individual rights, *versus* collective rights, 152
International Covenant on Civil and Political Rights (ICCPR), 3, 20, 220
International Covenant on Economic, Social and Cultural Rights (ICESCR), 4, 20, 220
  Article 1 of, 189
  Article 12 of, 50
  Haiti and, 112
  and human rights-science connection, 67
  in science classroom, 77
  US failure to sign, 19
International Declaration on Bioethics and Human Rights, in science classroom, 76

International Declaration on Human Genetic Data, 67
  in science classroom, 76
International Hotel (I-Hotel).
  See also Asian American leadership
  background information on, 198–9
  case study of, 188
  struggle for, 194–7
  student films about, 202
  student visits to, 202–4
  UDHR Article 25 and, 194–5
International Human Rights Education Consortium, 13
International & Multicultural Education (IME), 23, 25
international treaties/conventions.
  See also specific treaties/conventions
  human rights standards in, 3–4
  lack of US support for, 19–20
  science and, 67
  violations of, 51
Islam, FGM and, 218
Islamophobia, 87–105
  Aladdin as embodiment of, 91–3
  critical race theory and, 94
  defined, 88
  dominant narrative *versus* counter-narrative and, 94–5
  examining, 89–92
  in popular culture, 88
  rationale for teaching about, 88–9
  student responses to unit on, 95–6

Japanese American internment camps, in understanding UDHR unit, 131
Jhally, Sut, 222
jigsaw lesson, 138–40, 142
Jordan, June, 234
journaling
  for *Crucible unit,* 158
  in Haiti unit, 118, 120, 121
  in Islamophobia unit, 90
  in *Know Your Rights* unit, 137

in science classroom, 68, 79
for social problems course, 182–3
Juarez, Deborah, 16
junior high school/middle school, pedagogical tools in.
 See Islamophobia; science classroom

Kassindja, Fauziya, 221
Katz, Jackson, 222
Katz, Susan, 23, 25, 26
Kennedy, John F., 163
Kerley, Barbara, 62
Khan, Ali, 91
Kilbourne, Jean, 222
Killing Us Softly 3 (Kilbourne), 222
King, Martin Luther, Jr., 32, 35
Know Your Rights: Understanding the Universal Declaration of Human Rights (UDHR), 129–47
  ELL students and, 132–4
  essential questions for, 131
  Frayer-style Vocabulary activity and, 136, 145f
  pedagogical tools for, 131–47
  persuasive essay exercise in, 140–2
  reading guide and split dictation for, 136–8
  Story of Human Rights and, 134
  student definitions and, 135–6
  SWBAT approach to, 132–5
  UDHR jigsaw and presentation in, 138–40
  using *Farewell to Manzanar*, 131–2
knowledge, subjective nature of, 90
Koenig, Shulamith, 12
Koirala-Azad, Shabnam, 23, 25
Kony, Joseph, 232
Ku Klux Klan, 34
Kumashiro, Kevin, 25

Larrieux, Amel, 213
Lavalas Movement, 112, 113

leadership. *See also* Asian American leadership; critical leadership theory
  critiquing notions of, 192–3
  legacies of, 194–7
leadership development. *See also* Asian American leadership
  key terminology in, 195
leadership models, traditional, 192–3
Legacies of Asian American Leadership: The Fall and Rise of the I-Hotel, 197–205
legal framework, 7–8
  HRE and, 68
Listen to the Wind (Mortenson), 57–8
literacy instruction, *Know Your Rights and*, 132–44
Little Mermaid, The, 94, 98

Making Connections, 52
Malcolm X, 32, 35, 225, 233, 234
  on human rights as decolonization strategy, 227–8, 230
Martelly, Michele, 111
McCoy, Frank, 36
McMartin Preschool Trial, 161–3
media
  Islamophobia and, 90–1
  violence against women and, 222
memory, collective, refashioning of, 34–5
middle school. *See* junior high school/middle school
Milk, Harvey, 38
Miller, Arthur, 155, 162–3
Mine Ban Treaty, US failure to sign, 19
mob mentality, 161
Mortenson, Greg, 57–8
Mount Diablo High School, 150
Mumia Abu-Jamal, 227
Muntaqim, Jalil, 36
Muslims
  lack of everyday representations of, 91
  negative stereotypes of, 88
  (*see also* Islamophobia)
  racial profiling of, 92

National Association for the Advancement of Colored People, 20
National Center for HRE, 12
neoliberal "reforms," 20–1
Newton, Huey, 33, 38
Nigeria, BringBackOurGirls campaign and, 232–3
No Child Left Behind, 20, 229
  communities of color and, 70
North America Partners in Human Rights Education, 12
nutrition security, *versus* food security, 50

Oakland Community School, 228–9
Obama, Barack, 232
Occupation of Alcatraz, 230
Office for Democratic Institutions and Human Rights, and core HRE competencies, 10–11
Office of the UN High Commissioner for Human Rights, 6
oppression
  Black Panther unit and, 43
  pedagogical lens and, 89–90
  UDHR for examining, 88
  in US, 32
  use of education to promote, 151
Organization of African Unity, 230
Orlin, Ted, 13
othering, 90
Our World, Our Rights (AI), 53
Ozawa, Takao, 226

Padilla, Lindsay, 7
Parks, Rosa, 37
Parmar, Pratibha, 222
Participatory Action Research (PAR), 72
pedagogies
  red *versus* critical, 226–7
  types of, 8–9
people of color, and legal concept of "human," 226
People's Decade for Human Rights Education, 12

performing arts, 16–17
Philoxene, David, 228–9
photography, as pedagogical tool, 119–20, 123f, 126f
photovoice, documentation with, 51
police profiling/abuse, Oscar Grant and, 15
popular culture, Islamophobia and, 90–1
Possessing the Secret of Joy (Walker), 222
poverty
  exploring impacts of, 48
  health and, 50–1
power, in critical leadership theory, 200
power structures, changing, 192
praxis, Freire's concept of, 89
prejudice, awareness of, 10

race, social construction of, 68–9, 78–9, 82t, 83t
Race to the Top, 20, 229
RACE—The Power of an Illusion, 78
racial profiling, of Arabs and Muslims, 92
racism
  Asian American leadership and, 191
  in critical leadership theory, 200
Reading, Writing, and Rising Up, 39
Reagan, Ronald, 20
red pedagogy, tenets of, 226–7
Red Scare of 1950s, 163
religious freedom, in UDHR and CRC, 92–3
religious norms, gender roles and, 152
resistance, in critical leadership theory, 200
resistance songs, as pedagogical tool, 120–1
restavèk system, 112, 113, 114, 121–2
Reynolds, Dan, 150
Robinson, Cedric, 226
Robinson, Karen, 23
Roosevelt, Eleanor, 19, 32, 171, 194, 231
rubrics, in science classroom, 75–6

Said, Edward, 90
Salem witch trials, 162
San Francisco International High School (SFIHS), 129–47. See also *Know Your Rights: Understanding the Universal Declaration of Human Rights (UDHR)*
 central principles of, 130
 curriculum and instruction at, 130–1
 student body of, 129–30
school funding, communities of color and, 70
schools. See also specific grade levels
 HRE in, 6, 9–13
 negotiating HRE in, 70–3
science, human rights treaties and, 67
science classroom, 65–86
 California science standards and, 75
 case-study example of, 67–70
 HRE and, 7
 pedagogical tools in, 73–84
 student newspaper and, 79–80
scientific method, California State Standards and, 73
Scott, James, 230
Seale, Bobby, 33
segregation, *Brown v Board of Education* and, 37
Sélavi, That is Life: A Haitian Story of Hope, 122
service learning, HRE and, 175–7
service learning project, 180, 183
Sesan, Gbenga, 233
Smith, Linda Tuhiwai, 226
social change
 HRE and, 5
 UDHR and, 174
social conditions, basic, defined, 50
social justice
 HRE and, 23
 human rights and, 21
Social Problems: A Service Learning Approach (Dolgon and Baker), 180
social problems course
 description of, 179

 HRE in, 171–4
 human rights perspective on, 169–85
 learning outcomes from, 179
 pedagogical tool for, 179–83
 requirements for, 180, 181t–2t
 service learning and, 175–7
 service learning project for, 180, 183
 student empowerment and, 177–9
 weblog assignment for, 182–3
social rights, US and, 19
Spero, Andrea McEvoy, 16, 154
"Stand Up for Haiti," 123
standard of living. See adequate standard of living
Starkey, Hugh, 48
stereotypes
 of Arabs and Muslims, 91
 of Asian Americans, 191–2
 essentialism and, 192
 in Islamophobia unit, 99
Stop Kony campaign, 232
Story of Human Rights, 134
Stranger, The (Camus), 150
students
 in community colleges, 172
 factors in performance level of, 153
 human rights knowledge of, 76
 Islamophobia unit and, 95–6
 nontraditional, 170
 responses to HRE, 26
suicide rate, in Durkheim's sociology, 229
symbols, Black Panther unit and, 42

Talamante, Olga, xi–xvi, 225, 232–3
talking timeline, in Black Panther unit, 44
Taylor, Betty, 25
Teacher and Student Participatory Action Research (TSPAR)
 goals and achievements of, 72–3
 in science classroom, 80–1
test scores, 71
 HRE and, 230
 impacts of, 150

"The World As It Could Be" program, 16, 159–60
Thiam, Awa, 210
Thind, Bhagat Singh, 226
Things They Carried, The (O'Brien), 150
Tibbitts, Felisa, 25
Tough Guise Violence, Media & the Crisis in Masculinity, 222
traditions, gender-based, 152, 214
Truman, Harry S., 32
Tubman, Harriet, 226
Two Truths and a Lie, 149

U.S. Constitution, 11
  14th amendment of, 92
U.S. Supreme Court, civil rights cases of, 226
United Indians of All Tribes, 230
United Nations. *See also* Convention against Torture and Other Cruel, Inhuman or Degrading Treatment or Punishment; Convention on the Elimination of All Forms of Discrimination against Women (CEDAW); Convention on the Rights of the Child (CRC)
  and Decade of Human Rights Education, 66
  guarantee *versus* violation of, 226
  HRE and, 6
  HRE definition of, 5
  resolution banning FGM, 212
United Nations Decade for Human Rights Education (UNDHRE), 6, 12, 66, 154
United Nations Declaration on Human Rights Education and Training (DHRET), 6
United Nations Declaration on the Rights of Indigenous Peoples (UNDRIP), 227, 231
United Nations Educational, Scientific and Cultural Organization (UNESCO)
  HRE and, 6
  and human rights-science connection, 67
  in science classroom, 76
United Nations General Assembly, former colonies in, 230
United Nations Human Rights Council, international treaties and, 4
United Nations International Children's Emergency Fund, 220
United Nations Stabilization Mission in Haiti (MINUSTAH), violations by, 110–11
United Neighborhood Improvement Association (UNIA), 229
United States
  building HRE movement in, 3–14
  and Convention on the Rights of the Child, 49, 152
  and failure to support international treaties, 19–20
  Haiti and, 116
  HRE movement in, 11–13
  HRE organizations in, 12
  "human rights" and military/economic aggression by, 230–2
  human rights history of, 32–3
  occupation of Haiti by, 109–10
  Universal Declaration of Human Rights (UDHR) and, 19
Universal Declaration of Human Rights (UDHR), 10
  accessibility to young learners, 47–8
  Article 1 of, 92
  Article 2 of, 92
  Article 7 of, 92
  Article 9 of, 92
  Article 18 of, 92
  Article 22 of, 229
  Article 23 of, 229
  Article 24 of, 229
  Article 25 of, 48–9, 108, 115, 194–5, 229
  Article 26 of, 93, 108, 115, 151, 188–9, 229
  Article 27 of, 93

Article 30 of, 151
California State Content Standards
   and, 17
and creating culture of respect, 173
for examining oppression, 88
and Free the SF8 campaign, 35–7
human rights in Haiti unit and,
   119–20
human rights legal system and, 4
Islamophobia as violation of, 92–3
knowledge and applications of, 170–1
in school curriculum, 4–5
in science classroom, 75–6
teacher knowledge of, 17–18
teaching through *The Crucible*
   (see *Crucible* unit)
transformative impacts of, 16–17
understanding (see *Know Your
   Rights: Understanding the
   Universal Declaration of Human
   Rights (UDHR)*)
Universal Declaration on Bioethics and
   Human Rights, 67
Universal Declaration on the Human
   Genome and Human Rights, 67
in science classroom, 76
University of Minnesota, Human
   Rights Center of, 12
University of San Francisco, HRE
   graduate studies at, 22–3, 25
US Human Rights Educators
   Network, 13
US Network for Human Rights, 12–13

Valdés, Juan Gabriel, 111
Vietnam War, 32
violence against women
   female genital mutilation and, 209–24
   (*see also* female genital mutilation
   (FGM))
   US culture and, 222

Wahdan, Muhammad, 218
Walker, Alice, 222
war on drugs, communities of
   color and, 70
war on terror, 24
*Warrior Marks: Female Genital
   Mutilation and the Sexual
   Blinding of Women* (Thiam),
   210, 222
We Are All Born Free, 139, 142–3
Witness to Hunger, 51
women
   discrimination against, CEDAW
      definition of, 211
   violence against (*see* Convention on
      the Elimination of All Forms of
      Discrimination against Women
      (CEDAW); violence against
      women)
women's rights
   adequate standard of living
      and, 51
   versus human rights, 221
Women's Rights movement, 11
World Conference on Human
   Rights, 6
World Declaration and Plan of Action
   on Nutrition, 49–50
World Health Organization (WHO),
   221
   FGM definition of, 212
Writing Beyond Race: Living Theory
   (hooks), 78

Young, John, 36
Youth for Human Rights website,
   134
youth Participatory Action Research
   (yPAR), 72, 228–30

Zarrar, Malika, 218

The manufacturer's authorised representative in the EU is Springer Nature Customer Service Centre GmbH, Europaplatz 3, 69115 Heidelberg, Germany. If you have any concerns regarding our products, please contact ProductSafety@springernature.com

Printed and bound by CPI Group (UK) Ltd, Croydon, CR0 4YY
23/03/2026
02076682-0017